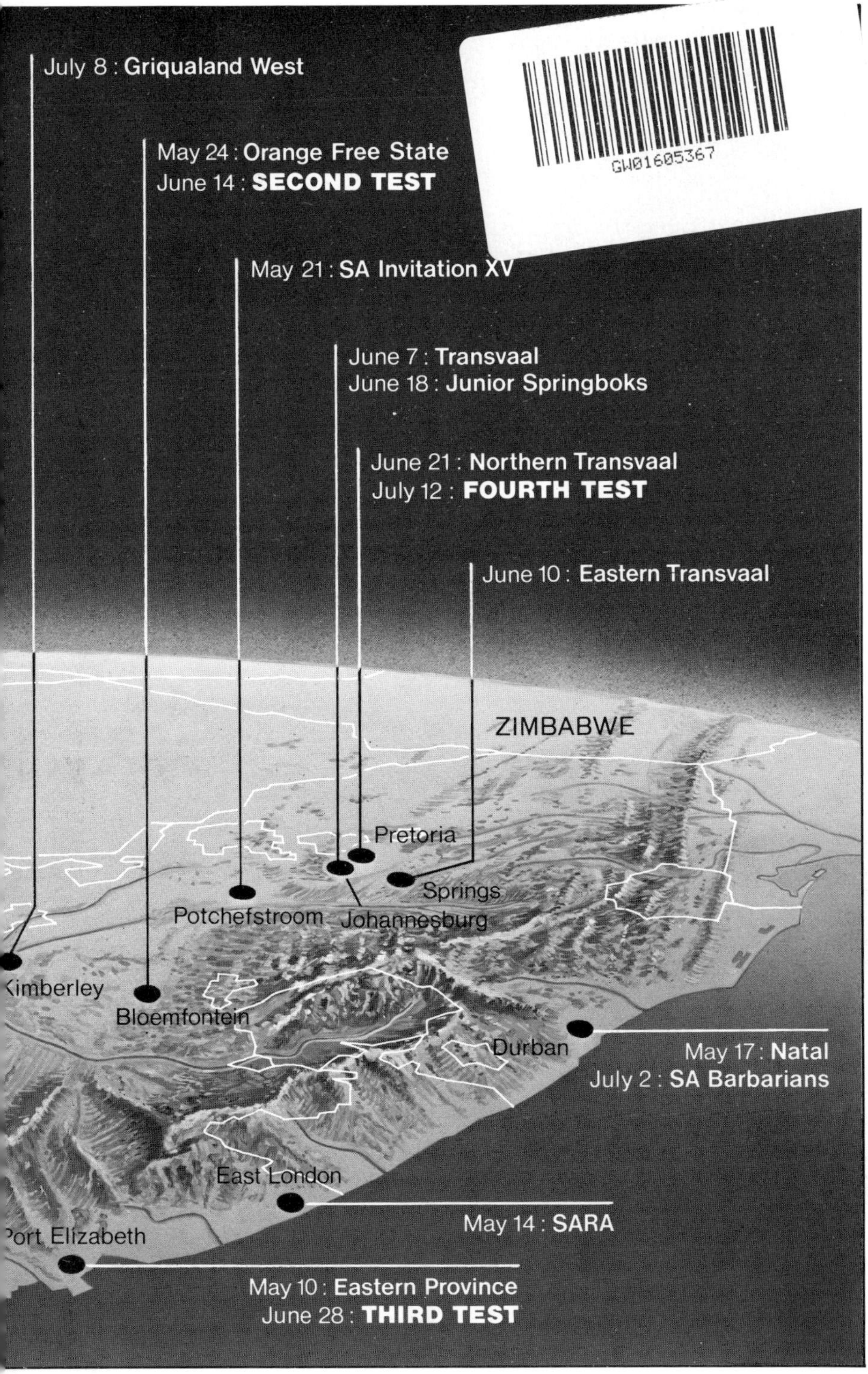

July 8 : **Griqualand West**

May 24 : **Orange Free State**
June 14 : **SECOND TEST**

May 21 : **SA Invitation XV**

June 7 : **Transvaal**
June 18 : **Junior Springboks**

June 21 : **Northern Transvaal**
July 12 : **FOURTH TEST**

June 10 : **Eastern Transvaal**

ZIMBABWE

Pretoria

Springs

Potchefstroom

Johannesburg

Kimberley

Bloemfontein

Durban

May 17 : **Natal**
July 2 : **SA Barbarians**

East London

May 14 : **SARA**

Port Elizabeth

May 10 : **Eastern Province**
June 28 : **THIRD TEST**

John Hopkins

BRITISH LIONS 1980

Statistics by Michael Nimmo
Photographs by David Rogers

WORLD'S WORK LTD

Hay

Davie

Campbel

Carleton

O'Driscoll

Slemen

Holmes

Renwic

Phillips

Wheeler

Quinnell

Beattie

Gravell

Ward

Patterson

Lane

Colclough

Blakeway

Woodward

Cotton

Morgan

Price

Beaumont

Rees

O'Driscoll

C. Williams

Martin

Orr

Tucker

Irvine

Squire

Stephens

G. Williams

Robbie

Richards

omes

Millar

odge

Murphy

nith

Matthews

But for the players, this book could not have been written. It was their tour and I was able to poke my nose into their affairs to acquire the necessary material only because they allowed me to. For their tolerance of my inquisitiveness, their innate courtesy and friendliness, I dedicate this book to them.

JOHN HOPKINS
August, 1980

Published by World's Work Ltd, Kingswood, Tadworth, Surrey
Typeset by CCC, printed and bound in Great Britain
by William Clowes (Beccles) Limited, Beccles and London
SBN 437 06851 X

Contents

CHAPTER ONE

Lions who went in hope and returned with dignity

The 1980 tour of South Africa by the British Lions was not solely a rugby tour. It was a 70-day, all expenses paid, anthropological study of one of the world's most troubled, most puzzling, most diverse and most interesting countries. And the 30 players from England, Wales, Scotland and Ireland who left London on the evening of 3 May, as well as the eight replacements who flew out at various times to join the party, would not have missed it for the world.

South Africa, where nearly 30 million people sprawl over an area larger than West Germany, France, Italy, Holland and Belgium combined, is also a country of breathtaking beauty. If you are not seduced by the banana country of author Alan Paton's Natal, or the midday stillness of the Willem Pretorius Game Park, which is actually only a second division game park, then the view of Cape Town as you circle Table Mountain or the muscular beauty of Stellenbosch cradled beneath saw-toothed mountains will stop you in your tracks and leave you wide-eyed and open-mouthed. The Republic of South Africa is so large and varied that some part of it will tug at your heart-strings, no matter how high you try to hold your defences.

The South African people the Lions met were almost invariably friendly, courteous, hard-working and riddled with uncertainty about themselves and their country. I lost track of how often a square-jawed Voortrekker type, his eyes creased by the long hours of sunshine, his hands as leathery as a saddle, would fix me with a firm gaze and ask, in those familiar flat tones: "How do you like our country so far?" It was the question we were asked more than any other—at every town we visited, in the bars, even in the shops. It was the 64,000 rand question.

It was probably just the same when W. E. Maclagan's team arrived in the Cape in 1891 on the first tour of South Africa by a British team, a tour underwritten, incidentally, by none other than Cecil Rhodes, the Prime Minister of Cape Colony. By then tours of Australia and New Zealand had been going since 1888. Maclagan's team compiled a record unmatched by any of the 10 British teams to visit South Africa since. They won all their 19 matches, took the Test series 3–0 and conceded the astonishing total of only one point—scoring was different in those days, of course.

Of the countries that can host rugby tours by the three major teams, the Lions, Springboks and All Blacks, South Africa is the most popular. It has untold wealth with which to pamper the players. Within the four provinces that lie between coastal Cape Town in the south west and land-locked Messina up on the Zimbabwean border stretches an area five times as big as Britain, with sporting facilities that are the envy of the world. A readily available labour force and huge natural industrial and financial resources keep the cost of living down to no more than three-quarters of that in Britain. The Mediterranean climate provides between seven and nine hours of sunshine daily throughout the year. Rain in the winter is rare. It rained on only seven of the 70 days while the Lions were in South Africa.

But there is of course a dark side to this paradise. South Africa's majority of 22 million blacks, 2.5 million coloureds and 750,000 Asians are oppressed by a minority of 4.5 million whites. This inequality and its resulting injustices are impossible not to see. "Whites only," say lavatory signs. Blacks may only enter certain "international" hotels, are given worse jobs, less pay and few rights. They have no vote and sometimes no home.

The official population of Soweto, which stands for south west township, that infamous urban slum 10 miles from Johannesburg, is 1.5 million. In reality nearer two million and maybe even more live there, many in abject poverty in houses that probably have no hot water or inside lavatory, and stand on streets that are unpaved and unlit.

Almost the whole world deplores the continued existence

of apartheid. Resolutions condemning South Africa have been passed in the United Nations, and the Gleneagles Agreement among Commonwealth prime ministers, aimed at discouraging further sporting contacts with South Africa, have left the sports-mad country with few opponents to play. South Africa have not appeared at an Olympics since 1960 and are barred from competing internationally at athletics, soccer and cricket.

The last rugby tour by the Springboks to Britain was in 1969/70. Since then they have visited France (in 1974) but maintained tenuous rugby links with New Zealand and Britain only by gratefully receiving the All Blacks (1970 and 1976) and the Lions in 1974 and 1980. Attempts to revive outgoing tours have been unsuccessful so far.

All South African teams are barred from Australia, a proposed Springbok tour of France in 1979 was cancelled at the last minute when the French government would not issue visas, and a scheduled tour of New Zealand in 1981 was already in 1980 under pressure from Stop the Tour movements and from the Leader of the Opposition in New Zealand. Little wonder, then, that the Lions' tour of 1980 was first agreed and then carried out amidst considerable political opposition.

So should the Lions have gone? On balance I still believe they should not. What is happening is that the more South Africa changes, the more it stays the same. Like silk chiffon, the changes are vivid enough to be seen, yet so flimsy they can easily be ripped apart. Despite some improvements, which included the appearance on merit of two non-whites for the formerly all-white Junior Springboks, I still saw much evidence that the *verkramptes* (unenlightened) were triumphing over the *verligtes* (enlightened), which seemed to be fuelling the black v white confrontation that the world is dreading.

On the morning of the fourth Test a leading American expert on African affairs, Steven Solarz, observed that since his last visit 15 months earlier, there had been a significant growth in the blacks' view that peaceful change was no longer possible and that the only way to bring about change was by violence. "One of the most deeply disturbing things I heard

It is impossible not to find something that will tug at your heartstrings in South Africa. A country of breathtaking beauty, it is also one where 22 million blacks (like the children below and right, photographed in Soweto) are dominated by 4.5 million whites. The Lions tour at least helped focus world opinion on what is wrong but Anglican Bishop Desmond Tutu said the presence of the team "had made the other chaps feel a little better". This was a view supported by Dan (Cheeky) Watson, pictured left, who lives in Port Elizabeth. Four years ago he won a Springbok trial but then threw in his lot with a black club. Watson's verdict on the tour: "The Lions have alienated many blacks".

over and over again from blacks was that they were ready to die for their liberation, whereas whites told me they were prepared to die to preserve what they had," he said.

The arguments for and against the Lions also raged inside South Africa among blacks and whites. As the black Anglican Bishop Desmond Tutu says later in this book, the Lions, by going to South Africa, "had made the other chaps feel a little better."

A plausible voice in support of this argument was that of Dan (Cheeky) Watson, a 29-year-old white who lives in Port Elizabeth where he runs two sports clothing shops. Four years earlier Watson was playing centre for Eastern Province, and had won a Springbok trial as a wing. But then he threw in his lot with a local black club who play on a bumpy and stone-strewn pitch in the local township of New Brighton. The club is affiliated to the South African Rugby Union, a body that refuses even to acknowledge Dr Danie Craven's SA Rugby Board. SARU seek non-racial, not multi-racial, rugby. Watson's verdict on the Lions tour was: "The Lions have alienated many blacks and implicitly told the SARB 'we approve of your policies.'"

There were other liberal whites in South Africa, who abhorred the Nationalist Government, but felt that "the more people who come here and show that apartheid won't stand up to the light of day the better." And there were blacks like Curnick Mdyesha of the SA Rugby Association, and coloureds like Cuthbert Loriston of the SA Rugby Football Federation, who welcomed the Lions. "Rugby is the biggest influence for change," says Abe Williams, secretary of SARFF. Change rugby and you change *them.*"

The Lions management, Syd Millar and Noel Murphy, naturally approved of the tour and Millar went so far as to say that if the SARB continued to tidy up their house to make their sport completely mixed from club level upwards he saw no reason why the Springboks should not return to international competition.

Their fellow Irishman Colin Patterson, who was visiting South Africa for the first time, was shocked at some of the blatant injustices he saw and heard about. He recalls that a black hall porter in one of the team's hotels had to work for 10 years before his wife and family could come and join him. "What really got me was the hypocrisy of some whites who said there was no apartheid and no inequality," said Patterson after he returned home. "When we were in the House of Assembly in Cape Town the Prime Minister stood up and talked of 'this democracy'.

"I didn't like what I saw of the relationship between the blacks and the whites. But would these feelings prevent me from going back? I don't know for sure. I don't think I would go back again on a 10-week Lions tour. I don't think I would go back for a five- or six-week tour." Then the pragmatism of a brutally honest top-class sportsman showed through as he continued: "But if I was offered an all-expenses paid trip for a fortnight with my wife just to play one game then I am not sure that I am not mercenary enough to take that and turn a blind eye to the things I don't like. And who wouldn't?"

Patterson and his teammates among the Lions of 1980 suffered many of the same experiences as previous Lions. They were badgered for souvenirs, telephoned for tickets, besieged for autographs. They were accompanied around South Africa by the largest group of journalists ever to cover a Lions tour—more than 50 writers, photographers and broadcasters. And everyone seemed to be making money. From 18 games watched by 616,000 spectators, South African rugby was expected to make a profit of R4.5 million (£2.5 million) after expenses and including advertising and television rights. The SARB would profit by R1.8 million (£1 million) as well as 50 per cent of the gate takings from the four Tests. The provinces were expecting anything from R600,000 (£333,300) for Western Province to Natal's R400,000 (£222,200).

Phil Bennett's Lions of 1977 in New Zealand had suffered a spate of injuries and an onslaught from the newspapers over there, and were depressed by the appalling bad weather. I described it as The Bad News Tour. Three years later Englishman Bill Beaumont led his team on what could be called The Bad Luck Tour. They had more character than Bennett's Lions, more humour, more charm. They were

FB - Full Back	THP - Tight Head Prop
LW - Left Wing	H - Hooker
C - Centre	CAPT - CAPTAIN
RW - Right Wing	T - Try
SO - Stand Off	Con - Conversion
SH - Scrum Half	Pen - Penalty
No8 - No8	DG - Drop Goal
F - Flanker	Rep - Replacement
SR - Second Row	Res - Reserve
LHP - Loose Head Prop	2½ - second half

Player		Sat 10.5.80 W 28/16 Eastern Province Port Elisabeth	Wed 14.5.80 W 28/6 S.A. Rugby Ass. East London	Sat 17.5.80 W 21/15 Natal Durban	Wed 21.5.80 W 22/19 S.A. Invitation15 Potchefstroom	Sat 24.5.80 W 21/17 Orange Free State Bloemfontein	Tue 27.5.80 W 15/6 S.A.R. Federation Stellenbosch	Sat 31.5.80 L 22/26 1. TEST Cape Town	Wed 4.6.80 W 27/7 S.A. Country Windhoek	Sat 7.6.80 W 32/12 Transvaal Johannesburg	Tue 10.6.80 W 21/15 Eastern Transvaal Springs	Sat 14.6.80 L 19/26 2. TEST Bloemfontein	Wed 18.6.80 W 17/6 Jnr. Springboks Johannesburg	Sat 21.6.80 W 16/9 Nth. Transvaal Pretoria	Sat 28.6.80 L 10/12 3. TEST Port Elisabeth	Wed 2.7.80 W 25/14 S.A. Barbarians Durban	Sat 5.7.80 W 37/6 Western Province Cape Town	Tue 8.7.80 W 23/19 Griqualand West Kimberley	Sat 12.7.80 W 17/13 4. TEST Pretoria	Appearances	Tries	Conversions	Penalties	Drop Goals	Points
B. Hay	S	FB			FB				FB	LW	LW Capt.	LW		LW	LW 1T		LW 1T	FB	LW	11	2	–	–	–	8
R. O'Donnell	I		FB	FB			FB 1DG	FB			FB		Injured 3rd min 2½							6	–	–	–	1	3
J. Carleton	E		RW	RW 1T		RW	RW 1T	RW			RW 1T	RW				LW	RW		RW	10	3	–	–	–	12
E. Rees	W	RW 1T	LW 1T		RW								RW 1T			RW		RW		6	3	–	–	–	12
M. Slemen	E	LW 1T		LW 1DG 1Con	LW 2T	LW 2T		LW												5	5	1	–	1	25
P. Morgan	W	C -30min SO				FB	LW		LW		C					C		LW 1DG 1T		7	1	–	–	1	7
R. Gravell	W	C		C		C		18min 2½ RW	C	C		C 1T		C	C		C		C	11	1	–	–	–	4
J. Renwick	S	Rep. Davies C 1Con 1Pen	C		C	C 1Con 1Pen		C	C 1T	Rep. Richards C	C		C 1DG			C		C		11	1	2	2	1	17
D. Richards	W		SO	C	SO	SO	C	C		C 1T inj. 21min 2½										7	1	–	–	–	4
C. Woodward	E		C 3Pen 1DG 2Con		C 1Con 4Pen		C		RW 1T	RW 2T 1Con 1Pen		C	Rep. O'Donnell LW 1Con	RW	RW		Rep. LW Irvine 1T	C		11	4	5	8	1	53
O. Campbell	I			SO 1Con 2Pen							SO 1Con 4Pen 1DG	Rep. Davies SO		SO 1Con	SO 2Pen		SO 2Con 4Pen 2DG		SO 1Con 1Pen	7	–	6	13	3	60
G. Davies	W	SO 1Con 2Pen 1DG Inj. 26min							SO 3Pen 1Con	SO 1T		SO 1Con 2Pen inj. 27 2½								4	1	3	7	1	34
T. Holmes	W	SH T		SH T		SH T inj 27 2½					SH off 27min									4	3	–	–	–	12
C. Patterson	I		SH		SH	Rep. Holmes 29min 2½	SH	SH		SH T	Rep. Holmes 29 min	SH			SH			SH inj. 6min		10	1	–	–	–	4
J. Beattie	S	No8		No8			F		No8 1T		No8		No8			No8		No8 1T		8	2	–	–	–	8
D. Quinnell	W	Rep. F Lane	No8 Capt. 2T		No8 Capt.		No8 Capt.	No8		No8		No8				F Capt.		F Capt.		9	2	–	–	–	8
S. Lane	W	F Inj. 55Sec																		1	–	–	–	–	–

J. O'Driscoll	I		F		F	F		F		F		F IT	F	F	F		F		F IT	11	2	–	–	–	8
J. Squire	W	F		F		No8		F		F		F	F Capt	No8 IT	No8		No8		No8	11	1	–	–	–	4
C. Tucker	I		F	F			F		F		F			F	F		F		F	9	–	–	–	–	–
B. Beaumont	E	SR Capt.		SR Capt.		SR Capt.		SR Capt.		SR Capt.		SR Capt.		SR Capt.	SR Capt.		SR Capt		SR Capt	10	–	–	–	–	–
M. Colclough	E		SR		SR	SR		SR		SR		SR	SR	SR IT	SR		SR		SR	11	1	–	–	–	4
A. Martin	W	SR		SR			SR		SR		SR		SR			SR		SR		8	–	–	–	–	–
A. Tomes	S		SR		SR		SR		SR		SR					SR IT		SR		7	1	–	–	–	4
P. Blakeway	E		THP inj. 10min																	1	–	–	–	–	–
G. Price	W	THP		THP	THP	THP		THP IT		THP IT		THP	THP	THP	THP		THP		THP	12	2	–	–	–	8
F. Cotton	E	LHP	Rep. THP Blakeway	LHP			LHP Rep 31min													4	–	–	–	–	–
C. Williams	W		LHP		LHP	LHP	LHP Rep. Cotton	LHP			LHP	LHP	Rep. Orr	LHP	LHP		LHP		LHP IT	12	1	–	–	–	4
P. Wheeler	E	H		H		H IT		H	H	H		H		H	H		H		H	11	1	–	–	–	4
A. Phillips	W		H		H		H				H		H			H		H		7	–	–	–	–	–
G. Williams	W				F	F			F IT		F					F		F		6	1	–	–	–	4
T. Ward	I						So 2Pen 1Con	So 5Pen 1DG					So			So 1T 1Con 3Pen		So 1Pen 1Con		5	1	4	11	1	48
I. Stephens	W						THP		THP		THP					THP		THP		5	–	–	–	–	–
J. Robbie	I								SH				SH	SH		SH	SH	Rep C.Patterson 1T 1DG	SH	7	1	–	–	1	7
P. Orr	I								LHP	LHP			inj. 7min LHP			LHP		LHP		5	–	–	–	–	–
A. Irvine	S									FB 1Pen		FB 1Pen	LW, FB 1T	FB 2Pen	FB	FB 1T	FB 1T 1DG inj. 23min 2½		FB 1T	8	4	–	4	1	31
P. Dodge	E												C 1T	C	C		C		C	5	1	–	–	–	4
S. Smith	E																			–	–	–	–	–	–

This chart was John Hopkins's technique for keeping track of players' facts and figures on tour. It is a common practice among journalists, revealing among other statistics, the games each player appeared in, the position he played and the points he scored in that game.

better managed, better coached and better led. But they lost the first three Tests, and the series, and their injuries were far worse.

They lost an average of one player every second game and, at an extra cost of £8,000 in fares, had to call for eight replacements, as many as had been needed for the previous three Lions tours. "What's up Doc?" was a question asked time and again of Dr Jack Matthews, the team's doctor, as explanations were sought for the war-proportion lengths of the injury list. "I've no idea," he was forced to reply. Time after time a knock on his door or the ringing of his telephone meant another Lion was calling to say: "I'm not all right, Jack."

The average age of the 30 Lions when they left London on 3 May was 26¾. Their average height was a whisker under 6ft, their average weight 14st 4lb. In all the 30 of them topped the scales at 2¾ tons, or 430 stone, or 6,021lb. There was precisely 12 inches between the tallest Lion, the 6ft 5in Colclough and the smallest, the impish, 5ft 5in Patterson, and at 17st 5lb and 11st respectively they were also the heaviest and lightest men in the party. Eight were still bachelors, two were engaged—Clive Woodward and Alan Phillips both planned to get married within weeks of returning, Woodward on July 19 and Phillips two weeks later. The remaining 20 were married.

Dr John O'Driscoll from London's Westminster Hospital, solicitor Colin Patterson and chartered surveyor Andy Irvine provided the 1980 Lions with a core of professional men, and the representatives of the traditional craftsmen were Clive Williams, a plasterer, and Jim Renwick, an electricity linesman. Three firms employed two Lions—Gremer Chemicals (Derek Quinnell and Bruce Hay), the Gateway Building Society (Jeff Squire and Gareth Davies) and the Distributive Industries Training Board (Fran Cotton and Steve Smith, the last of the replacements flown out). From a nation of shopkeepers came Tony Ward, another replacement, and Allan Martin, who each had sports shops in, respectively, Limerick and Port Talbot.

The team's entrepreneurs ranged from Alan Phillips (window and office cleaners) and Terry Holmes (scrap metal and demolition merchants) to the biggest of them all, the Angoulême (France) based Maurice Colclough, who has a mini-empire with property in Australia, is a director of a firm renting out amusement-arcade games, and managing director of a firm hiring out holiday cruisers on canals and rivers in Western France.

Inevitably there were good fliers as well as those for whom flying was an ordeal. "Once I'm up I'm okay," said Fran Cotton, edgily looking out of the window as our Boeing 747 took off from Johannesburg on its way to Durban. "In small planes I worry less, because if something goes wrong it can float down, but if anything goes wrong on this thing it'll drop like a stone." With a shudder he told the story of North West Counties on tour in South Africa in 1979. "We were on this bloody great plane and it was very slow in taking off. We taxied along the runway for ages, and everybody suddenly realised something was wrong. Then Jim Sydall broke the silence. 'It's all right boys, we're going by road.'"

John Carleton remarked one day "I could never take flying for granted, it's too frightening, I don't understand it. A plane full of 250 people and all that luggage, and it races to the end of the runway and then just glides up into the air. It's fantastic, unbelievable, and I just don't have any idea of how it happens."

A Lions tour is an endurance test of morale, character and self-discipline, with extra hurdles dotted unexpectedly along the way. The hurdles may be having to share a room with the noisiest snorer (Hay), the tidiest Lion (Renwick), the untidiest (Colclough), the most superstitious (O'Donnell), and the most homesick (Ward, who wrote 80 postcards), and remembering things like returning room keys to reception so that a room-mate is not locked out. On tour even organising your laundry becomes a major logistical problem. More serious trials are coping with the constant whirl of training, eating, travelling and the nerves of match day.

The players had the often-gruelling training sessions when they could work out their frustrations. Millar and Murphy had no comparable outlets. The night after the game against Natal, which the Lions had come through to win in the last five minutes, coach Murphy restlessly roamed the Elangeni Hotel in Durban. He was wearing his red Lions shirt open at the neck, having put his tie in his pocket, his Lions blazer, and the black and white check trousers the Lions called their Rupert Bear trousers. He looked, and felt, exhausted.

"I woke up at 6.00 this morning and wrote half a dozen letters," said Murphy. "I hardly slept at all the first week because of the pressure. I couldn't wait to get the first match over. On match days I always wake at dawn and lie there worrying about the team, have I made the right choices, what's the weather going to be like, should I mention this in my team talk?

"I don't eat a thing during the morning, I'm in the changing room for an hour before the game, and it's so hot in there, calming the boys. Then, when I get back to the hotel after a game, I'm so tired all I want to do is go to bed. I reckon I could sleep from 6.30 on the night of a match round to breakfast the next morning."

The Lions stayed in 12 different hotels in their 10 weeks for periods as short as three days or as long as eight. They didn't much like one gargantuan and inefficient hotel where waiters would waken innocent guests at five in the morning bearing laden trays: "Your breakfast sir," they would announce to the startled and sleepy guest. Alarm calls tended either not to come, or to come at the wrong time.

We all had our own favourite hotels, which we came to regard as home. Mine was the Landdrost in Johannesburg and I didn't realise I had become so attached to it until I was stuck at Cape Town airport trying to get a flight back to Johannesburg. In case I failed I had booked a room in Cape Town. And, as it happened, I also had a room in Pretoria. The moment came when I had to make a choice between ending the long wait at Cape Town and moving into a nearby hotel, or taking a chance on getting a seat on the last flight to Johannesburg. Like a small lost child I found myself whimpering: "Let's chance it. I want to sleep in my own bed tonight."

At 8.30 am on Monday 14 July the Lions landed at Heathrow. We had all seen Alan Paton's Beloved Country,

In South Africa the Lions criss-crossed the Republic, and stayed in 12 different hotels in their ten-week tour for periods as short as three days or as long as eight. The scenes above are typical. On tour even organising your laundry becomes a major logistical problem.

and experienced the "dreadful calm" of white society in South Africa of which novelist Nadine Gordimer has written. We had criss-crossed the Republic, made a three-day raid into South West Africa/Namibia and visited the oldest city, Cape Town, and its joint capital Pretoria as well as nine other towns or cities.

In the end, was it worth the candle? The Lions had left Britain in hope and returned with dignity. They had become only the second side of modern times to win all their provincial games and they would kick themselves for ever that they hadn't done better in the Tests. And what about their moral and political scruples? "I believe the tour did help," said Peter Wheeler. "If nothing else it focussed world opinion on what is wrong with South Africa."

CHAPTER TWO

How the decision to tour was made

At 10.15 on the morning of Friday, 4 January 1980, Micky Steele-Bodger bounded up the steps of the East India and Sports Club in St James's Square, London. The East India Club, a porticoed, early 19th-century building, is on the west side of the tranquil square. It was here on the night of 21 June 1815, that a messenger brought news of Wellington's victory at Waterloo to the Prince Regent, the Prime Minister and the Foreign Secretary who were dining at the club. The historic announcement was then passed on from a balcony on the first floor to an expectant crowd milling in the square below.

The club's involvement with rugby began when England's selectors found it a convenient place to meet and select their teams. That practice has now died out, but the connection with rugby remains. The International Board, rugby's world-wide governing body, have a room at the club decorated with plaques of member countries, and other British rugby committees hold meetings there as well. It was here, for example, that the tribunal met to sentence the Welsh flanker Paul Ringer the day after he had been sent off in the international against England at Twickenham in February 1980.

As Steele-Bodger came through the wooden swing doors, photographer Frank Herrman and I got up to meet him. I had arranged to interview him there to complete the research necessary for a profile I was writing of him in *The Sunday Times*.

"Sorry I'm late," he said, dumping his bag at the reception desk. "The train was delayed. Apparently someone had jumped off a platform in front of the engine and we were held up for nearly 20 minutes." He turned to the desk, pulled a

Micky Steele-Bodger at the East India and Sports Club in London. Where a messenger brought news of Wellington's victory at Waterloo, Britain's best-known rugby administrator is at home. There, early in 1980 he was arguing the case for the Lions' tour of South Africa: "If sport is left alone it will break down all the barriers."

pair of spectacles out from his top pocket, slipped them on to his nose, and looked to see which room he was staying in.

"Morning Bob," he said cheerily to the distinguished-looking man in a black uniform behind the desk. "How are we today?"

"Very well, sir, thank you," replied Bob. "There's a letter for you, sir."

Steele-Bodger squinted at it, and then put it into a side pocket of his jacket. "See you in a minute," he said to us as he turned to pick up his bag and climb the stairs to his room.

Michael Roland Steele-Bodger is arguably the best-known rugby administrator in Britain. He was born in Tamworth on 4 September 1925. His father, a vet who had moved to the Staffordshire town from Peterborough a few years earlier, had two practices and later he gave one to each of his two sons. Micky went to Rugby School, like Rupert Brooke and William Webb-Ellis before him. At Cambridge he captained the University, and when he came down he played for Harlequins, Moseley and among other wandering clubs, the Co-optimists.

He won nine caps for England as a wing-forward in 1947 and 1948 before an injury to his left knee forced him to use crutches for a year and ended his playing career. He was only 23. He quickly moved into administration where he was not hindered by having a double-barrelled surname; remember Poulton-Palmer, Kendall-Carpenter, Cove-Smith and Horrocks-Taylor? Soon he found himself booted and spurred by rugby's establishment.

He became an England selector when he was 28, one of the youngest ever. By 1973, aged 48, he was President of the RFU and about to begin his stint on the International Board. That same year he was invited by the then Minister for Sport, Denis Howell, to sit on the Sports Council. In August 1979 he began a second term of three years on that council. For a time he was secretary of the Barbarians, one of the most famous of all clubs; now he is vice-president.

He could scarcely be more involved in the game than he is, yet his real power-base in the game in Britain is his influence on the two committees that arrange and organise major tours to and from Britain. He has been chairman of one of them, the Four Home Unions Tours Committee for three years. The other committee is, confusingly, called the Committee of Home Unions. This early January day Steele-Bodger was in London to attend to some domestic RFU business. As a past President of the RFU he was one of the 50-plus members of the RFU's main committee who had been called to a special committee meeting at the Hilton Hotel. The main subject to be discussed was whether to support the proposed tour of South Africa by the British Lions in the summer of 1980.

Arguments for and against this tour had been raging for months. Normally a manager and coach are appointed at least one year in advance, as were the management of the 1977 Lions tour of New Zealand, George Burrell and John Dawes. But by the midsummer of 1979 no appointments had been made, and the tour of South Africa looked a dead duck. People had other things on their minds.

Ian Botham captured his 100th wicket and shortly after scored his 1,000th run in Test cricket, Bjorn Borg won a fourth successive singles title at Wimbledon, and Severiano Ballesteros won his first British Open—despite bashing the ball all over Royal Lytham golf course. Entranced by these three brave young sportsmen, while also watching closely to see how Europe's first woman Prime Minister was getting on, we all forgot South Africa for a time.

All except the members of the Home Unions and Tours committees, that is. These two committees are among the least known yet the most powerful in British rugby. They are the praeposters of the game in Britain, organising between themselves incoming tours, and outgoing tours by the British Lions to South Africa, Australia and New Zealand. The members of these committees are generally the most senior representatives of their country, often former presidents, and sometimes they sit on the International Board as well.

The chairman of the Home Unions Tours committee is Micky Steele-Bodger. The other English representative is Albert Agar, who sits with Steele-Bodger on the IB and represents Middlesex on the RFU's main committee. On the tours committee these two are joined by Tarn Bainbridge and

Duggie Harrison, former presidents of the RFU. Wales are represented on both committees by Hermas Evans and Gwilym Treharne, Ireland by Harry McKibbin, who was assistant manager of the 1962 British Lions team that toured South Africa, and Ronnie Dawson, who was coach of the 1968 Lions there. Cliff Wilton, vice-President of the SRU in the 1979/80 season, and George Burrell, manager of the 1977 Lions to New Zealand, represent Scotland on these two committees.

Coincidentally the secretaries of both committees are Scotsmen: John Hart, capped once as a wing on the famous day when the Springboks won 44–0 at Murrayfield in 1951, is both secretary of the International Board and of the Committee of the Home Unions; John Lawrence, secretary of the Tours committee, is a former RAF officer, a talented all-round sportsman and chief accountant, and one of three assistant secretaries of MCC.

In the late summer of 1978 many of these men went to South Africa to attend an International Board meeting, and while they were there they investigated the extent of apartheid in South African rugby. They felt there had been significant improvements.

Then in April 1979 the newly-formed South African Rugby Board, now comprising the South African Rugby Football Federation, the South African Rugby Association and the former all-white South African Rugby Board, published a statement. It claimed, among other things, that the SARB comprised all races; that coaching courses for all races were to be organised; that there would be provision of equal facilities and opportunities for players and spectators of all races; and, most importantly, that national teams, including the Springboks, would be chosen on merit from all races after mixed trials, and would be selected by a committee composed of representatives from all racial groups.

Both the IB and British rugby authorities were anxious to get South Africa back into world rugby. "The South Africans have done enough, they've improved their rugby. What more can we ask of them?" was the feeling in Britain, which had, anyway, maintained contact with South Africa. The South

African Rugby Federation's team, the Proteas, had played six matches in England in 1971, the first overseas tour ever undertaken by a coloured team; and England had played the Proteas, and the Leopards, the SARA's team, when touring South Africa a couple of years later. Llanelli, Newport and the North Western Counties were three of the teams that toured in South Africa in the summer of 1979.

All this was sufficient to convince the Four Home Unions committee that the time was right to invite the South African Barbarians to visit Britain. An unofficial approach prompted an enthusiastic response, and in July an official invitation was issued and accepted in principle. By now the South Africans were forcing the pace a little, and some of their leading sports officials had attended an International Olympic Committee meeting in Montevideo.

What seemed to have been overlooked was the embarrassing end there had been earlier in the year to an attempted tour of France by an all-white team from the Transvaal. Local authorities in France refused to allow their grounds to be used for matches, and so the team, which was already in France, had to return prematurely to South Africa. The French Foreign Minister and the Sports Minister both called the tour "untimely".

At the same time the two French ministers set their faces firmly against the proposed tour of France by the Springbok national team in the autumn of 1979. No sooner had Albert Ferrasse, President of the FFR (French Rugby Union) heard of the Government attempts to stop the Springbok tour than he went on television and announced trenchantly: "I refuse to withdraw my invitation to the Springboks because I find it completely wrong that sport should be mixed with politics."

As the FFR and the French Government angrily faced up to each other, the announcement of the South African Barbarians eight-match tour of Britain was made. The story broke over a quiet August weekend. Some of the key paragraphs in the announcement were: "Racial discrimination is rejected by a majority of people in these islands and sportmen, including rugby players and administrators in the

UK and the Republic of Ireland, are no different in that respect. However, over the years the Home Rugby Unions in their relations with South Africa have adhered to a policy of 'continuing contact', firmly convinced that internal changes in the administration of the game in South Africa would be more likely to come from communication between men of goodwill rather than from threats and isolation.

"There is now evidence that this policy has achieved the desired effect and ... in recent times teams from the Home Unions have played against multi-racial sides in South Africa, and this invitation to the South African Barbarians is extended in recognition of that fact and of the enormous advances which have been made in South Africa in the organisation and playing of the game.

"It is believed that unless this progress is more widely recognised outside South Africa, the playing experience and advancement in the game by all players, particularly the coloured and black players, will be adversely affected."

The tour created a problem for Hector Monro, the Minister for Sport in Mrs Thatcher's new Conservative Government, which opposed sporting contacts with South Africa. Monro, 56, a former flanker and forward for the South of Scotland, and now MP for Dumfries, had managed Scotland's tour of Australia in 1970 and was President of the Scottish Rugby Union in 1976. His protests were ignored and at the same time Dr Danie Craven announced with some jubilation that he and Albert Ferrasse had reached an agreement that the Springboks would tour France.

This was not to happen. The French Government moved fast and firmly, making it a requirement that from 1 September all South Africans had to have visas to enter France. When the South Africans duly applied for these visas they were turned down. Said the French Foreign Minister, Jean-Francois Poucet: "Apartheid is seen by black Africa as a grave affront to dignity. This is not a question of politics but a fact of life."

In Britain, meanwhile, the Sports Council threatened to cancel their annual £200,000 grant to the RFU and Hector Monro raged against the Barbarians' tour. "It has many inflammatory overtones and I intend to do all I can to discourage it from taking place," stormed the Minister. Monro was worried at the prospect of violent anti-apartheid demonstrations similar to those that had marked the Springboks tour of Britain ten years earlier and also that the tour would flout the Gleneagles Agreement which was an accord, signed by Commonwealth Heads of Government in 1977, discouraging sports contacts with South Africa. He was also concerned that to allow a South African Barbarians tour of Britain and then a Lions team to tour South Africa could force a confrontation with Russia over Britain's participation in the Olympics in midsummer 1980. He realised it could even provoke a walk-out from Moscow similar to that by nearly 30 African countries on the eve of the Montreal Olympics in 1976.

Monro called the tour "ill advised" in a letter to the rugby authorities, but received a dusty answer. HART, the Halt All Racist Tours group, and SANROC (South African non-racial Olympic Committee), another powerful anti-apartheid movement based in London, promised demonstrations against the tourists; and a resolution deploring the contravention of the Gleneagles Agreement was drawn up by John Disley, the former British Olympic athlete and a vice-chairman of the Sports Council.

The rugby authorities were unmoved by this criticism. They had made their decision after hearing reports from those teams that had visited South Africa during the summer. Middlesex and Surrey were two such. Indeed, Middlesex had drawn 28–28 with a multi-racial Barbarians side containing six coloured and black and nine white players. John Hart of the Committee of the Home Unions, said "The tour can demonstrate that South Africans now play rugby together, no matter what colour they are. The causes that provoked anti-apartheid demonstrations during the 1969 Springboks tour have now been removed."

Opponents of the tour simply didn't believe this. They were irritated at what they considered the obvious cosmetics of a party consisting of eight whites, eight blacks and eight coloured. "... that the Barbarians' team will consist of an equal number of whites, Africans and coloured is surely ample evidence that ethnic consideration and not merit will receive priority in selecting the team," wrote Sam Ramsamy, the chairman of SANROC, in a letter to the *Guardian.* The Liberal leader David Steel called for the cancellation of the tour and described the team as a travesty of sport and merely "window dressing".

Donald Woods, former editor of the *Daily Dispatch*, an outspoken anti-authority newspaper in South Africa, who was banned and then escaped to Britain, laid into the rugby authorities as well. He suggested that it was naive to believe that sport could be separated from an apartheid society and . . . "Sports apartheid will not disappear in South Africa until all traces of racial discrimination are removed from every aspect of life in that country. And that can never happen under a white government," wrote Woods in the *Observer.* "No white government in South Africa could hold on to its power base while dismantling the entire apartheid structure on which the powerhouse is founded."

In Britain, the Conservatives refused to go any further than expressing their concern at the tour. The Irish Government, however, brought pressure to bear on the IRFU, and eventually the invitation to the Barbarians to play two matches in Ireland was withdrawn. This was not surprising. Some years earlier an Ireland hockey international had been refused permission to tour South Africa by his employers, the Irish Army. And later, those candidates for the 1980 Lions tour who worked for the Irish Government, including second-row forward Moss Keane, were not to be given permission for their names to go forward for selection.

By mid-September the anti-apartheid groups had laid their plans for disrupting the South African Barbarians' tour, relying mainly on volunteers from the National Union of Students. The first game was due to be played against Devon in Exeter on 3 October. One of the ploys they planned was to release rabbits on the pitches. This brought the heated reply from John Lawrence, secretary of the Tours committee who was travelling with the Barbarians: "If they release rabbits we'll release ferrets." This in turn brought Lawrence a wigging from the local branch of the Royal Society of Prevention of Cruelty to Animals.

Even in South Africa not every one welcomed the tour. South African Kevin de Kerk, who had been capped eight times for the Springboks and would have been the most experienced member of the Barbarians team, withdrew at the last minute. "When you are unwelcome in someone else's house you don't go barging in," said the big second-row forward.

Another opponent was Cuthbert Loriston, President of the South African Rugby Federation for 20 years. "I don't agree with the composition of this party," Loriston told the *Guardian*'s John Rodda. "Teams should go from South Africa on merit, which would mean that this one would be all white. I did not stop our men going, because had I done so it would have been regarded as sour grapes that I am not on the tour party. What should be happening is that the coloureds, blacks and whites should have their own tours. The Proteas tour in 1971 of which I was team manager, helped us develop our game and we've improved a lot since then. But we are a long way behind the whites. Take our forwards. Either our locks have mobility and no weight, or weight and no mobility. Our boys just want to be backs. We've got to develop forwards. Let us go our way and then some time in the future a South African national team picked on merit can go on tour."

The Barbarians party of 24 players, three officials and a team doctor arrived at London airport on Monday morning, 1 October, after a 28-hour journey from Cape Town. Plain clothes policemen mingled with travellers at Heathrow's terminal three, and uniformed officers searched cars entering the access tunnel to the airport. A knot of demonstrators shouted "Racist Barbarians go home," shouts of disapproval that were echoed in an editorial in the *Guardian.* But the *Daily Telegraph* editorialised: "... and like every group of visitors to this country the team deserves our welcome."

A few hours later the engine of the bus taking the team to their hotel in Torquay began to make ominous knocking noises as it travelled down the M4. No sooner had the driver pulled on to the hard shoulder to search for the cause than the entire bus burst into flames and black smoke rose into the sky. The players jumped out of the doors and windows and John Lawrence, who had got out and then climbed back in to retrieve his coat, slung a parcel out of a window. It shattered on the road outside and two bottles of best Scotch trickled over the road. Other losses were small: a movie camera, a typewriter, and Lawrence's address and telephone book.

Dr August Cohen, the team's doctor, was just wondering whether to scramble through the emergency exit and risk aggravating an old back injury, when he had his mind made up for him. The giant second-row forward Hennie Bekker picked him up bodily and threw him out of the half-open window. Sabotage was ruled out when it was discovered that a piston had broken and caused the engine to overheat.

A reserve bus arrived quickly to collect the party, and when it finally pulled into the hotel car park in Torquay, practically the entire staff of the hotel stood on the lawn waving a welcome to the Barbarians while five demonstrators shouted protests.

By a juicy coincidence, the Sports Council were meeting in London that same day to vote on a motion put forward by Paul Stephenson, the only black member of the council, to penalise the Rugby Union for issuing its invitation to the Barbarians. The motion was not carried and Stephenson walked out in protest. But the Sports Council did decide they would regret "any action by governing bodies of sports which contravenes the letter and spirit of the (Commonwealth Heads of Government) Gleneagles and Lusaka agreements." And at this meeting the Council agreed to send a fact-finding mission to South Africa in January 1980.

Attempts were made from the start to integrate the team's three nationalities. On their first night in England six of the eight white Barbarians shared rooms with black or coloured team-mates. The language chosen for coaching was English even though only two of the 24 spoke it as their first language, and even though as a party they often sang in Xhosa, for example.

That first day, manager Chick Henderson held a press conference. "It was hoped to include a couple of black players

In 1979, the South African Barbarians visited Britain. A carefully proportioned group of white, black and coloured players, its composition said its critics proved only that ethnic consideration and not merit was the priority in choosing the team. As a result the tour was subjected to demonstrations, the biggest of which occurred at Exeter on 3 October when the Barbarians met Devon.

MY SON IS DEAD!
TELL THE FREE
WORLD HOW HE WAS
KILLED, AFRIKAANERS

against the Lions in 1974," he admitted. "But the story leaked out and a government minister intervened. Since then we have made a lot of progress and we hope for more from this tour. All our players, black, white and coloured, need the experience of playing in your country. I confess that demonstrators might have had a point when the last all-white Springbok team toured here ten years ago, but not now we have a mixed team."

As time passed Henderson revealed himself to be highly capable at the public relations side of his job. A white South African, he had been born in Johannesburg in February 1930, and at 19 he became the youngest forward ever to represent the Transvaal. Then he went to Oxford University where, in the mid-fifties, he won both a Blue and nine caps for Scotland, marking his name in the record books by scoring a try against each of the other home countries. While in Britain he played for Richmond, Coventry and the Barbarians.

As the opening match against Devon at Exeter approached Henderson and his assistant manager Dougie Dyers, a 42-year-old coloured who worked as a building contractor and had captained the Proteas, worried that their team had been over-matched. Henderson felt that they were about the standard of a London club, yet the opposition included English counties and some of the leading clubs in Wales. As it happened there was little justification for this concern, particularly as they won their first match convincingly.

The police had anticipated there would be enormous demonstrations to coincide with the game at Exeter, on Wednesday 3 October, and had mounted a large security operation. Alsatian dogs were on patrol from the Tuesday and extra police were drafted in from villages and hamlets all over the south-west, to cope not only with anti-apartheid demonstrators but also counter-demonstrations by the National Front who threatened to stage another rally at Camborne where the Barbarians were to play their second match.

By lunchtime on the Wednesday 400 protestors had gathered in Exeter's High Street and were handing out banners, and singing and chanting songs to tunes played on a portable gramophone. The police watched warily from the other side of the road and checked spectators entering the County ground.

John Lockyer, the captain of Devon, received several abusive and threatening telephone calls at his home. Referee Peter Hughes, a dentist in Manchester, spoke to both captains an hour before kick-off and Henderson warned his men that, in the event of demonstrators reaching the pitch, they should avoid any confrontation and walk away if there was trouble. This was unlikely for as the players ran on to the pitch a cordon of 75 police ringed the field, facing the 2,500 spectators. Among the corps of officials and alickadoos in the stand was Micky Steele-Bodger.

Nearly 20 minutes had gone before four demonstrators burst out from the terraces. Two were caught quickly and the other two were removed by the police when they reached the pitch. Rain started to fall and at half-time the Barbarians, who included seven whites, five of them in the forwards, led 18–3. They had scored a lovely try by full-back Solomon Mhlaba, another try by centre Tim Koni and a third by forward Ewoud Malan, all three converted by Errol Tobias, their stand-off. Devon's three points came from a dropped goal by stand-off Neil Thomson.

In the second half the score moved on steadily, the Barbarians going further ahead—they led 27–6 after less than ten minutes of the half—but a late rally by Devon, encouraged by their disappointed supporters, made the final score 27–18. Devon's last two tries, which were both scored by left-wing John Hoskin and converted by Tony Watkinson, came after the Barbarians had lost their hooker Malan, one of their try-scorers, with pulled calf muscles.

Three days later the Barbarians played Cornwall at Camborne and were again shielded from the small group of demonstrators by a large number of police. Thirty anti-apartheid demonstrators had earlier arrived in Plymouth to drive to the game in a hired coach, only to find four members of the local National Front already on the bus and waving sticks. The anti-apartheid demonstrators had to hire cars and vans to get to Camborne.

The tour progressed without any scenes to compare with

The pitch on which the South African Barbarians played Devon in 1979 was cordoned by police but two demonstrators did reach the playing area, only to be promptly removed. The Barbarians won 27–18.

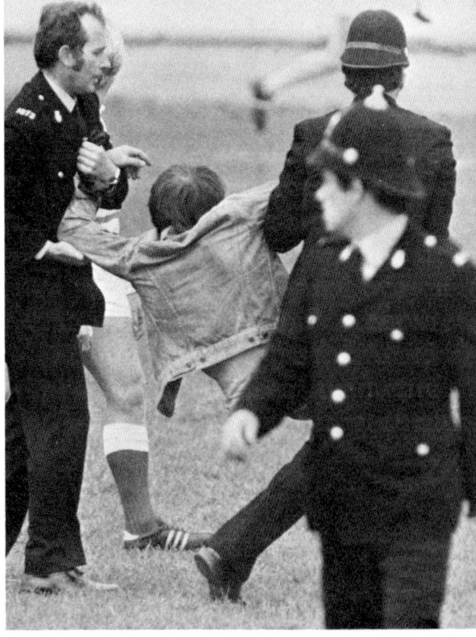

the demonstrations of the 1969/70 Springbok tour, though no game went entirely without incident. At Galashiels in the border country between England and Scotland, 300 policemen were on duty when the Barbarians faced the Scottish border club. A few days later and a few miles away at Hawick, two men got on to the pitch and 300 anti-apartheid demonstrators picketed the ground. Down in Wales, police reported that ¾-inch long roofing nails had been scattered on the pitches of the Newport and Llanelli clubs where the Barbarians were to play later.

The tour ended on 26 October at Newport, where the Welsh club, which had been in a long slump, had a rare victory. The South African Ambassador, Dawie de Villiers, captain of the Springboks on their tour of Britain 10 years earlier, watched the Barbarians go down 21–15. After the game he urged the Lions to go ahead with their South African tour in 1980. "I hope the Barbarians tour will prove to be a turning point in South African sport," he said. "I think a lot of people are getting sick and tired of small groups dictating to sportsmen."

The results of the Barbarians had been better than their manager had anticipated. Of their seven matches they had won four and drawn one against opposition ranging from two of England's weaker county teams to composite sides in Scotland that contained several internationals. They scored 140 points—an average of 20 in each game—and 20 tries.

At their best they were spectacular, capable of missing simple tackles and then retaliating furiously with a blitz of attacks. Against Coventry, for example, they trailed 10–0 within 15 minutes only to rebound and score 27 points in 33 minutes in the second half and eight tries in all. Victory by 41–24 earned them a standing ovation from a crowd of 3,000.

At their worst they were weak, as against the Co-optimists on a slippery pitch at Hawick, where they scored only one try while conceding four. This was their first defeat, and it was partly due to the fact that they could pick only two white players instead of their more normal six or seven. The game was played on a Sunday, and though two more whites came on as replacements others were not available for selection because their religion prevented them from playing on a Sunday.

Just before flying home, Chick Henderson said that his tour report would be strongly in favour of issuing an invitation to the Lions and that he was optimistic that the tour would take place. He felt that as his team had had a relatively quiet tour of Britain the feelings of antipathy towards South Africa were dying down. It was more likely, however, that the sophisticated police methods, which cost the taxpayers and the rugby Unions over £300,000, had ensured the tour's comparative peacefulness.

The Four Home Unions had regarded the Barbarians' visit as a water-testing venture, and its relative success convinced them that there was no reason why they shouldn't continue their policy of maintaining contact with South Africa.

But outside rugby there were many who totally disagreed with this view. The proposed Barbarians tour had been embarrassing for Mrs Thatcher at the Commonwealth Heads of Government meeting in Lusaka in August. Then, when that tour had come and gone, the Foreign Office found themselves just as embarrassed as the Rhodesia conference at Lancaster House dragged on from September to December, and it daily became more clear that the Lions tour was going to go ahead.

Opponents of the tour watched the black nations comprising the Supreme Council for Sport in Africa, who were due to meet in Yaounde, West Africa, just before Christmas, to see what revenge would be exacted on Britain for rugby's unbending attitude. One threat was that the black African countries would boycott the Moscow Games, just as nearly 30 countries had done at the Montreal Games in 1976. Other suggested reprisals included ending all sporting relations and trade in sports good between African countries and Britain.

The committee members of the Four Home Unions were due to meet at the East India and Sports Club on 25 November 1979. Ringing in their ears as they all travelled to the meeting was another loud denouncement of the proposed tour by Hector Monro, who made "a desperate plea" to them to call it off. Also, Sports Council chairman Dick Jeeps had written to the secretary of the Four Home Unions committee suggesting they discuss the possible effect of the Lions tour on other British sport.

As the eight-man committee met in the East India Club that Sunday in November, the betting was that they would stall for time. A decision to tour South Africa had to be unanimous, otherwise the team could not represent the British Isles. Yet there were two clear signs that were thought would cause the committee to delay. The first was that they hadn't yet received an invitation from South Africa. The second was that they had been thrown a lifeline by the Sports Council's decision to send an investigating commission to South Africa in January. Sure enough, after the meeting it was announced that a decision had been deferred.

They were stalling for time and hoping that if they waited then some of the pressure might lift. Whether by good luck or by good judgment this is indeed what happened. The meeting of the Supreme Council for Sport in Africa ended after the Russians had clearly dissuaded the Africans from threatening to mount another walk-out at the Olympics if the Lions tour went ahead. The Russians wanted to get as many of the eligible nations represented at Moscow and they persuaded the Africans to point the rifles of their protests at other targets such as the Commonwealth Games in Australia in 1982. This was, of course, before the invasion of Afghanistan.

At Christmas time each of the four Home Unions reconsidered whether they should or should not approve the Lions tour.

The IRFU had a meeting scheduled for early in January but were so sure of their position that one IRFU committee member said: "I would be more than surprised if the vote were anything other than strongly in favour of the tour." The Scots were just as keen. A few months earlier the President of the SRU, Jimmy Ross, received tumultuous applause when he spoke at an official SRU dinner in Edinburgh "of our interest in playing rugby football against any people, black or white." The SRU did not vote in committee on this subject because it was considered to be a foregone conclusion in favour of the tour.

Greater debates were going on in Wales and England. On 3 January the WRU were due to hold one of their regular monthly meetings, and it was not anticipated that the Lions tour would be brought up officially. "In principle the WRU agreed to tour ages ago," said one committee member. "We'll wait and see what the RFU do. If they vote in favour of the tour they will agree with us. If they vote against it there will be no tour anyway."

As it happened the WRU did vote on this issue and by a small margin decided to support the proposed tour. That left only the RFU.

The 54 members of their committee were summoned for a special meeting at the Hilton Hotel on 4 January. In the weeks before, a number of these committee members were genuinely against the tour. "One can't stampede through the world without taking notice of other people's feelings," said one. "Bridge-building is OK at the right time, but there is no point in building a bridge if torrents of water are going to wash the poor old bridge away," said another. A third committee member who opposed the tour acknowledged the weight of public opinion that had grown up against it. "Two months ago I wanted the Lions to go," he said. "Now I am being affected by other sports and by people who keep saying to me 'Can't you wait?' or 'Must you go?'."

Still, one third of the committee (18 out of 55) were for the tour going ahead. These men had several common themes. "We won't give in to blackmail, never have done, never will do," was one. There was genuine concern at the prospect of ignoring the South Africans, old friends, which was thought to be inconsistent and hypocritical in view of the support by the British for rugby in South Africa over the past ten years. "The South Africans have done everything we've asked them to do in rugby. They're members of the IB. We can't desert them now." Finally there was the dogmatic viewpoint: "I don't think the Russians will allow the Olympic Games to be interrupted in any way. They want it to be their showpiece."

No one was more secure in his own mind than Micky

Steele-Bodger. He had had plenty of time to think about the issues and he had dug his trenches, positioned his artillery. Now he was ready to face his attackers.

That January morning he sat in the International Board Room at the East India and Sports Club, his back to the French windows which overlook St James's Square, and puffed rather nervously at a cigar. "I would be very sorry if anybody lost the opportunity to play sport," he said, resting his head on his hand and allowing his careworn features to settle. "But rugby football was the first sport to invite a coloured team from South Africa to visit this country—the Proteas in 1971. The following year England played representative games against the blacks and coloureds and against mixed sides in South Africa. The managers of those sides that visited South Africa last summer all reported favourably to us. They also said that the blacks and coloureds had asked us to go.

"Basically my tenet is that if sport is left alone it will break down all the barriers that are erected by politicians. If you only play sport against those who are politically acceptable, then that rather narrows the field doesn't it? These days people are saying 'let's hit them through sport.' Sport is the new form of warfare. There are no casualties, it's less expensive and there is plenty of prestige."

Just before the RFU met at the Hilton, John Disley, a vice-chairman of the Sports Council, criticised Steele-Bodger. "Rugby is not a democratic sport," he said. "It is so inward-looking that it is very, very hard for someone like Micky to realise that other sport has moved on from its Victorian base. I think he is blinkered but that is also an indictment of his sport, which is also bigoted."

Despite this criticism, Steele-Bodger was in a breezy mood as he hailed a taxi to go to the Hilton. The letter he had been given by the hall porter was a last-minute request from Hector Monro to reconsider once again the repercussions of deciding to vote in favour of the tour. The repercussions included the almost certain disruption of the Commonwealth Games in Brisbane, Australia, in 1982. Steele-Bodger knew that only the RFU could stop the Lions tour now and as he settled back in the taxi he felt quietly confident that his request for the tour to go ahead would be endorsed by the RFU.

He was quite right. The issue had been resolved so clearly in everybody's minds that, according to one committee member, there was practically no debate at all. "Everyone who spoke just got up and explained why they thought the tour should go ahead," he said. At the end the vote among the 55 members was nearly unanimous in favour of the tour. The RFU President Alec Ramsay explained later: "There is an old and traditional friendship between British and South African rugby, and we decided it was best to encourage their moves by maintaining contacts."

He was asked about the effects the decision might have on other sports, and he said it was unfair to blame rugby people. "The blame should be attributed to countries who don't have the same political freedoms as us, and who do not allow for individual choice by sportsmen. It can't be right to punish rugby for doing something that is perfectly legal. We did what we thought best and it is both a legal and popular decision."

CHAPTER THREE

Picking the pride of British Rugby

The announcement that the Lions' tour was to go ahead was made to criticism and applause that reverberated from Britain to South Africa and back again. British newspaper headlines ranged from "a union of men in blinkers" (*Observer*) to "The Springboks are back to stay—Craven" (*Daily Mail*). Though the majority of rugby followers were heartened, white South African rugby officials, the Tory Monday Club, and Dr Craven were the only ones to welcome the news officially. "It's the fulfilment of a dream," said Craven.

Britain's former Foreign Secretary, Dr David Owen, accused Mrs Thatcher and Lord Carrington of failing to uphold the spirit of the Gleneagles Agreement. Sir Denis Follows, chairman of the British Olympic Association, said rugby had ignored the views of other sporting bodies. And Peter Hain, the long-time campaigner against apartheid in sport, promised further protests to try and stop the tour.

In Africa, Hassan Howa, President of the South African Council of Sport, said he hoped the Lions would not go. He felt that if they did, then the South African sports administrators and the Government would think there had been enough changes and no more would be made. Howa also argued that the concessions made by the South African Government were merely attempts to get their sports teams accepted back in world sport. How could blacks be the equals of whites on the sports fields, only to be humiliated by apartheid once they came off the field, he asked.

In Britain strong arguments were put forward for and against the tour, and *The Times* neatly captured the two extremes. In an editorial on 8 January the paper suggested that "the rugby authorities have set their own narrow interests above what the Government has suggested to be a wider interest, and above the losses that may be sustained by many other sports which hope, unlike rugby, to send representatives from the United Kingdom to the Commonwealth Games in Brisbane in 1982 and to Moscow this year."

After the publication of the Sports Council's report on sport in South Africa, rugby men in Britain felt more justified in their support of the tour. The report suggested that while rugby in the Republic followed the Government line by developing in separate groups it also provided facilities for matches across grouping lines.

And on 10 January, columnist Ronald Butt, writing in *The Times*, sprang to rugby's defence. "If the British Lions are accused of selfishly jeopardizing more important sports, what about their minority rights?" asked Butt. "And what about their conscientious conviction that they are having a good effect on multi-racial South African sport? Why should they come to heel at the Sports Minister's say-so?"

The argument was soon overshadowed by the world-wide repercussions of the Soviet's invasion of Afghanistan and American President Jimmy Carter's subsequent attempts to co-ordinate a boycott by the Allies of the Moscow Olympics. These two events, and the holding of the American hostages in Teheran, dominated the news night after night—and they deflected and obscured much of the criticism that would otherwise have been aimed at rugby's authorities, as when the Lions toured South Africa in 1974. Instead of whether the Lions should go to South Africa, the question was: "Should Britain pull out of the Olympics?"

And so rugby men kept their heads down and turned their attention to the international championship, and to picking the 30 Lions needed for the tour. No more time could be lost in choosing the management. Syd Millar, the burly, genial Irishman, agreed to become manager.

He had initially been asked if he would be available as long ago as June, 1979. His answer then was "No." He was just about to move house, and his children were involved with exams at school. Additionally, he had considerable commitments as managing director of a building materials firm employing 200, the largest sand-producing firm in Northern

Ireland. But in December, when he was approached again, the pressure had eased slightly and he was able to say "Yes."

"I had to ask myself, 'could I afford the time and did I want to do it?'" Millar explained one day early in March. "I decided I could, and yes, I did want to do it. My children understand the demands of rugby. My two boys play, and my wife always used to stand on the touchline. My eldest boy was born when I was in Windhoek with the Lions in 1962. My wife sent a telegram but it didn't reach me for five days. I think she thought I wasn't interested in the news."

You need only glimpse Syd Millar to realise that he had played prop forward. He has the short thick neck and broad shoulders of a man used to playing in the front row; there is a suspicion of a cauliflower ear, too. He is down to earth, tends to look slightly dishevelled, speaks with a hint of an Irish burr, and can be disarmingly charming. He has a distinctive mannerism of putting on his spectacles and then just as quickly taking them off again. "Syd is street-wise," says Andy Ripley, the former England No. 8 who was a Lion in 1974. "He can take care of himself. In my book he is an all-round good guy, one of the best in rugby. Anyone on tour with Syd Millar has a head start."

Millar played 37 times for Ireland between 1958 and 1970 and has considerable experience of South Africa, too, having toured there with Ireland in 1961 and the British Lions the following year and again in 1968. His fourth visit to the Republic came when he coached the brilliantly successful Lions of 1974. They were undefeated in their 22 games and won the Tests 3–0, with the fourth and last being drawn. They were the first visiting team ever to win a full-scale series in South Africa this century. In July and August 1977 Millar was in South Africa again, this time as manager of a Rest of the World party that played a number of celebratory games to mark the opening of the new Loftus Versfeld stadium in Pretoria.

To accompany Millar, Noel Murphy was chosen as coach. Murphy comes from Cork in southern Ireland and with 41 appearances between 1958 and 1969 was his country's most capped flanker until Fergus Slattery edged past him in 1980.

The triumvirate chosen to control the Lions: The captain, Bill Beaumont (*far right*), noted for his stoicism, manners and perennial optimism. The coach, Noel Murphy (*right*), nicknamed "Noisy", gregarious, who comes from Cork and had the distinction until 1980 of being Ireland's most capped flanker. The "street-wise" manager, Syd Millar (*below*), from Northern Ireland, who played 37 times for his country between 1958 and 1970.

Murphy was the obvious choice to be coach. Wales's John Lloyd was just about to start his first season, Englishman Mike Davis had taken over the national team only in March 1979, and Nairn MacEwan's Scotland teams hadn't won a match in the championship since 19 February 1977.

Murphy is a director of Musgrave Ltd, a cash-and-carry firm in the Republic of Ireland with an annual turnover of £60 million. The branch in Cork is typical of their outlets. It sells everything from wines and spirits to furniture and clothes in a vending area of more than 100,000 square feet, with parking space for at least 500 cars.

There are two interesting facts about Noel Murphy. The first is that he is a teetotaller, a wowser as the Irish would say; the second that even among as garrulous a nation as the Irish he is reckoned to talk rather a lot. As a result he has been nicknamed Noisy.

"Noisy" Murphy's wife's name is Noelle and their children (five boys and one girl) are between 10 and 18. Murphy, a Catholic, and Millar, a Protestant, represented a united Ireland. "I said to Syd we're going to be all right," joked Murphy the day the team was announced. "The Lions team was announced on St Patrick's Day and the day of the last Test is July 12, Orangeman's Day. We've got the best of both worlds."

These two Irishmen have some similarities, too. Both are gregarious, Millar played in nine Tests while on tour with previous Lions' teams and Murphy eight, and both had had to cope with questions about the political problems in South Africa. While Murphy insisted on keeping his views to himself, Millar was more open.

"Boycotts rarely work," said the manager. "I believe it is better to say to them 'we are coming to see you' rather than to ignore them. From 1974 until I was last there, in 1977, the changes they made were very radical. Non-whites were playing with whites. Non-whites attended after-match functions and there were blacks at a supper dance I went to in Cape Town. These things sound very small to us over here, but they are very significant over in South Africa."

The selectors had been appointed too: Budge Rogers from

England, Welshman Keith Rowlands, and Alec Harper of Scotland were joined by Kevin Flynn, the Irishman who had scored that dramatic try in injury-time to defeat England at Twickenham in 1972. Millar was chairman and Murphy was on the selection committee, though he had no vote.

As the selectors fanned out to watch the opening matches of the championship, France looked the side to beat following their sparkling 24–19, four tries to two, victory over the All Blacks in Auckland on Bastille Day the previous summer. They had also convincingly beaten Rumania, 30–12, in December, whereas Wales had struggled a month or so earlier against the Rumanians before edging home 13–12 at Cardiff.

The captaincy of the French team had settled on the blond flanker from Toulouse, Jean-Pierre Rives, who has assumed it with the authority and ease of a man donning a favourite old jacket. His team-mates had taken to him so well that they quickly began to play his style of rugby. The game now was to move the ball to the wings, to use every man on the field, and as a result the wings were beginning to score more tries than for years.

Wings in the whole international championship had scored 14 tries in 1973 but only five in 1978. Rives changed all that for France, so that in eight games on tour in New Zealand in 1979 their wings got 11 tries between them, and the backs in all scored 20 out of 23. "The strength of a rugby team is in its 15 players," said Rives, absent-mindedly pulling a hand down through his long hair. "It is ridiculous not to use all 15 players. Some people say to play open rugby is not to win, but I think that to attack and to play open rugby is not to lose."

Rives is the most colourful captain in European rugby, a free-spirited bachelor whose approach to the game is as Corinthian as C. B. Fry's approach to cricket some 80 years ago. A charming host, he made it seem quite natural the day after France had beaten Rumania to drive two visiting British journalists 15 miles into Toulouse from Montauban where the game had been played. Fog blanketed the road and his throaty Alfa Romeo covered the journey sedately, except when he mischievously turned to enquire "Vous prenez le risque?" and then jammed his foot on to the accelerator.

I spent three days in Paris just after the New Year and saw Rives several times. He was keen to practise his English because he had an American girl-friend, and this was the language they spoke to one another. During our conversations he sometimes searched for the right word, tilting his head upwards and looking around. Once or twice he simply couldn't find a word he wanted. "I am sorry," he would say then with a winning smile. "I speak so poor English."

We were having drinks together one night in the Nikko, a Japanese-style hotel on the Left Bank where he stays when he is in Paris. I asked him who he knew in England, who his friends were. He began ticking the names off on his fingers.

"I know Archee Bishop. I sat next to him at a dinner last season and I drink too much. You know him, you know Archee. Archee Bishop of London."

I half nodded, having a feeling that I ought to know this person yet not quite being able to place him in my mind's eye.

"He is a fine man," Rives continued. "He speak better French than I do." It was only some time later that I realised he was referring to the Archbishop of Westminster, Cardinal Basil Hume, a keen rugby enthusiast who had nearly won a Blue to Oxford.

I flew back from Paris invigorated that such charming men like Rives still existed in rugby and wrote in *The Sunday Times* that France's captain was "an Edwardian figure. In his wheat-coloured jacket with its patched elbows, he needs only a pair of pince-nez on his nose to pass for a librarian from his native Haute-Garonne. Over the marble floors of the Hotel Nikko he moves quietly, diffidently, his head slightly stooped forward, his hands often in his jacket pockets. He is excessively polite, gallant and philosophical and, unusually among rugby men, practically a teetotaller. He exudes gentleness and it is no surprise to hear him explain that over Christmas and the New Year he had looked after his cousin's children: 'I sat in a fauteuil and they ran all around me. It was wonderful.'"

France's first opponents in 1980 were Wales who, moving into a new decade, were less sure of themselves than for years. With J. P. R. Williams's emotional retirement at the end of the previous season, the last of their world-famous players had gone. Now flanker Jeff Squire was captain and John Lloyd, the former prop forward, was coach after John Dawes had given up that job to become coaching organiser. Ray Williams, Dawes's brilliantly successful predecessor, was in line to become secretary of the WRU in 1981, and was preparing to spend the season before he took up his new post by organising the WRU's centenary celebrations.

There had been changes at the famous Wales ground as well. The east terrace had been razed during the summer and rebuilt and topping it off was a spanking new scoreboard supplied by a building society—The Principality Building Society, naturally.

Wales had the advantage of playing France there in Cardiff, which was consoling, but their Celtic tendency towards pessimism made Wales's supporters worry about the game against Ireland in Dublin at the end of the season. And with reason, for the Irish had toured Australia in 1979 and won two Tests; Wales were beaten in both Tests they had played in Australia in 1978.

Ireland's confidence was rising, thanks in no small part to the emergence of the tiny, gritty and impishly fast Colin Patterson at scrum half. He scored five tries in seven internationals before Ireland arrived at Twickenham for their opening match of the 1979/80 championship season. The other reason for Ireland's optimism was the kicking of stand-off Oliver Campbell, which was little short of phenomenal. The ginger-haired Campbell kicked 28 of his country's 36 points in their two Tests in Australia and then, just after the New Year, he scored 26 out of 30 points for the Whites in the Irish trial.

The Scots were in the midst of a dreadful run that precluded realistic thoughts of a revival. They hadn't won any of their previous 10 games in the championship, and though there was pace and talent among their backs, which was to blossom marvellously as the season passed, their forwards were callow. They desperately needed the strength, skill and experience of three-times British Lion, Gordon Brown, who had not played for Scotland after returning from the 1977 Lions tour because of a string of injuries.

Who could have guessed that within three months England would beat Scotland and win the Grand Slam? For if the truth be told, England, for all the optimism of their new chairman of selectors Budge Rogers and coach Mike Davis, had looked dreadfully ordinary against the All Blacks at the end of November. One year all but one day after being humbled 16–6 at Twickenham by the New Zealanders, a better England team were beaten 10–9. Two penalty goals in the second half by full-back Dusty Hare took them to within one point of the All Blacks but the trouble was that there was then practically no sign of them overtaking the opposition. England looked dull, unskilful and unadventurous. No wonder their last home victory over New Zealand was way back in King George V's reign, January 1936, in Obolensky's match. Was it, I suggested, that the New Zealanders' desire to conquer, whether it be mountains or rugby opponents, motivated them to play to greater heights than, say, Englishmen?

So the decade ended badly for England and a rotten decade it had been, too. Starting on St. Valentine's Day 1970, and finishing on 24 November 1979, England played 50 games against International Board countries. They won 15 and lost 32, scored 553 points while conceding 738 and they could manage barely half as many tries as their opponents, 57 compared with 103 against them.

An odd statistic is that England seemed to get no noticeable advantage from playing at Twickenham. While Wales were unbeaten at Cardiff in a championship match during the seventies, England had an average of slightly less than one victory each season when playing at home—eight in all. Away from the shadows that Twickenham's huge stands seemed to cast over them, England won seven internationals, defeating, among other countries, South Africa and New Zealand.

Yet the eighties bought new hope, and within three months hundreds of England's scarred supporters gathered outside the changing room at Murrayfield chanting "We want Bill Beaumont." England had made a promising start to the championship campaign by murdering Ireland at Twickenham, three tries to none. Then they carried on for 40 minutes in the same intimidating way in Paris to set up their ultimate victory by 17–13. As France had already been defeated by Wales, the French were now bottom of the table. Ireland, meanwhile, recovered some of their aplomb in front of their own supporters and defeated Scotland 22–15.

Then came the appallingly rough England–Wales match at Twickenham, when Welsh flanker Paul Ringer was sent off for a late and dangerously high tackle on the English stand-off John Horton. According to one count there were eight fouls in 13 minutes, the majority, though not all, by Welshmen. "It was a bloody disgrace," said Welshman Cliff Morgan later. Even the spry Lord Wakefield, who could remember some lively games in the early decades of the century, admitted "It was an absolute shocker." Wales, though down to 14 men after a quarter of an hour, scored two tries, but Dusty Hare kicked three penalty goals, the last, the one that gave England victory, coming in injury time.

While this sordid affair was going on at Twickenham, Scotland and France held a huge crowd spellbound at Murrayfield. With 12 minutes remaining France led 14–4. Then an imp of genius touched Andy Irvine and he scored 16 points—two tries, two penalty goals and one conversion to complete a spectacular turn-around that gave Scotland their first victory of the season and France their third successive defeat.

There was such an outcry the week following the Twickenham game that when Wales played Scotland at Cardiff on St David's Day, even the presence of the Prince of Wales, a daffodil in his buttonhole, could not exorcise the gloomy spirits that haunted the national stadium. Scotland's frail front row, with two and a half caps between them, were crushed by Wales and the problems spread outwards like ripples. Over 70 minutes had gone before Scotland scored—a scintillating try by Jim Renwick after a move that had begun in their own 25. Nevertheless, the Scots were defeated 17–6.

France ended their season by narrowly avoiding their first whitewash for 23 years. Had Ireland won, it would have been their first victory in France since 1972. As against Scotland, the French squandered a 10-point lead but this time two tries by Gourdon, a conversion and two penalty goals by Aguirre and a dropped goal by stand-off Pedeutour saw them home by a whisker, 19–18. It was Toto Desclaux's last game as coach, and it was probably Jean-Pierre Rives's most disappointing season. The French forwards hadn't played well and the team had suffered from contrary decisions by the selectors.

What a contrast there was now between Rives and Beaumont. Rives, on his 27th birthday on New Year's Eve, had been the captain of the moment, leading what was expected to be the team of the championship. Beaumont's team, meanwhile, were struggling to get over that defeat by New Zealand and seemed to be cast yet again in the role of gallant losers.

In defeat, Beaumont won many friends. Men admired his stoicism, his manners and perennial optimism. "Never mind, one of these days we'll show them," seemed to be his explanation for another unconvincing England performance. And his politeness and rather doleful, battle-scarred face won him the hearts of many women who found his shyness and slight awkwardness compulsively attractive.

By the beginning of March 1980, though, those victories over Ireland, France and, most cherished of all, Wales, had put England under Beaumont's captaincy within sight of every possible record. Beaumont had shown maturity as captain and scarcely anyone anywhere begrudged the big friendly Lancastrian his success.

It was his 28th birthday six days before the Calcutta Cup match and he was physically at a peak: 6 ft 3½ in, broad-shouldered and slim-waisted. His neck measured 17 in, his waist 34 in and he took size 11 shoes. Though he weighed 17 stone he had a spring in his step. There was an enviable air of security about him. As well as being about to equal the record of captaining England 13 times he was becoming England's most capped lock-forward, exceeding John Currie's 25 appearances.

Beaumont had been visibly growing in confidence all season. When Fylde played Northampton the week after

England had beaten Wales, he was given a standing ovation as he ran on to the pitch, and before he could get back to the changing room at the end of the game he had to sign hundreds of autographs. "You are much more confident now," his pretty wife Hilary said to him at dinner a few days before the game against Scotland. "You like responsibility, and you've really taken to it. You've become more sure of yourself, and now you have a lot of authority. Those girls at your factory are really frightened of you."

Before the Scotland match England led the table with six points from three victories. Wales came next with four points while France, Ireland and Scotland were third equal with two points. Dreams of glory were forming in Englishmen's minds as their team prepared for the Calcutta Cup match.

Wales set off for Dublin with rather less optimism. Their apprehension was well founded, for they were trounced 21–7. Campbell kicked three conversions and one penalty goal which gave him 46 points for the championship, a record for one season, and Ireland beat Wales for the first time for 10 years. With only two victories, Wales had suffered their least successful season since 1973/74 when they could only beat Scotland and draw with Ireland and France.

On the Friday before the Calcutta Cup, the foyer of the North British Hotel in Edinburgh was packed. Five of England's selectors and Mike Weston's attractive wife squeezed into a booth in the basement restaurant for a long leisurely dinner. Later Weston was to refuse all drinks, saying "Thanks, no. I want to keep a clear head for tomorrow. It's going to be a great day."

And he was right. The speed of the game was breathtaking, the sportsmanship marvellous, the quality of rugby above average. England scored five tries and Scotland two to make it the highest-scoring game ever between the two rivals. Even the most dyed-in-the-wool Scot would have raised his bonnet to Beaumont's men. England's right wing John Carleton scored two tries and left wing Mike Slemen one within the first 30 minutes. With Hare converting two, England led 16–0. It was the Ides of March and a slaughter was imminent.

In the second half the Scots attacked ceaselessly, often from wildly unlikely situations, and in doing so they took the capacity crowd to the edge of their seats, up on to the tips of their toes. Giant Alan Tomes scored a try and then John Rutherford sliced cleanly through, Irvine converting both tries. But with Carleton scoring his third try, England were too far ahead. They retained the Calcutta Cup, won the Triple Crown for the first time since 1960, and the championship for the first time since 1963. Most of all, their four victories gave them their eighth Grand Slam, 23 years after they had won their seventh.

And as the crowds chanted "We want Bill," Beaumont emerged looking pleased though slightly embarrassed, his hair still damp and tousled, and took his place on the team bus. What a transformation from the seventies.

That night, as the celebrations were under way in the North British Hotel, Lions' coach Noel Murphy and selectors Kevin Flynn and a disappointed Keith Rowlands flew in from Dublin where they had been watching the Ireland–Wales match. The next morning, Budge Rogers, looking pale from a tummy upset and somewhat hungover from the champagne, bumped into Murphy. "Congratulations," said "Noisy" in characteristically exuberant tones while pumping his friend's hand. "It couldn't have happened to a nicer bloke—other than me of course." He put his arm around Rogers's shoulders and squeezed hard. Rogers smiled bravely and winced.

As the Lions' selectors met upstairs, Beaumont was wandering around downstairs, accepting congratulations and making arrangements with Hilary for driving back to their home in Preston. He was wearing a check shirt and greyish-green trousers. Crossing one leg over the other and lazing back in an armchair he admitted: "It's a dream, and it hasn't all sunk in yet. A chap in the lobby has just told me that at the start of the season he put a fiver on England and got odds of 14–1. 1980 was our season. Nobody can take that away from us now.

"I think we played our best against Ireland and France," Beaumont continued. "Against the Irish we were the underdogs. They had just come back from Australia where they had won both Tests, and they were very confident. They were going for everything. Our forwards played exceptionally well against Ireland, though I think that perhaps the best rugby of all was the 20 minutes on either side of half-time against France.

"I do resent the slighting of this side. People have made us out to be a poor side and pretty boring, but any team that can score ten tries in four games and 30 points in one match away from home can't be that boring."

Later that afternoon Beaumont climbed into his blue Fiat and drove slowly home. Seven days past his 28th birthday, he was tired and contented. Not only had England won the lot, but under his captaincy the North had beaten the All Blacks and Lancashire had won the county championship. In fact, Beaumont had lost only three games all season, including appearances for his club, Fylde. He remembers thinking to himself that it wasn't bad for a man who had played for Fylde's sixth XV at full-back only eight years earlier. And he was now certain to be chosen to captain the Lions, though the official announcement would not be made until the next morning.

At the start of the season the captaincy had seemed to be between Beaumont, Welshman Jeff Squire and most people's No. 1 choice, Ireland's Fergus Slattery, an intelligent and articulate man who had been a Lion in New Zealand in 1971 and again in South Africa three years later. But then Slattery announced that he couldn't afford to take time off from his thriving estate agency in Dublin, and Beaumont and Squire were free to fight it out among themselves.

Squire, the manager of the Pontypool branch of a building society, led Wales well against France, spurring them just when their spirits were flagging. Then came Wales's defeat by England amid the uproar about rough play, and Squire's chances lessened significantly. They disappeared with Wales's disastrous performance in Ireland.

The only trouble was that Beaumont wasn't everyone's choice as captain. At times during the season his play and his captaincy had seemed to be immature. Critics suggested that he had had an enormous advantage when leading Lancashire, the North and England, from being surrounded by experienced forwards such as Cotton, Neary and Uttley, all former England captains, and in internationals from hooker Peter Wheeler too. And these same critics cited tactical failure against Wales at Twickenham, when England had not stretched the depleted Welsh forwards across the field. But Beaumont had solid support from, among others, the legendary 1974 Lions captain, Willie-John McBride. "It must be someone who has gone through the campaign," said the big Irishman firmly. "I see no need to look further than Beaumont."

Minutes after midday on Monday Micky Steele-Bodger sat down at a baize-covered table in front of two microphones and three television arc lights. Flanked by John Lawrence, secretary of the Tours committee, Millar and Murphy and peering over the top of his half-moon spectacles, he read out the team.

FULL BACKS: B. H. Hay (Scotland), R. C. O'Donnell (Ireland).

WINGS: J. Carleton (England), A. R. Irvine (Scotland), M. A. C. Slemen (England).

UTILITY BACK: P. Morgan (Wales).

CENTRES: R. W. R. Gravell (Wales), D. S. Richards (Wales), J. M. Renwick (Scotland), C. R. Woodward (England).

OUTSIDE HALVES: S. O. Campbell (Ireland), W. G. Davies (Wales).

SCRUM HALVES: T. D. Holmes (Wales), C. S. Patterson (Ireland).

PROPS: P. J. Blakeway (England), G. Price (Wales), F. E. Cotton (England), C. Williams (Wales).

HOOKERS: A. Phillips (Wales), P. J. Wheeler (England).

SECOND ROW FORWARDS: W. B. Beaumont (England) (Capt.), M. J. Colclough (England), A. J. Martin (Wales), A. J. Tomes (Scotland).

FLANKERS: S. M. Lane (Wales), J. B. O'Driscoll (Ireland), J. Squire (Wales), C. C. Tucker (Ireland).

NO. 8's: J. R. Beattie (Scotland), D. L. Quinnell (Wales).

The name that caused a buzz of surprise was that of Colm Tucker, the Shannon flanker. Tucker's sole appearance for Ireland during the 1980 championship was as a replacement in the game against France. But the 27-year-old was a member of the Munster team that had beaten the All Blacks in the autumn of 1978 and had won two caps for Ireland that season. He was 6 ft 1 in and weighed just over 15 stone. If anyone was, he was Murphy's choice.

Tucker, a brewery worker, had come into the reckoning following the withdrawal of England's two flankers, Tony Neary and Roger Uttley. Neary, a partner in a busy solicitor's firm in Manchester, had an unexpected work-load thrust on to him at the last minute and felt he could not afford the time off. Nor could Roger Uttley, whose firm Forward Health had just been taken over. Steve Fenwick, the Wales centre, who had toured with the Lions in 1977, was another significant player who was not available for the tour. He, too, could not afford to take time away from his industrial cleaning company.

Irishman Moss Keane, a Lion in 1977, was not allowed to send his name forward for selection because his employers, the Irish Government, opposed sporting links with South Africa. For the same reason Wigan Borough Council refused to give leave of absence to schoolteacher John Carleton, the England wing, for him to make the tour. So Carleton resigned his teaching post.

Of the 30 players who were chosen 12 were Welshmen, eight English, five Scottish and five Irish. Their average age was 26¾, with Fran Cotton the oldest at 32 and Peter Morgan the youngest at 21. Cotton, Irvine and Quinnell were on their third Lions' tour. Twenty of the 30 had never played for the Lions before and nearly half the party had seven or fewer international caps. Beaumont was the first Englishman to captain a Lions side since Doug Prentice 50 years earlier.

The doubts about the 1980 Lions concerned the two full-backs, both of whom were primarily defensive and neither able to kick goals. Englishman Alastair Hignell, who could, at a pinch, play scrum half or centre, was unlucky. His cricketing skills of handling and throwing have made him the safest defensive full-back in Britain and would have helped him deal with the inevitable hail of Garryowens from South African teams. He could kick, too.

Centre Ray Gravell, capped 17 times for Wales, entered the running when the selectors decided they needed a big man in the three quarters alongside David Richards, Clive Woodward and Jim Renwick who were to provide the pace. Gravell and fellow Welshman Derek Quinnell were the only two who had not played for their countries during the 1979/80 international season.

It did not take long for the composition of the team to spread around the country. Derek Quinnell heard it on his car radio as he was driving to Cardiff and soon made for a telephone to ring his wife Madora. Peter Morgan was told by a friend he met at a garage after he had been training on the beach in Broadhaven, West Wales. And Beaumont heard it slightly ahead of the official announcement because just before noon Noel Murphy rang to tell him.

Once the news was out Beaumont was inundated with congratulatory 'phone calls. At the family's 100-year-old cotton mill in Chorley, Lancashire, where he is sales and marketing director, Beaumont helped man the switchboard to cope with the flood of incoming calls. For hours on end all the lines were engaged. Finally, he made some callers wait while he telephoned Hilary at the school where she teaches, to tell her the news.

He had no respite from the 'phone when he went home that night, nor the next night, and finally he had to take it off the hook. He cast his mind back to the North Western Counties tour of South Africa in August 1979 and remembered the magnificent hospitality, the balmy weather and the people who had said they hoped they would see him with the Lions in 1980.

At that time he didn't think there was any chance of the tour by the Lions coming off and, thinking they wouldn't be in South Africa again for some time, he and Hilary made the most of their sightseeing. They went to the National Women's War Museum in Bloemfontein, looked with a mixture of awe and fear at huge frozen whales at a research laboratory in Durban, and spent some time in a small game park near Pretoria. But then at that time, August 1979, Beaumont would not have thought that England would be about to win the Grand Slam either.

CHAPTER FOUR

An uproar disturbs the Springbok camp

Six thousand miles or so to the south of Britain, the seven South African selectors sat down to choose 60 players for the trials that would mark the start of one of the busiest of recent seasons for the Springboks. A team from South America, the Jaguars, were due to arrive shortly to play seven matches, including two internationals, and to leave the very day the Lions flew in to Johannesburg. The four Tests against Bill Beaumont's Lions would be the first major series in South Africa since the visit of the All Blacks in 1976.

At this eve-of-season meeting the selectors also had to bear in mind that the Springboks hoped to tour South America later in 1980 before rounding off the year with a short tour to France, including two Tests. "We want men who think" said Colonel G. P. 'Butch' Lochner, convener of the selectors. "Men who are able to sum up the referee, their opponents, and conditions on the field, and then be able to improvise."

When the names of the four trial teams were announced there was an uproar. True, nearly half of the 60 players came from Western Province and Northern Transvaal, the teams who had shared the Currie Cup the previous year and, in all, there were 17 Springboks included. But there were also six non-whites, and three of them were considered not good enough to have been selected at the expense of some white players. It was as if the selectors had bent over backwards to try to prove that South African rugby was multi-racial.

In doing so they offended many people. The morning after the teams were announced the *Rand Daily Mail* said angrily: "The Springbok rugby selectors last night violated the principle of merit selection".

Full-back Solomon Mhlaba and another black, Timothy Nkonki, a right wing, and the coloured centre Charles

Williams, had all toured Britain the previous autumn with the multi-racial South African Barbarians. Yet there was a strong feeling that they weren't better players than a number of whites, and simply weren't potential Springboks. As if to support this view not one of the three managed to impress in the trials.

The choice of the coloured players Hennie Shields, a centre, and Nicky Davids, a fast and elusive wing, was welcomed, however, and so was the selection of the best of them all, Errol Tobias, a stocky stand-off who was soon to make history by becoming the first non-white to play for his province, Boland. There was even talk that Tobias might be the next Springbok stand-off.

Tobias had struggled all his life. He was born in Caledon, a township in the Cape Province 150 miles east of Cape Town, in March 1951 and he began playing rugby as a seven-year-old at the township's Holy Trinity School. The pitch was a stretch of weeds and gravel. At first, he played full-back, and after leaving Holy Trinity he worked his way up from the thirds of a club called Progress to the first team. The change to stand-off was an experiment that worked brilliantly.

When he was 20 he was selected for the Proteas, the South African Rugby Federation's team that toured Britain late in 1971, and his development as a stand-off continued steadily though unspectacularly for eight more years. He made his next significant improvement in 1979 on the Barbarians tour of Britain, where his devastating breaks past one opponent after another would often send buzzes of excitement around the grounds. After returning to South Africa, Tobias chased the game's highest honour there—a Springbok jersey—with determination.

He lives with his mother, wife and daughter in a two-storey house he built himself in Caledon. To get to training for his club, province and for the SARFF, he often has to drive 250 miles each week, racing away from his job as a plasterer to travel an hour or more each way. This constant travel and training did not diminish his loyalty for the game in South Africa. "We have a lot of talent in this country and the Lions tour will wake the players up a bit," Tobias said in April. "I think the Springboks have a 65 per cent chance of winning the Test series."

After the trials Tobias was beaten to the stand-off position for the two Tests against the Jaguars, the selectors instead choosing the very promising 22-year-old Naas Botha of Northern Transvaal. Botha had only recently appeared on the national scene, having become the leading match winner and points scorer in first class rugby the season before, and people had only just become accustomed to the pronunciation of his two Christian names—Hendrik Egnatius, "Naas" (to rhyme with pass). In 1979, aged 21, he scored 241 points in first class rugby, 154 of them in Currie Cup games, and all but seven of his first-class matches in this unusual season were for Northern Transvaal. Botha is a gifted athlete who played for his province at softball (a form of baseball), and while at Pretoria University he represented the South African Universities at baseball. But it was the right-footed goal kicking of this tousle-headed, fair-haired young player, particularly his drop kicking, that was to bring him into the public eye and into the Springbok team to play the Jaguars in the first Test, at Johannesburg at the end of April.

The Jaguars were a new name on the international rugby circuit, a band of 22 Argentinians and one player each from Paraguay, Brazil, Uruguay and Chile plus half a dozen officials and five players' wives. They had been invited to visit South Africa to help the Springboks prepare for the arrival of the Lions and were financed by £35,000 worth of sponsorship from the South African Dairy Control Board. Their name, Jaguars, was clearly chosen to show they were different from the Argentinian Pumas, but nonetheless, in both Tests, they fielded a team made up entirely of the relatively experienced and trusted Argentinians. The Brazilian, Pedro Miranda-Cardosa, acquired some notoriety by not playing in a single match on tour because he simply wasn't good enough, but otherwise, the standard of the team was high. They won their first four matches, scoring at least 30 points in each, and they prepared for the first Test with high hopes.

The South Africans, on the other hand, were worried. These were the first Test matches they had played for nearly three years and there was considerable doubt as to the true ability of their team. Yet they were burning for revenge over Britain after being humiliated by Willie-John McBride's Lions six years earlier.

It's history now and there aren't many South Africans who don't know that the 1974 Lions were the most successful side ever to visit their country. McBride's men scored more points than any other touring team and in that 28–9 victory in the second Test gave the Springboks the biggest hiding they had ever had in a Test match.

This time the Springbok selectors prepared more thoroughly, determined to avoid panic changes such as they made in 1974 when they chose 32 players for the first three Tests. They were only too aware that they had been outscrummaged by the Lions in '74, and they had seen on television that the Lions of 1980 would not include many very large men. So they chose one of the biggest and heaviest set of forwards ever to represent their country for the first warm-up Test against the Jaguars in Johannesburg. The eight men, who included two new caps, averaged just over 16 stone, nearly a half stone heavier per man than the England pack, the heaviest in the 1980 Home international championship.

The Springboks made a sprightly start to the Test. In the third minute, as spectators were still settling in their seats, scrum-half Tommy du Plessis scored a try that Botha converted. Six minutes later Botha kicked a penalty. Nine points is a big lead to hand to a team like the South Africans and the only response the Jaguars could make came just before half-time when their captain Hugo Porta kicked a penalty.

The second half was livelier. First came a good try by Springbok wing Ray Mordt, which Botha converted. But then came the ultimate embarrassment for the South Africans, a nation renowned throughout the rugby world for their scrummaging power. At a scrum five yards out from their own line they were pushed back and back until Gabriel Travaglini, the Jaguars No. 8, was able to score a push-over try. The lead was reduced to only six points now—15–9—and the way the Jaguars cut loose in the last quarter that score would have been a fair result.

The sheer weight those big South African forwards were carrying around increasingly became an embarrassment to them. Like clockwork toys running down, they became noticeably slower the longer the second half went on. But with only a couple of minutes remaining Botha kicked upfield from near his own goal-line, two Jaguars over-ran the ball as it bobbled temptingly around, and Springbok wing Gerrie Germishuys darted in, picked it up, and raced 55 yards to score a soft try. Naturally Botha converted it to make the final score 21–9.

A week later the two teams met again in Durban and both had made changes. The Jaguars brought in Juan-Pablo Piccardo in the centre for Loffreda and switched Ernesto Ure to lock in place of Marcus Iachetti. In Ure's place at flanker they chose Silva. The only change the Springboks made was to drop Transvaal strong man Johan Strauss at tight-head, and bring in Daan du Plessis of Northern Transvaal.

There was a crowd of about 35,000 in Kings Park, Durban, and the scoreline of 18–9 to South Africa definitely flattered them. The Jaguars had an astonishing superiority in the set scrums, where they won five tight heads to one, and edged clear in both the line-outs and mauls, but they could not score a try. They just could not make enough of the possession they won.

Botha played a sterile, unadventurous game, not passing the ball until nearly 40 minutes had gone. Yet no-one could really call him a villain. By the end of the game he had kicked three dropped goals, equalling the world record, to make certain of victory. In his first two Tests for South Africa he had scored 26 of his team's 42 points.

"Not good enough, Boks" said the newspaper headlines after the match, and suggestions were made that Beaumont's Lions would have an easy time unless the overweight Springboks could improve drastically by the time of the first Test at Cape Town at the end of May. Critics asked whether Botha, a kicker of extraordinary ability, was the right man to play stand-off. He had, after all, scarcely used his backs at all. Why was it too that the Springbok forwards were so decisively beaten in the line-outs and mauls in the second Test, not to mention the scrums, which they lost by an astonishing five tight heads to one?

Yet despite the general criticism, some experts felt the home team had done well. "No other team in the world but the Springboks would have beaten the Jaguars", said Danie Craven. He added, in a menacing comment to the Lions: "Don't talk until you've beaten us." Another view came from Mark Loane, the Australian back row forward, who has played for his country in Tests in Britain and back home, and who now works in Natal and represents that province. He said: "The Springboks won by nine points in a hard international game. That's good enough for me."

It was to these discordant notes that the Lions flew in to Jan Smuts Airport in Johannesburg half an hour early on Sunday morning, May 4. There was one late change in their party. Andy Irvine, the brilliant Scottish full-back who had been selected as a wing, had failed a fitness test for a hamstring injury and had had to return to Edinburgh.

The loss of Irvine was considerable, for both his attacking play and his goal kicking had been exceptional in South Africa in 1974 and again with the Lions in New Zealand three years later. In South Africa, though playing in only two Tests and 15 games in all, he scored 156 points, including 42 in two games. He was the Lions' highest points scorer ever in South Africa and ran in five tries.

Three years later he played in all four Tests in New Zealand as full-back and in his 18 games he scored 11 tries, five coming in one carefree afternoon against King Country/Wanganui. Another try was as brilliant as anyone could want to see. He caught the ball just on halfway near the right touchline after a clearance kick had missed touch and then ran through the entire opposition to score near the posts. As he trudged wearily back, the entire ground rose and gave him a standing ovation.

In Irvine's absence it was decided to call up wing Elgan Rees of Neath, a Lion in 1977, who was staying at a nearby hotel with the Welsh party who were to fly out to North America the next day. It was rapid promotion for Rees. One week earlier he had been expecting to spend the summer at home after missing selection for the Welsh team. But then Gareth Evans, the Newport captain and another British Lion in 1977, was injured and Rees was hastily added to the party. Having heard of his selection for the Lions, he rang his wife and then his boss in Swansea to check he really could take 10 weeks off work instead of a month. That done, he moved over to the Lions' hotel.

The worry now was that without Irvine the Lions were being unwise in starting a tour with only two recognised international kickers, Ollie Campbell of Ireland and Gareth Davies of Wales.

The 16-hour flight to Johannesburg passed quickly, and after arriving at Jan Smuts Airport where they were met by a few hundred spectators, the Lions were taken to Vanderbijlpark, an industrial town 43 miles south of Johannesburg. They soon realised that coach Murphy and manager Millar intended to work them very hard at the start. Within hours of registering at their hotel on the banks of the river Vaal, which separates the Transvaal and the Orange Free State, Murphy ordered a fierce, hour-long training session under 75-degree sunshine.

New Lions and old gathered in their bright red tracksuits and training shoes, many of them carrying their boots in little red and blue bags shaped like the bum-bags which skiers strap around their waists. There wasn't a cloud in the sky nor a breath of wind to cool them and soon they were all gasping in the thin air. "Take short quick breaths," Murphy would shout as he limped arthritically among his men. "Come on lads, get up off your haunches. Walk proudly." Often Murphy would say to his gasping players: "You mightn't get water during a game, lads. Come on, get going."

By midweek some of the players were looking worn. Monday's and Tuesday's twice-daily sessions had been so fierce that they couldn't eat breakfast or lunch for fear of being sick later on. The training had to be hard, for some of the team had last played six or seven weeks earlier. Murphy realised, too, not only that this would be the last time he would have two complete teams to work with (injuries would affect his future training sessions) but also that this was the

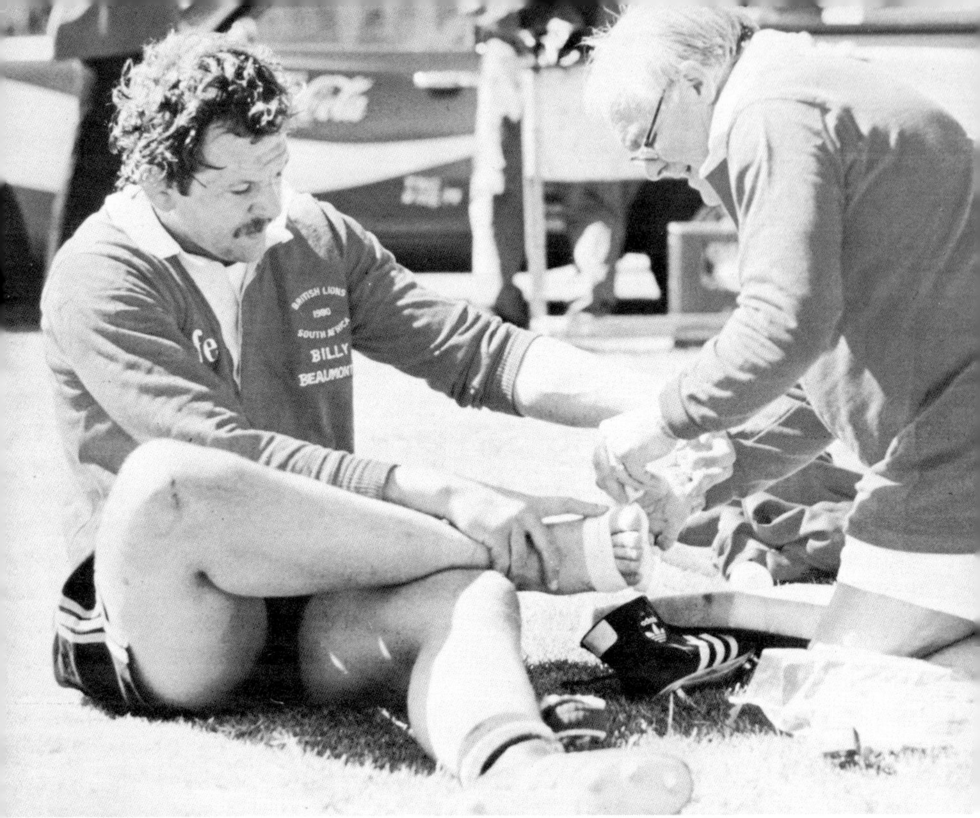

Shortly after their arrival in South Africa, the Lions were involved in a fierce, hour-long training session at Vanderbijlpark, an industrial town 43 miles south of Johannesburg. After the workout, which took place in a temperature of 75 degrees, Bil Beaumont had his feet attende to by the Lions doctor Jack Matthews, and prop forward Clive Williams took a well-deserved drink. The training sessions were unrelentingly hard early on and almost every player lost weight. It was just a well because Eastern Province against whom the Lions playe their first match, gave the visitors a torrid welcome (opposite page), which even the obvious elan with which scrum-half Terry Holmes fed the ball out to a teammate, an Allan Martin and Derek Quinnell reached up at the line-out, could not erase. Within 60 seconds Stuart Lan had suffered a dislocated right knee, the first of a string of injuries that were to plague th Lions on tour. The British Isl won this first match 28–16.

WALK TALL
TEXAN

ONS 3

time when he had to impress himself and his coaching methods on the Scots, Welsh and English players who didn't know him so well as his own Irish players.

He drove them really hard in training, one minute cajoling them with "Well done, lads", the next minute storming at some of them for lack of effort or concentration. On one notable occasion Syd Millar took over the scrummaging practice and gave the forwards a taste of the discipline he had imposed upon his Lions when coach six years earlier. Explained Murphy: "If you've got one of the most knowledgeable men in the world on forward play on your side then you use him, don't you?" adding with a mischievous smile: "There's not much else he's any use for."

The result of this fierce training was that almost everyone lost weight as they sweated under the burning sun. The big forwards shed pounds and pounds. By nightfall they were so tired all they could do was drink cups of tea and sit around the hotel lobby watching the comings and goings of other guests, or playing the noisy gambling machines that were placed just outside the lifts. And, after all that sun, Ray Gravell's nose turned strawberry red. Stroking it tenderly, the Welshman joked "My wife will call me Rudolf—among other things of course."

It was here that Mike Slemen revealed he had thought seriously about turning down the invitation to tour with the Lions. His wife was due to have their second child in September, and early in the year Slemen honestly felt it would be unfair if he was away for so long in the later months of her pregnancy.

"It wasn't that we had had any problems with our first, a boy," explained Slemen, a schoolmaster at Merchant Taylors' Crosby, one night as he chewed biltong (dried meat) at a braai (barbecue) in the grounds of the hotel. "It's just that I would have been worried lest anything went wrong. But then with England getting the Grand Slam, and my own rugby going so well, we decided that I would have to go if I was asked. I'm 28 now and my rugby is very important to me. In the end, it was the wife who persuaded me to go."

On a Lions tour the captain and the management have

their own rooms. Other Lions sleep two to a room, and as they looked around their new homes they couldn't fail to see that the conventional hotel notices were in both English and Afrikaans, as was the Bible that was open on a table in each room. Stuck on each window was a notice that read: "To keep the flying hawhaws (insects) out we advise you to close the window—and turn off the lights."

Each morning the Lions had a choice of two English-language morning newspapers, which both carried front page pictures of them the day after they arrived, and an evening paper, also in English, as well as one morning paper for blacks, which scarcely mentioned the Lions at all. The Lions ate their meals in their own room at the front of the hotel, away from the enquiring gaze of resident holidaymakers, businessmen and autograph hunters; and black waiters stood silently by as the Lions queued up holding out their plates, waiting to be served. Beams of gratitude wreathed the waiters' faces one day when a kindly Lion slipped them some cans of beer.

Training eased off, rain fell, and one midweek afternoon half a dozen players visited several nearby townships. At Sharpeville, 11½ miles south of Johannesburg, they stood on the very spot where the riots had begun 20 years ago.

It was eerie to look at the spot now: a vast stretch of stubbled grass, flanked by a tarmac road with reddish earthen tributary roads running off it. On the other side of this African meeting place were rows and rows of one-storey houses. There are 68,000 registered inhabitants of Sharpeville today (and many more unregistered) and they live in six thousand houses. Not one house has electricity, and all but a handful have running water available only from taps outside. Lavatories, more often than not, are tin pails.

The Lions stood outside the police station for only a moment before they were surrounded by dozens of children who spoke only South Sotho, a language of the Lesotho homelands. John Beattie sidled up to one small boy and slipped two coins into his little hands. The child jumped and shrieked and was besieged by his friends. "I'm sorry, I haven't got any more money," said Colm Tucker as these youngsters good-naturedly ambushed the big flanker on his way back into the bus. "What's goodbye in Afrikaans?" asked Beattie thoughtfully from his seat at the back of the bus.

"Totsiens," some one said.

"Totsiens," the Lions shouted as they waved goodbye.

Then it was time to pack and move on. The lobby of the hotel the Lions were leaving was ringed with red travelling bags that were stamped, in white letters, with "BIRUT to South Africa 1980" (British Isles Rugby Union Team) before the luggage was swept up and taken to the airport. Soon the lobby of the hotel the Lions were arriving at would be similarly ringed with bags, and other residents would have to pick their way through what looked like a temporary and overcrowded lost property office.

In Port Elizabeth the customary cocktail of champagne and orange juice awaited the players as they walked into their hotel, and the papers were full of pictures of the Lions, on front and back pages. A coloured schoolteacher brought 35 of his pupils 500 miles from Cape Town to meet his heroes. The Lions were down at sea level now and breathing was easier as they approached their important opening game.

Eight of the 1977 Lions were included in the team to play Eastern Province and, as tradition demands, the captain was the touring party's captain, Bill Beaumont. He, his second row partner Allan Martin and the entire front row of Fran Cotton, hooker Peter Wheeler and tight head prop Graham Price had played in Test matches in New Zealand (Price in all four) as had flanker Jeff Squire. Behind the scrum Scotsman Bruce Hay at full-back was the only previous Lion. As expected no time was wasted in pairing Terry Holmes, the powerfully built Welsh scrum-half with Ireland's goal-kicking phenomenon Ollie Campbell. But then at training on the day before the match Campbell withdrew with a nagging hamstring injury and his place was taken by Gareth Davies of Wales, Holmes's partner in the national team.

Eastern Province were dismissed by some as being little more than "a Second Division side" but they gave the Lions a torrid greeting at Port Elizabeth. The sun was glorious, the pitch green and firm, the sky clear but there were many moments of horrid disorganisation and heart-stopping uncertainty before the Lions suppressed a game home side, who scored two good tries and lacked only poise and skills in certain key positions. The question was, was it a Pyrrhic victory?

Both flanker Stuart Lane and Gareth Davies had to leave the lovely grassy amphitheatre within 25 minutes. Lane dislocated his right knee before 60 seconds had passed and possibly had damaged a cartilage. It was to be announced the next day that he would be sent back to Britain and a replacement flanker would be requested. Davies, the dark-haired, Welsh-speaking stand-off who was born just down the road from the great Barry John, and went to the same school, seemed at first to have been more seriously injured. After carving a glorious break between Province's two big centres, and thus creating a try for Slemen on the left wing, Davies was helped off with a suspected dislocated left shoulder. Shades of John himself in South Africa 12 years earlier.

The injuries didn't end there. Eastern Province were disrupted too by having to replace right wing Hermanus Potgeiter, their only Springbok, and centre Hennie Lotz, even though they constructed two fine tries.

The first began with a strong run down the left wing by replacement Tino Kankowski followed by a quick heel from a ruck 20 yards from the Lions' line. Then Province, with the full width of the field at their disposal, swung the ball smoothly down the back line, made the most of the arrival in the line of full-back Hannes Pretorius, and created space for Heunis to score in the corner.

At half-time Lions led 21–10, which gives you some idea of the frantic pace of the opening 40 minutes. Three tries came in the last 18 minutes of the half. By the final whistle each side had scored a further try and the Lions had widened that margin by one point. But if it sounds a convincing victory then it most certainly was not. It was ragged, at times disorganised and only occasionally did Province allow the Lions to show any signs of class. Province went close to scoring at least three times in the second half. It was all so far removed from the highly organised, well disciplined practice the Lions had been doing all week.

Bruce Hay at full back was buffeted from pillar to post, teased by some fine kicks by Province's stand-off Gavin Cowley, forced into errors and at other times pressurised so hard, once by Potgeiter, that he was lucky to get the ball away at all. Elsewhere in the first half passes were being dropped and players caught in possession.

By the time Davies left the field, after 25 minutes, he had personally set the Lions on their way to victory by scoring one conversion, two penalties and a dropped goal. It was only his second game since the beginning of March, but he nevertheless looked calm and practised. When he went off Peter Morgan moved in to stand-off and Jim Renwick came on as centre. Morgan gained slowly in confidence after starting badly by having a kick charged down and slicing two left-footed kicks.

Eastern Province wheeled the Lions consistently, a disturbing practice, and one that had happened in New Zealand in 1977. On occasions the back row of Jeff Squire, Derek Quinnell, who replaced Lane, and big John Beattie, had an inordinate amount of work to do. It was as well that Squire had looked so sharp in training and played so well, and that Quinnell, who only two days earlier had been unable to train because of a suspected hamstring injury, could turn in such a fiery and spirited game. And Beattie was impressively bumptious in his first game for the Lions, once picking the ball up from a maul and racing earnestly 20 yards at Gavin Cowley, his shoulder down, his face set in fierce determination.

After half-time Eastern Province found themselves being slowly ground down. There was a flurry of tries, one by Rees after a neatly-timed pass from Morgan. Then came the reply, two minutes later by the big, strong centre Dennis Campher. Head down, he charged over from 10 yards out, brushing aside Morgan's tackle.

Now the margin was only nine points and any lack of concentration like those in the first half would have been disastrous for Beaumont's side. But now they settled in a rhythm, slowing down the pace and driving away from line-outs and mauls. They conceded nine penalties in the second half, while receiving six, and, as the end approached it was

Renwick, with a beautiful kick from 45 yards, who took the Lions far out of reach.

There was still time for Thys van der Merwe, the home side captain, to have a run at the line and only a sturdy shoulder charge by Terry Holmes on the flanker saved a try. The danger still wasn't over. Burger won the first line-out, Human the second but time and again Squire or Quinnell or Beattie or Holmes managed to stop them as they strove to drive the five yards to the Lions' line. Now, at last, the Lions' defence was firm and they won 28–16, three tries to two.

As they celebrated their first victory of a new decade, the Lions cast their minds back over their first week in South Africa. Sharpeville haunted some of them. To say they found it both interesting and yet depressing would be an understatement of British proportions.

They remembered the words of prop forward Phil Blakeway, who was scheduled to play his first game for the Lions the following Wednesday. "Do you know about punk rock?" Blakeway, already cast as one of the team's jokers, asked an attractive, tanned lady at a cocktail party to celebrate the Lions' arrival in Port Elizabeth. "You do? Our manager is one. We call him Syd Vicious."

That Saturday night Millar was not so much Syd Vicious as Syd Relieved. After all, as he pointed out after the game and amidst some stern criticism, the Lions *had* won.

CHAPTER FIVE

A visionary voice in a troubled land

He is nearly 80 now, a small vigorous man who speaks precisely and clearly in a rich voice. His shoulders are slightly rounded, as much from hours spent reading and writing as from old age. He is keen and alert, cock sparrowish almost, with a slightly stern face that sometimes cracks open as an unexpected shaft of humour breaks through.

"I am supposed to be presenting the sash at a debutantes' ball tonight," said Alan Paton, speaking slowly and staring out of a window. "This ball is very largely Indian and I thought I would at least be asked to kiss the girls but the programme has arrived and it's not down. I intend to complain very strongly."

The author of *Cry the Beloved Country* was talking in the study of his home just inland from Durban. "I used to play rugby," said Paton, shaking his head so that waves of his silvery hair jumped down on to his forehead. "I used to play scrum-half. I was never very good. I was in the second XV at school and university, that sort of standard, but when I joined the Liberal Party in 1953 I made my decision to boycott rugby. I decided not to attend another rugby match until there were equal opportunities for all races in South Africa."

"Would you like to come and see the Lions play Natal tomorrow?" we asked him, offering to get a ticket. He seemed quite keen at the idea. "I recognise the improvements that have been made although I don't think for one moment that we have reached a complete change in the country's sporting policies." He sat quietly for a moment, pondering our offer.

"I'll have to make a telephone call first," he said, hustling out of the room.

Above the slight buzz of traffic on the Pietermaritzburg to

Alan Paton, nearly 80, whose book *Cry the Beloved Country* appeared to world-wide acclaim soon after the war, watched his first live rugby match for nearly 30 years when the Lions played Natal, beating the province side 21–15. He used to play rugby, as a "never very good" scrum-half but resolved, when he joined the South African Liberal Party in 1953, to boycott the game and not attend another rugby match until there were equal opportunities for all races in South Africa. Persuaded by British visitors to attend the game against Natal, he did so, he said, because "I recognise the improvements that have been made although I don't think for one moment that we have reached a complete change in the country's sporting policies."

Durban road we could hear him talking in an adjoining room. Then he came back and sat down behind his desk.

"That's all right," he said, looking pleased. "I've got a ticket thank you very much. I'll be there."

And so Alan Paton watched his first live rugby match for nearly 30 years. Natal, his province where he had been born just after the end of the Anglo-Boer War and had lived the major part of his life, forced the Lions to a thrilling finish. With six minutes remaining the Lions led 15–9. Natal scored a magnificent try that was converted and then, in injury time, the Lions scored another try for victory by 21–15.

Alan Paton's study is clogged with the artefacts of a public figure and writer. Newspaper and magazine cartoons hang on the walls and several of the shelves behind his desk contain only copies of his own books—*Apartheid and The Archbishop. Too Late the Phalarope* and *Hofmeyr*, his biography of Jan Frederick Hendrik Hofmeyr, the man who seemed certain to succeed Jan Smuts. The room is cool, dark and blessedly quiet.

It was soon after the war that Paton's first book, *Cry the Beloved Country* appeared to world-wide acclaim. *The Observer* wrote of its intelligence, simplicity and compassionate sincerity. "Alan Paton has thought deeply and impartially and has put his heart into this subject but he has made it bigger than argument or emotion; I don't think you will soon forget the resigned sorrow of its closing pages."

At that time Paton was the principal of a reformatory school for black children just outside Johannesburg. It was, he recalls now, the most terrible place he had ever seen. In the 11 years he was in charge he introduced graduated freedom, as it has been described, pulling walls down and allowing boys who had proved themselves trustworthy to have free access to the adjoining 900-acre farm. To the best behaved of all, he granted permission for them to visit their homes. It was a highly successful experiment. Out of every hundred, all but a handful of these poor black children returned on time and those who didn't, who were late, turned up sooner or later.

But following the election of the Nationalists in 1948, Dr

Hendrik Verwoerd, then Minister of Education, abolished the whole school. Paton now talks with contempt of the introduction of laws that were to become cornerstones of Nationalist policy. The law preventing mixed marriages was introduced in 1949; the Group Areas Act, stipulating where non-whites can and cannot live, followed one year later. After Verwoerd had introduced his Bantu Education Act in 1952, Paton realised that apartheid was no mere election slogan but a new and systematic ideology of racial exclusiveness that regarded racial purity as the highest good. He likened the country to a fortress. "Each day, each month, each year the Nationalists make it stronger," he wrote at that time. "They make the walls thicker; they make them higher. Yet in the long view, no one believes that their fortress will endure. Sooner or later it must yield. But till then inhabitants must all be on guard."

There were many long hard years when he was punished for his outspoken and critical views. "Do you know what being banned means?" he asked. "It means you can't even go to your children's birthday party. You can't attend any gathering at all and you must stay in your house from six each evening until six the next morning." He edited a publication called The Long View, which spoke out bravely against the Nationalists. He was president of the Liberal Party in South Africa until May 1968 when it was disbanded under persistent official pressure.

This deliberate persecution of Paton by the Nationalists makes it ironic that Paton should now live in a village that bears the name of that party's present leader, Prime Minister P. W. Botha. Paton lives in Botha's Hills.

These days, he hears and sees changes all around. "I know they are small and insignificant but they are changes. The number of people dying while being detained by the police has dropped since the death of Black Consciousness leader Steve Biko. Look, Doctor Craven is a changed man from what he was five years ago. The Lions coming here will encourage more changes. I believe the Jeeps report was too sanguine but I also believe it's not possible to window-dress in South Africa any more."

These changes had come about, he said, because of three great events in the seventies—the fall of Caetano in Portugal, Soweto in 1976, and what he described as an awakening on the part of Afrikanerdom.

"You know the history of the Afrikaner is remarkable," said Paton, settling back in his chair. "He was knocked into the dust in 1902 in the Anglo-Boer War and he picked himself up. He established his Nationalist party in 1914. He came to partial power in 1924 with Herzog but they came into real, final power in 1948. And there is absolutely no doubt that they intended to build a new heaven." He gave a little smile: "Afrikanerdom has now realised that the great plan isn't going to work.

"What will happen?" he mused aloud. He foresaw several possibilities.

"One is that P. W. Botha will retreat back to where he came from. He has got a very short temper and he doesn't like criticism. Also he has the typical Afrikaner nationalist attitude towards the rule of law. He doesn't regard the law as something of great value that should be cherished at all. It's something that you use at your convenience. But I don't think that Botha will retreat. When a man says at a public meeting, as no prime minister has said in the whole history of South Africa, not even Botha and Smuts and Herzog, that he wants to build a country where there will be safety and security for every child, white, black or brown, then I am prepared to believe that's what he wants.

"The second possibility is that Botha could get himself kicked out by his right wing," Paton continued. "The one thing you mustn't do is break the party. For an Afrikaner the party, the Broederbond, the Church, the language, the culture, they stand above any other value such as the rule of law, the freedom of the press. These are minor virtues and if they interfere with the safety of the *volk* then they must be cleared out of the way."

"The third possibility would be of internal revolution and the taking over by black radicalism. I myself don't see that happening unless the fourth factor comes into operation, and that is outside intervention. If there were outside intervention then the third factor would come into operation very quickly. Within 24 hours I would guess."

We said we'd heard talk of revolution being the only answer and of it being only a matter of time before it came. For several moments he looked out over the neat lawns, the lush trees and down towards the sea. Then he turned back to face us.

"If such a revolution were attempted and there were no outside intervention, it would be destroyed within a few days. It wouldn't stand a hope. I don't say this with pride because it would be terrible. But people who talk like that sound as though they're consumed with bitterness. I understand a person who is consumed with bitterness, but bitterness doesn't help one appraise the situation rationally.

"When I speak of these things I always say 'Look, I can't speak too rationally because I have a love of my country. I want to live there and I want my children and my grandchildren to live there, and this colours everything I say.' Nevertheless I try and be as rational as I can. If you are consumed by bitterness you can't be rational. It's psychologically impossible."

The conversation turned to a new topic. He had just finished the first of a trilogy of novels about South Africa covering the country between 1952 and 1958. He was already at work on the second, from 1958 to 1970, and he said he hoped to be fit enough to finish the trilogy, bringing it up to 1980.

"I'm in a good patch at the moment," he said with some justifiable pleasure. "I did 2,000 words one day last week and I know I'm writing well because I wake up in the middle of the night and construct whole passages. I don't need to get out of bed to write them down. It's so clear I can easily remember it the next day."

Was there a title, I asked? He nodded.

"You know a lot of people come here to see me, people from Sweden, Germany, America and they all say 'But it's beautiful.' And I reply 'Yes it is, isn't it?' I think I am going to call my book 'But it's beautiful.' That's not bad is it?"

It was time to go. He had to prepare for his debutantes' ball.

The sting of the midday sun had gone from the blue-green hills. A servant padded in barefoot to take away the tea cups he had thoughtfully replaced on a tray by the door. Momentarily we gazed out from the verandah outside his study down to the Indian Ocean, which was just visible in the distance 20 miles away. "When we first came we could see Durban almost every day. Now there is so much smog about that we can see it only on very clear days."

"A colour bar," someone joked and he laughed as he led us back through the house and out to our car. On a wall outside the front door was a basket piled high with big rich avocado pears. One by one we signed his visitors book in the hall while he stood by the door and offered each of us one as we filed out. "You must leave them for a few days," he said. "They still aren't quite ripe." We shook hands with the small man and as he walked up to the car with us he flicked his hair up out of his eyes. He was still waving as we drove out through the gate.

CHAPTER SIX

Test for Supermen and a miracle try

As the Lions travelled around in those hot and sunny days of early May, the name that was whispered menacingly at them wherever they went was that of Naas Botha, the South African stand-off. Botha was the latest in a long line of match-winning goal-kickers and, on his own, had become the single greatest threat to the Lions for the first Test in Cape Town at the end of the month.

Botha had reached that elevated position early on. He was 22 in February, and though he had been playing for Northern Transvaal for two seasons he had represented the Springboks only in the two Tests against the Jaguars. It was significant though that in his 59 first-class games for Northern Transvaal, he had been on the losing side only six times. Many of the victories were won by his kicking, which was so good now that he was being cast as the natural successor to the great South African kickers of the past, Okey (The Boot) Geffin, Piet Visagie, Keith Oxlee and, most recently, Gerald Bosch.

Hendrik Egnatius Botha is a little under six feet tall, a slight figure who weighs less than 11 st, and has a thatch of blond hair and a moustache. His handshake is firm though not strong, his voice soft, his manner confident, his English somewhat mangled. He is a dapper sort of man who likes to wear well-ironed rugby shirts and shorts, and off the field he fusses with his watch to keep it in position on his left wrist. He drives as he dresses—calmly and tidily. There is little about him to suggest that he can kick a rugby ball almost as far as anyone ever has, including such giants as the 15 st former All Black Don Clarke.

His punts soar up, up and away, like a well struck golf ball, ending 65, 70 or even 75 yards away. His place-kicks are conventional, struck with the right foot swinging smoothly

The Springboks' amazing kicker Naas Botha in the jersey of the Lansdowne club in Dublin, where he stayed brie
in 1977, and whose drop kicks have been described thus: "It's bang as he catches it and then boom with his foot a
then the ball is gone, climbing, climbing, climbing."

through the ball in the contemporary round-the-corner fashion. Yet he made more of a name for himself with his uncanny ability to swivel on the run, aim and then drop a goal, often in the last minutes, as he did to give Northern Transvaal a draw with Western Province in the final of the 1979 Currie Cup.

In the Tests against the Jaguars, Botha scored 26 of the Springboks' 42 points—nine coming from those world record-equalling three dropped goals in one match, the second Test in Durban. "His drop kicks are so fast," notes former Lions coach Carwyn James. "It's bang as he catches it and then boom with his foot and the ball is gone, climbing, climbing, climbing."

Whether succeeding with swiftly-taken dropped goals or with his measured style of place-kicking, Botha's consistency is remarkable. In his first three games in May he missed only two kicks at goal in more than four hours and he gathered, as a result, 51 points from eight dropped goals, seven penalties and three conversions. Truly he is a Dead Eye Dick, perhaps the most accurate and longest kicker there has been in world rugby for 30 years.

Photographer David Rogers and I went to see Naas at his parents' single-storey house in Terblanche Avenue, Pretoria. The house is surrounded by a garage and lawns where water sprinklers were playing. Suburban Pretoria is stiff with Bothas. Over the hill a half mile away Prime Minister P. W. Botha has a home.

Naas Botha was born on 27 February 1958. He was an outstanding sportsman at the Hendrik Verwoerd High School in Pretoria and before he was 17 he had run the 400 metres in 51 seconds and broken two minutes for the 800 metres. But after his schooldays, he was hampered in his running by an injury he suffered when surfing in Durban. A big wave crashed on to him and left him with a back that stiffened whenever he ran more than a mile or two. Consequently, his training had to be based mainly on sprinting.

As he grew up he was surrounded by the memorabilia of his sports-mad nature and was captivated by his two heroes: Frik du Preez, the giant Springbok second row forward with the speed of a sprinter, who captained Northern Transvaal, and Welshman Phil Bennett. "Frik were a character in South African rugby and Phil is the best fly half I have ever saw," Botha explained, scrambling his syntax, as he spoke in a slow soft voice.

He was living with his older brother Darius, his father, who had a heart attack a few years earlier and was by now in retirement, and his mother. His life is dominated by sport. In addition to his rugby, his baseball and his softball prowess, he gives tennis lessons at the university of Pretoria, where he is studying physical education and psychology.

Having visited North America in January 1980 he was planning to return to University there on a sports scholarship, preferably somewhere warm like Florida. First though, he had to get his BA from Pretoria University, and then do the compulsory two years' national service.

When we met him he was wearing the familiar red, yellow and black jersey of the Lansdowne club in Dublin, where he had stayed for a month in 1977. He remembers watching Tony Ward and Ollie Campbell play in an Irish trial and, on that same trip, his brother Darius, normally a wing, packed down in the second row for Lansdowne alongside Moss Keane, the Irish international and 1977 British Lion.

Naas disappeared into a room at the back of the house for a moment before he reappeared carrying a handgrip and several footballs and with a pair of blue and white beach sandals on his feet. We drove in his white Datsun 1600 to a nearby field and for 15 minutes he practised his drop-kicking and place-kicking. He was very precise in his movements. He kept his head well down, swung his right foot back slowly, and then followed through smoothly. For once, though, he was less than accurate by his own high standards. He succeeded with only two out of five place-kicks and missed all three drop-goal attempts.

Back in the house Botha settled back on the sofa, swung his left leg over his right, and began to talk. Phil Bennett influenced him so much with his pin-point punting that Botha copied the style of the little Welshman. "You mustn't lean forward like this," he explained, getting up, picking up a new ball and swinging his right foot at it. "You must keep your head back to get the ball in the air and give it distance. That's when you get your leg straight and the way you get power from your thighs.

"It's all a matter of timing," Botha continued. "If your style is right, then your timing is right. Some guys is throwing the ball here," and he held the ball to his left, "and is leaning over his body and kicking like that." He jackknifed himself forwards and sideways. "That's wrong." He moved the ball down nearer his feet. "You must put the ball down and pull back."

As he prepares to take a place-kick Botha carefully lines up the ball at the posts, aiming the stitching slightly towards the right upright. He always stoops rather than crouches over the ball. Then he walks back, at the most five or six yards, more often only two or three, turns and runs up to the ball. He believes it is crucial to the success of his kick that he points his left foot at the posts. If he put it down pointing in any other direction he would off-balance himself. "The other guys don't know it, but I think that's one of the main things of place-kicking," he says. "If your left foot is not just so, then the ball just doesn't go to the posts. I am working on that this year, and I think that's why I am kicking better. I'm kicking further and more accurately."

South Africans generally greeted their new prodigy with acclaim for his kicking but with reservations about his passing and his tactical brain. Tommy Bedford, the former Springbok forward, who had seen him play on 10 occasions by mid-May, ruled: "He may be very capable, and he may be under orders, but I have only once ever seen him do anything other than kick. There is no evidence so far that he can run with the ball." Gerald Bosch, Botha's predecessor in the green and gold colours, added: "He has got the potential and he's a match-winner, but in the Durban Test (against the Jaguars) he missed touch 11 times and that is unforgivable. Under pressure he was weak, too, and he let the ball out when his centres were in trouble."

We left Botha in the late afternoon as dusk was gathering. He had been a considerate host, driving us around in his car and serving us tea when we returned to his parents' house. As we drove off, he hurried out of the house carrying a bag of kit. He was going to a Pretoria University practice. He gave a cheery toot on his car horn and was gone.

The Lions had meanwhile settled into the Elgro Hotel in Potchefstroom, a small town south west of Johannesburg. Those who had been in New Zealand three years earlier were struck by the likeness between this hotel and the ones they had stayed at in 1977. The Elgro was no more than four storeys high, had a couple of bars, a small reception area with the hotel switchboard just behind, and a large dining room on the first floor. When the Lions' party arrived almost all the rooms were taken, the switchboard whirred continuously with international calls, and the staff hurried thither and yon under considerable stress.

Peter Wheeler said one night in the bar: "We don't seem to have as much time to ourselves as we did in 1977. Perhaps it's because the places we are staying in are bigger and there is more to do. In many of the small towns in New Zealand all we could do was to go into the bar and drink—'specially as it rained so much."

The conversation moved to South African players and, particularly, the very fast flanker, Rob Louw. Someone recalled how Louw, when playing for the South African Barbarians in Britain, had picked the ball up in his own 25 and raced three-quarters of the field to score a brilliant individual try against Coventry. Wheeler cut in quickly. "Coventry always are a bit vulnerable to that tactic though," noted the Leicester captain amid roars of laughter.

The game at Potch against a South African Invitation XV was the Lions' fourth of the tour. Slowly they were improving and victories in their opening matches over Eastern Province and the South African Rugby Association had been followed by an encouraging first-half against Natal in lovely Kings Park. But the Lions fell away after half-time against Natal, in the 80 degree heat that shimmered over the Indian Ocean, and it was 15–15 as the game entered injury time. Forty thousand spectators banked up in tiers around the pitch as in a Roman amphitheatre, sensed a draw and roared their hearts out, but then the Lions' stand-off Ollie Campbell, the whey-faced Irishman playing his first game of the tour, set up a move that ended with John Carleton darting over for a try in injury time.

As had become the pattern already, this victory was achieved only at a cost. So far it had been one injury each game. Davies (dislocated right shoulder) and Lane (torn ligaments in right knee) were the casualties in Port Elizabeth. Phil Blakeway's ribs, injured in England's game against France in Paris in February, hadn't had time to mend and were broken in East London and now, two days after the Natal game, Campbell's troublesome hamstring finally gave way again at training.

More injuries were to come, yet already the 1980 Lions were being branded as one of the most unfortunate of all touring teams. The only piece of luck that came their way during these opening weeks was the announcement of a change in the tour's agreement. Now any number of spare players (known either as replacements or supplementaries) could be flown out from Britain if it was felt that injuries were placing too great a demand on other players. It would be possible therefore for a player to join the team, play a few games and then return home. On all previous tours, once a replacement had arrived then the injured player was off the tour and, in most cases, would go home.

At Potchefstroom Syd Millar was negotiating for two replacements, a prop for Blakeway and a stand-off for Campbell. Lane's replacement, Welshman Gareth Williams, had arrived while the players were still in Durban. It soon became known that Wales's reserve tight-head prop, Ian Stephens of Bridgend, was on his way from North America, where he was touring with the Wales team. A round-faced, barrel-chested man, Stephens had worked as a casemaker for a firm in Taff's Well, Gwent, but he had resigned just before flying out with Wales and he arrived in South Africa after his hectic journey with no job, few prospects, and a proud but anxious wife and two children back home.

The other replacement was Tony Ward, the dark-eyed Irishman who had been Campbell's predecessor in Ireland's team until he was spectacularly unseated during his country's tour of Australia in 1979. Ward, who owns and runs a sports shop in Limerick, had played nine internationals, scored in every one in totalling 77 points, and been nominated as Britain's Player of the Year before his demise.

Neither Stephens nor Ward would be ready to play his first game for a week, and in the meantime Millar organised his team for Potchefstroom under the captaincy of the piratical-looking Welshman, Derek Quinnell. The big No 8 had begun growing a beard, only to shave it off a few days later as the first tufts appeared. Quinnell, who was nicknamed Sloppy on the 1971 Lions tour of New Zealand but was now known more often as DQ, was proving himself to be an inspiring leader. When captain, he had scored two tries the previous week, making him briefly the team's leading try scorer. Nobody knew just how inspiring he was going to have to be for the fourth game.

The Invitation XV was packed with potential Springboks. The captain was 29-year-old Wynand Claassen, an architect who spent his spare time oil-painting and sketching and had captained Natal against the Lions. His team had practised together on the Monday before the match and a number of them were bidding for places in the Springboks' XV for the first Test. The leading Test candidates among the backs were the centres Hennie Shields, the coloured player, and David Smith, who played for Zimbabwe, and the tiny scrum-half Divan Serfontein, who had toured Britain with the Barbarians. In the forwards there was the hooker Willie Kahts, tight-head prop Martiens le Roux and the menacingly named Transvaaler Moaner van Heerden at lock, while No 8 Thys Burger was this time playing on a flank.

Long before the kick-off Olen Park buzzed with anticipation. The South African selectors were there, and able to see Clive Woodward go through a little routine of wiping his hair back into place and talking to the ball before he kicked at goal. Most times it worked, for he finished the game with one conversion and four penalties. The game was also notable because when the Invitation side went ahead 6–3 in the 24th minute it was the first time the Lions had been behind on tour. It was a switchback sort of game and before the end the Lions trailed four times. There were moments when it seemed certain they would fall to their first defeat in South Africa for 12 years. But then, with less than 10 minutes remaining, they began a movement that ended with them scoring one of the most talked-about tries of all time to snatch a memorable victory.

The move began ordinarily enough with a throw-in at a line-out by hooker Kahts. John O'Driscoll palmed it back from the end of the line-out, and scrum-half Colin Patterson, who had a brilliant game, spun it away to David Richards, who darted upfield. Flankers O'Driscoll, breaking from the line-out, and Gareth Williams were in support and when they were stopped Quinnell eventually got the ball away and Patterson took it to the left to Richards, who missed out Woodward to get the ball more quickly to Mike Slemen on the left wing, and full-back Bruce Hay.

Hay was caught by scrum-half Serfontein, another ruck formed and again Patterson got the ball back. This time Richards moved play to the right, on to Woodward, to Quinnell, to Renwick and finally to Rees out near the touchline. Rees's path was blocked 30 yards out, so he cut infield and was stopped on the 25. For the third time in this single movement Quinnell was at hand to dig the ball out, this time seemingly from half the opposition's forwards.

Patterson moved to the left, towards the main grandstand, passed on to Richards, on to Woodward, who ran to his right and then raced back left before being tackled by left-wing Timothy Nkonki, one of two non-whites in the Invitation XV.

Slemen pounced on the loose ball as a man pounces on his hat after it has been blown off on a windy day, and passed infield to Gareth Williams who, once tackled, had to release the ball.

The ball ran loose and Nkonki hacked it upfield. It looked all over for the Lions now. In fact, it looked as though the Invitation XV would take play to the other end. But Richards swooped from somewhere to flick the ball up to Jim Renwick. The inspiration was with the Lions now, for whereas normally

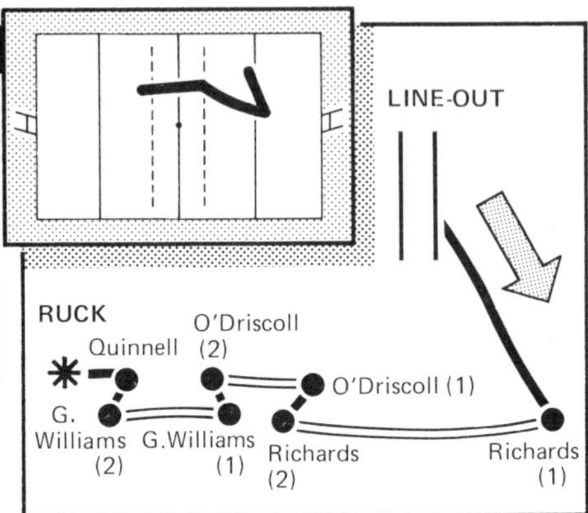

David Richards, receiving the ball from Patterson, darted upfield and the miracle try scored by the Lions against the S.A. Invitation XV on 21 May was underway.

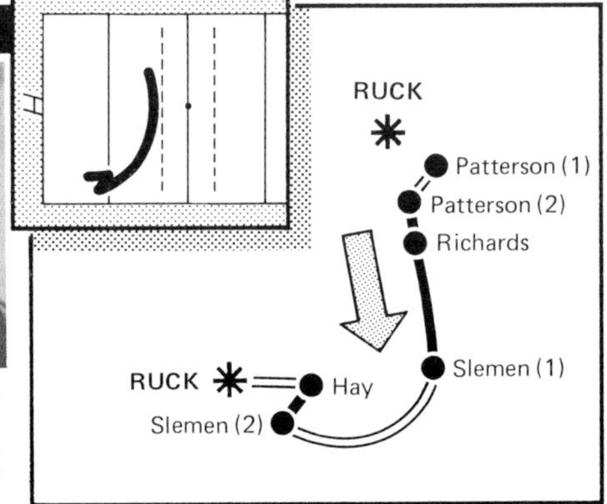

Bruce Hay, who received the ball after Richards had missed out Woodward to get it more quickly to Slemen on the left wing, was stopped by the opposition scrum-half.

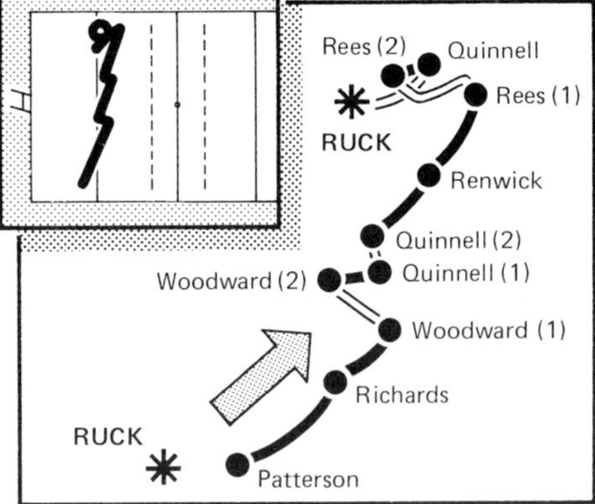

Derek Quinnell was at hand three times in this single movement to dig the ball out, on the third occasion seemingly from half the opposition forwards.

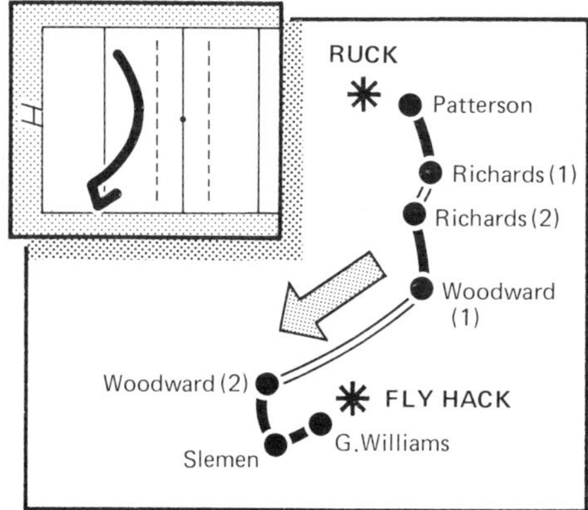

RUCK : 45 sec

Colin Patterson, who had started the whole move, here swung to the left. When four pairs of hands later Gareth Williams was tackled, the ball was hacked upfield by an opponent.

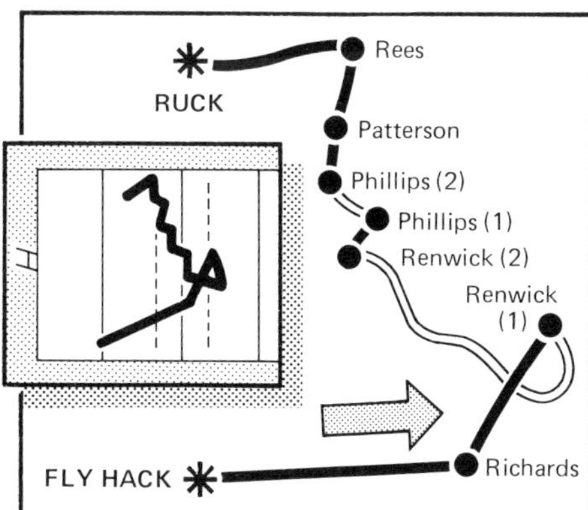

FLY HACK : 59 sec

Jim Renwick, kept things flowing with a touch of inspiration, resembling seven-a-sides. Without a teammate behind him he ran, instead of opting for the usual kick to touch.

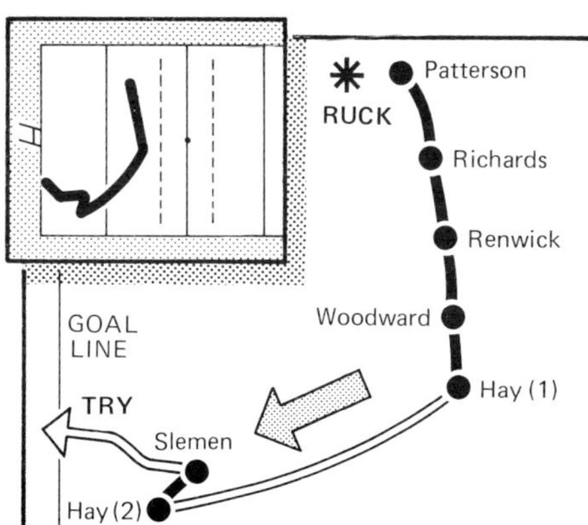

RUCK : 1 min 23 sec

Mike Slemen, the last Lion in an astonishing chain, ran around a despairing tackle and touched down. Behind him Hay raised both arms exultantly.

TRY : 1 min 36 sec

Renwick would probably have kicked for touch—there wasn't a teammate behind him—this time he decided to have a tilt at the opposition, as he would in sevens. He jinked twice, heading first to his left before switching to his right where he passed to hooker Alan Phillips. Little Patterson appeared at Phillips's elbow to take the pass, moved it to Rees, and the wing, in a repeat of his move a few moments before, cut infield from the right. This time he was tackled by Moaner van Heerden just outside the 25.

A ruck formed, and again the Lions won it for Patterson to dart off once more. In the crowd one could sense that something extraordinary was unfolding in front of us and we began to slide towards the edge of our seats. The scrum-half passed to Richards, and the ball went on to Renwick and to Woodward, and then Hay barged into the line again full of running. Hay had been overweight at the start of the tour, but he used his extra poundage to good effect now by crashing through two tackles and then somehow turning to slip the ball inside to Slemen. The left-wing, seeing his teammate was near the touchline, showed his innate footballer's brain by cutting infield on a diagonal slash towards the posts. He took Hay's pass beautifully, ran around the despairing tackle of Wynand Claassen and touched down. Twenty yards behind him Hay, still on his knees, raised both arms exultantly.

It was one of the greatest of all tries. Syd Millar said he had never seen anything like it. Johan Claassen, the former Springbok coach, said it was the best he had ever seen. To my mind this one, which lasted 1 minute 36 seconds and involved 32 pairs of hands, rated above the magnificent try by the Barbarians against the All Blacks at Cardiff in 1973 because it came after 72 minutes of play in a highly competitive match at stamina-sapping altitude.

As Slemen touched the ball down, some British journalists were in tears, four South African players were on their knees gasping for breath, and the 23,000 spectators in Olen Park rose to their feet to give the Lions an ovation that lasted for several minutes. "All 15 of us scored that try," Quinnell remarked later.

The Lions sang well that night. They had looked defeat in

In the Lions' match versus Orange Free State, Terry Holmes, passing the ball out from the scrum (above), dislocated his right shoulder. The following fixture, against the SARF Federation side, was a niggly battle in which winger Clive Woodward (below) was glad to be able to race with the ball.

the face and had cheated it in spectacular fashion, and this deadened the disappointment of another injury, to Elgan Rees. They had made a raid into rural Afrikanerdom, where two British journalists were spat upon, and where the first language used in shops is Afrikaans, and come out triumphant. Carleton and Slemen, the two Lancastrians, who were the best of friends, laughed and joked about it later. Finally Carleton turned to his teammate and said with a stern face: "Slem you buggered up that move."

"What do you mean?" asked Slemen, feeling hurt.

"You should have run in under the posts," replied Carleton.

By this time on tour, midway through the third week, David Richards, one of the heroes of Potchefstroom, was emerging as a practical joker and, consequently, had been nicknamed Dennis the Menace. As is often the case he was an unlikely-looking person for this role. He is curly-haired, charming and Gallicly good-looking, a baby-faced dapper dresser who works for a finance company in Swansea. When we had dinner together one night he ate snails and talked knowledgably of the merits of South Africa's Bellingham Grand Cru white wine, compared with, say a German hock or a French wine from the Loire.

One of his favourite tricks was to set off fire alarms, and when one went off during the Lions' visit to Parliament later in the tour naturally every one asked, knowingly, "Where's Dennis?" He was also a good mimic and able to keep a straight face long enough to sustain a telephone conversation. He caught both Bill Beaumont and Ollie Campbell with late-night calls by pretending to be a newspaper reporter who still had a small hole to fill, and wanted to write a well-informed piece about the Lions. But his greatest success was with another Potchefstroom hero, Mike Slemen.

The phone rang in the Liverpudlian's room one night and Mike, sleepily, put it to his ear. "Mr Slemen, I'm from the local paper" said Richards, easily falling into the appropriate accent and combining the right amount of inquisitiveness with the necessary apologies for ringing so late. "I understand you're the Lions' best back?"

"Yes, I have scored five tries so far," replied Slemen, unwittingly falling head first into the trap.

Riding high, the Lions moved on to Bloemfontein, seat of the South African Appeal Court, to play the Orange Free State. It would be their second game in four days at altitude and they were beginning to get used to the odd symptoms of life at this height—slight sore throats and sniffly noses in the morning, and a frustrating inability to recover their breath after a burst of activity.

Said Ray Gravell, the big bearded centre, "After 20 minutes I'm absolutely stuffed. Goodness knows how the forwards do it, fighting for the ball, running around the field and shoving in the scrums." And John O'Driscoll, the flanker, confirmed: "I can't breathe, can't do anything. I find it very, very tiring to start with. It's pant, pant, pant. You never seem to be able to catch your breath. As the game goes on you somehow get accustomed to it and it never gets any worse. But the trouble is it doesn't get any better either."

For the first few weeks Dr Jack Matthews made the players take three or four slow sodium (salt) tablets each day, but as the tour wore on the practice died out. "I don't think they're up to much," Matthews said later. "As long as you drink plenty of water, put salt in your food and eat lots of fresh fruit then you'll be okay."

Some of the players used one little trick to help them combat that irritating dryness in their throats and mouths. Before each game they rubbed dollops of Vick on their lips, around their mouths, up their noses and into that square in the base of the throat directly beneath their Adam's apple. It gave them something to moisten their lips on during lulls in play and the vapour helped keep their noses clear. Irishman Colm Tucker did all that and rubbed Chapstick on his lips as well. But Peter Morgan didn't like Vick under his tongue. "I spat it out straight away," he said. "It was revolting. I didn't want that in my mouth during the game."

South Africa is the only one of the eight International Board countries where a touring team must take altitude into account. In agreeing the 1980 itinerary the Four Home Unions decided that it would be better for the Lions to do their early tour training at the punishing height of 6,000 feet above sea level, while they were still fit and able to cope. Remember how at Vanderbijl Park coach Murphy used to shout at his men "Come on lads, I want you to break through today." He realised that if at the start of the tour the players could get used to the thin air, the bright clear light that is so striking up in the high veld and, most of all, the difficulty in regaining their breath, then that would be one less worry for him later on. The last thing he wanted was to have a group of players, some injured and some with colds, climbing up to the 5,000 or so feet above sea level of Potchefstroom or Bloemfontein.

Murphy would have preferred all the matches at altitude to have been lumped together, and played one after another, but he knew the South African Rugby Board would not agree to that. The next best thing was to make sure the Lions had as few of those debilitating changes from sea level up to altitude as possible, and this was done. For example, after the first Test the team were to stay up at a height of at least 5,000 feet for a run of six games, including the second Test, before they descended to sea level for the third Test at Port Elizabeth. All that though, was still ahead of them as they arrived in Bloemfontein late in the afternoon of Thursday, 22 May.

In the game against the Orange Free State two days later they tied a lead weight around their necks by trailing 7–0 at half-time but then sprang back to score 14 points in as many minutes after half-time, finally winning 21–17 after a few unnecessary alarums and excursions. Sadly, the injury jinx struck again, this time at Terry Holmes, the fiercely combative and strong scrum-half. He dislocated his right shoulder midway through the second half. In five games the Lions had lost three of their first-choice half backs, and were forced to send for Irishman John Robbie, a scrum-half, who happened to be in Zimbabwe touring with a team called the Goshawks.

The day after the Orange Free State game, the Lions flew down to Cape Town, leaving secretively soon after dawn in order to avoid demonstrations that, allegedly, were being organised to mark their arrival. All over the country non-white students had been boycotting their schools, protesting against the inequality of their educations. And while the Lions were in Bloemfontein, 20 people had been arrested and a schoolgirl shot dead in riots in a local township. In the wind and rain of that bleak Sunday, police threw road blocks around Cape Town airport and half a dozen policemen were stationed around the team's hotel.

The danger for the Lions came not from student demonstrators but from the South African Rugby Football Federation's team who were to play the Lions in the breathtakingly beautiful Danie Craven Stadium at the University of Stellenbosch east of Cape Town. The SARFF are the union for coloureds and their team, known as the Proteas, had toured England in 1971. It was always known that they would have to be strengthened by the inclusion of some white players in order to make it less one-sided, but Syd Millar was shocked when he learned that the front five forwards were all from Western Province, the joint holders of the Currie Cup.

Later Millar spoke out angrily about "some incidents that I hope I won't see repeated on a rugby field. I don't blame the referee, I blame the selectors." He was angry at the way so many of the midweek teams to play the Lions had been strengthened, turning traditionally easier games into something approaching Test matches. Most of all he was angry at what had happened in this particular game to the big and popular prop forward Fran Cotton.

The Lions had won 15–6 but it was a niggly game, far worse than England against Wales at Twickenham according to one player who had appeared in both. Every one of the first few scrums ended with Cotton and the SARFF tight-head prop Hempies du Toit wrestling each other to the ground.

Cotton had complained of feeling shivery, as if he was getting flu, after sitting on the replacements' bench during the game at Potchefstroom the previous week. He had gone straight to bed and spent the next three or four days with what was later diagnosed as cellulitis of the left leg. A cellulitism is an inflammation.

He had run a high temperature for a day or so, and before the game at Stellenbosch Dr Jack Matthews asked him whether he felt fit enough to play.

Shortly before half-time against the SARF Federation Invitation XV, the popular prop forward Fran Cotton was le off the field, in pain and clutching his chest. "A chap like that doesn't come off for no apparent reason," said th Lions' team doctor, and Cotton was rushed to hospital.

"I'm all right, Doc," Cotton replied. But it was clear soon after the start that he was far from himself. He had looked pale and drawn as he ran on to the field, and after the game started he often trailed around some distance behind play.

"Are you okay Fran?" asked teammate Allan Martin at one point during the game. "I've got these pains in my chest, and I'm have trouble breathing," Cotton replied. It became so difficult that he was unable to think of anything else, and a few minutes before half-time he was led off the field clutching his chest. In the changing room he gripped Noel Murphy's wrist tightly, and said he was frightened because he didn't know what was happening to him.

Matthews and a local doctor both examined Cotton at the doctor's surgery in the town. They then rushed him into the nearby University hospital. "I was very worried" Matthews recalls. "A chap like that doesn't come off for no apparent reason and he did have low blood pressure and chest pains. And he had been running a temperature. His heart could just have given up."

At the hospital, Cotton was immediately given an electrocardiogram, which showed that something was abnormal. A blood test revealed that his enzyme count was high, which, says Matthews, sometimes indicates coronary thrombosis. "Clinically I thought he had had an attack of cardiac ischaemia (not enough blood getting to the heart). His blood pressure was very low. A differential diagnosis was that it was a pulmonary embolism (a clot in a lung). I didn't think he had a phlebitis, which is a clotting of the veins in a leg, although I wasn't 100 per cent sure, because you could get a deep phlebitis that you wouldn't notice unless you made intense investigations."

Meanwhile, Beaumont delegated the after-dinner speech to the captain of the day, Derek Quinnell, and with Millar set about trying to track down Cotton's wife Pat. She and their 14 week-old daughter Rachel, were staying with her parents in Morpeth in the Northeast of England. Beaumont also rang his wife Hilary in Preston to enlist her help. The race was on to get hold of Pat and tell her what had happened before she read it in the papers or heard it on the radio.

Cotton spent that night in a four-bed ward on the first floor of the whites-only section of the hospital, while his friend and fellow prop-forward Phil Blakeway sat at the end of the bed fending off intruders. Cotton said later: "It broke my heart lying there. I was so far from home, and I thought I was never going to see my wife and family again."

The next morning he was taken by ambulance to the Groote Schuur hospital in Cape Town and straight into intensive care where he had another ECG, another blood test and numerous other tests. His ECG was still abnormal but his enzyme count had dropped, which was the first concrete sign that perhaps he hadn't had a heart attack after all. While he was being wheeled around the hospital the heart transplant pioneer Dr Christiaan Barnard spotted him and came over to say hello. "What are you doing in here?" he asked.

"I'm not sure," replied Cotton. "They're still trying to find out."

"Well, if you need a new heart, then just come up and see me on the floor above," Barnard said cheerily as he bustled off on his ward round.

The senior cardiologist at the Groote Schuur was Elwyn Lloyd, who had hooked for Oxford while at University there in the mid-sixties. It was at his direction that Cotton was given another series of tests, which included an ordinary blood count and another ECG. Lastly, Cotton had a heart catheterisation in which a tube was inserted into his groin and up into his heart. Fluid was pumped in and an arteriogram taken of the heart to find out how the coronary arteries stood out. They were normal. To everyone's relief it was certain now that he hadn't had a heart attack at all and he was well enough to be discharged on the Friday morning, less than 72 hours after the match. At lunchtime he walked into the dining room of the team's hotel, looked around rather sheepishly and muttered: "Back from the dead."

"I've had pericarditis," he explained later. "As I understand it, the heart is in a sac surrounded by fluid, which is called the pericardium and my pericardium was infected. This meant it was bloody dangerous for me to do anything in case the infection spread to the heart muscles which could cause myocarditis, an inflammation of the heart muscles causing a weakening of the heart. I was told that the cure was four to six weeks rest and that if I wanted to play rugby after that, then there was no reason why I shouldn't. What I will do is to start the pre-season training with Sale and see how that goes. That is what I intended to do anyway."

With seven of their original party out of contention for Test places because of injuries, the Lions' management were spared from having to make some ticklish decisions. For example, they had only one fit scrum-half, Patterson, and one fit stand-off, Ward, though Ward would be playing only his second game in as many months. They chose the superstitious Irishman Rodney O'Donnell at full back ahead of Bruce Hay, and Jim Renwick in the centre with David Richards because it was felt that his distribution was better than Clive Woodward's. The forwards were easier. Cotton's illness meant that the front row that had played the last three Tests in New Zealand would have to be broken up, but otherwise five of the pack had played in Tests in 1977—Quinnell, Squire, Beaumont, Price and Wheeler. There was great experience among the forwards. Dr John O'Driscoll, the owlish-looking Irishman, was given the task of policing Naas Botha.

The South African selectors made six changes in their team that had defeated the Jaguars. They included new caps in centre David Smith, scrum-half Serfontein, hooker Kahts and Martiens le Roux, the tight head prop, all of whom had played for the Invitation XV in that pulsating game at Potchefstroom. And they persisted with their tactic of playing the lock forward Theuns Stofberg as a flanker.

That Friday night the talk all over Cape Town was of the next day's Test. Drivers travelling along the road that girdles Table Mountain hooted their car horns and shouted into the darkness "up the Boks". In the cavernous, panelled dining room of the 19th century style Mount Nelson hotel, columns of anxious conversation rose towards the ornate ceilings. South Africa's 150th international (the previous 149 had been played against 10 different countries) was to be played 90 years to the day after the famous Newlands ground had staged its first match.

The First Test

The match was played 90 years to the day that the famous Newlands ground in Cape Town had staged its first match, and the Springboks won 26–22. An epic encounter in which the South Africans scored three tries in 12 minutes in the first half, it had the crowd in a frenzy and caused the French referee to exclaim afterwards: "Mon Dieu, it was a Test for Supermen." During the game Ray Gravell, being tackled by two Springboks (above), replaced John Carleton, who had injured his ribs. Bill Beaumont, winning the ball at a line-out (right), had played, like the rest of the Lions' forwards, with a controlled fury. But it was to no avail, and after the final whistle the Lions had to take in another piece of bad news: their stylish winger Mike Sleman had decided to return home.

It was a game to match the occasion. It began with the strange sight of more than 100 policemen leashing their Alsatian dogs as they took up positions around the edge of the pitch, the highly visible warning that they would not allow any demonstrations by rioters such as had hit the Cape Peninsula all week.

The pitch was firm and dry, though short of grass in patches. As the sun disappeared over the edge of the stand and barely 40 seconds had gone, Ward's first penalty attempt slid narrowly wide. It was the only one he was to miss all afternoon. For the next 20 minutes the Springboks were harried, twice having to defend at line-outs on their own line and often depending on prodigious kicks by Botha to keep them out of trouble. Twenty minutes passed in the twinkling of an eye.

At the end of this spell there was no score. Then Ward, his right leg heavily bandaged because of an haematoma, made one of two crucial mistakes. A kick across field landed in Pienaar's outstretched hands. Pienaar was considered his country's best attacking full-back and now he showed why. He slipped past the Lions' midfield defence and kicked ahead, and Rob Louw, a flanker who played better and better as the game wore on, grabbed the ball on the 25. He charged at O'Donnell, and though O'Donnell made a brave tackle, he carried the Irishman over the line for a try which Botha converted.

Ward pegged back the lead with a penalty from 35 yards, but then Botha incisively opened up the Lions' line again. As he took a pass from Serfontein he looked to be in two minds. Should he hoof the ball far upfield, or should he chip-kick it over the heads of Richards and Renwick? He chose the latter and O'Donnell was caught in no-man's land as the ball bounced in front of him, while Mike Slemen, rushing in from the left wing, was too late to reach it. The ball bounced favourably for centre Willie du Plessis to gather, run over, and score between the posts. Botha converted. Just before half-time Moaner van Heerden gathered a ball that had rebounded off O'Donnell's legs and charged, head down, to score in the corner after running 20 yards. The Springboks could do no wrong, though penalties by Ward on either side of van Heerden's try kept the score to 16–9 at half-time.

Slowly the balance of power tilted to the Lions after half-time. Their forwards were able to bring off those rolling mauls they were so good at, ripping the ball away and spinning off upfield. There was a controlled fury about their play that sent shivers down the spine. A fourth penalty by Ward narrowed the gap to 16–12.

Midway through the half O'Donnell, up in the three quarters, kicked neatly to touch five yards from the Springboks' line, and at the ensuing line-out—a Springbok throw-in, too—Price barged over for a try after a muddle and the score was level. Four minutes later the Lions went ahead. From the midst of an army of green and gold Springbok shirts 20 yards out, Ward dropped a goal with his left foot. The turnaround had been astonishing. The Lions had scored 13 points off the reel and now led 19–16. It was inspiring rugby.

But perhaps this dominance left its mark? In the last nine minutes South Africa scored two tries. Germishuys caught the ball in his own 25—another bad kick by the Lions—and ran to his right. Pienaar was there, and so was the ubiquitous Louw who passed the ball on to right wing Ray Mordt. He threw an overhead pass infield to Germishuys who balanced it on his fingertips and then drove fiercely over the line with two defenders clinging to him. Botha converted this try and the score was 22–19 to South Africa. The crowd were in a frenzy, one minute cheering their heads off, the next falling desperately quiet. Two minutes after Germishuys' fine try, the Lions equalised when Serfontein fell offside at a scrum and Ward's fifth penalty of the afternoon, plus that dropped goal, took him to 18 points—nine in each half—a record for a Lion in a Test series in South Africa, beating by one point the mark previously held by fellow Irishman Tom Kiernan.

Now the game tilted back to the South Africans. It was a moral victory for them anyway, with their four tries to one, even though the scoreline read 22–22. But they were about to make victory secure. Mordt came in from the blindside wing, Germishuys kicked through and a maul started a yard from the Lions' line. I don't suppose there was a person in the crowd of 50,000 who was cool enough to remain seated as captain Morné du Plessis plucked the ball out of the maul and gave it to Serfontein for the little scrum-half to dart over from point-blank range. Botha missed the conversion, but it didn't matter.

In this pulsating game, the Springboks had scored three tries in 12 minutes in the first half, and the Lions 10 points in seven minutes after half-time. "Mon Dieu, it was a Test for Supermen," said French referee Francis Palmade.

As the defeat sank in, the Lions heard another bit of bad news. The stylish winger Mike Slemen had decided to return home to be with his pregnant wife, who had just been admitted to hospital, and their ill young son. He had thought of going earlier, but was persuaded by Noel Murphy to stay until after the Test.

The Lions were to miss him as much for his sense of humour and for organising the complicated accommodation roster as for his growing rugby skills. He had always been a good ball player, good enough to have played at stand-off for St. Luke's College, Exeter, when he was training to be a teacher, before making the change to a wing. He should by rights have gone to New Zealand with the Lions in 1977. On the hard grounds of South Africa, three years later, his progress was rapid. By the time he left he had played in five games and scored five tries as well as dropping a goal and converting one try. Time and again, when there was a penalty on the left side of the field, it was Slemen's right foot the Lions would choose to boot the ball 50 or 60 yards into touch.

He was the outstanding back among the Lions of 1980, a world-class wing, and everyone was sad to see him go.

CHAPTER SEVEN

Among the Bushmen of the Caprivi Zipfel

THE single-engined Cessna droned over the arid scrub and then banked steeply to descend on a narrow landing strip among the eucalyptus and teak trees. Out of the 80-degree sunshine, South African Army officers in green-camouflaged lorries were waiting for their visitors.

It was a few days after the first Test, which the Lions had lost 26–22, and nine of us journalists had left Windhoek, the capital of South-West Africa/Namibia, early that morning and flown 500 miles north east. None of the Lions could come with us. They had to stay in Windhoek in preparation for the game on Wednesday, 4 June, against the South African Country XV.

For nearly three hours we had passed over little more than scrub until we had landed at the western end of the Caprivi Zipfel, the Caprivi Strip, a slim finger of land that points eastward all the way to the Zimbabwe border. To the north were the Angolan guerrillas, UNITA, and the guerrillas of SWAPO, the South West African Peoples Organisation; to the south and east was Botswana.

The strip was razor thin—some 12 miles from north to south and perhaps no more than 120 from west to east. It became part of SWA/Namibia through a quirk of history. On 1 July, 1890, the British Government, who felt that the strip would give them access from SWA to Zambezi, agreed, nevertheless, that the area could fall under German influence. Subsequently it was named after the German, Count von Caprivi.

Our hosts, 31 Battalion, had had their base at Camp Omega since 1977. It was neatly landscaped with paths bordered with poincettia and bougainvillea bushes dotted here and there, and guinea fowl running wild. Outside the officers' mess was an aviary and an ostrich cage where Agatha, the battalion's mascot, pranced and preened.

The prime purpose of 31 Battalion was to act as a training unit for recruits from the indigenous population, the Bushmen, some of Africa's most primitive people. Commander Piet Hall, the CO, explained: "We are an ordinary infantry battalion doing normal counter insurgency work. The battalion was formed in 1974 to make use of the bushmen and of their tracking and survival skills. Our patrolling is purely preventative. There hasn't been any enemy activity in the western Caprivi for six or seven years."

Although SWA/Namibia is at war with the neighbouring guerrillas, Hall's role is less of a soldier than that of a 19th century missionary ministering to the two tribes, the Barakwena and the Va-sekele, from which his recruits are drawn. There are 700 Bushmen troops, 750 women dependants, 1,400 children and 250 other dependants, and Hall's men teach them everything that will help them to raise their standard of living. Hall himself arranges divorces, and arbitrates in family arguments.

Bushmen have no idea of how to use a lavatory or have a shower. Their education is virtually nil. They can't read or write. The two tribes, who don't speak the same language, can't speak to each other. They are underfed from living off "veldfood" and they are physically vulnerable. There is a school and six teachers to look after the children of school age. The camp's hospital has one sister and one doctor, and Hall's wife teaches the Bushmen's wives simple knitting and sewing. Church services are held three times each week and twice on Sundays.

"Of course there is criticism of what we are doing," says Hall, a deeply suntanned man who wears sunglasses and smokes incessantly. "The criticism is based on the spoiling of the noble savage. What those people don't realise is that the noble savage is in a mess. As many as seven or even ten children used to die each week after arriving here because they suffered from malnutrition or cold. Now the deaths have dropped to one or two each month."

This humanitarian attitude towards non-whites in

SWA/Namibia contrasts strongly with the attitude of whites towards non-whites in South Africa. Amid great controversy, the Abolishment of Racial Discrimination Bill was put before the SWA Assembly, causing the leader of the National Party, Mr A. H. du Plessis to say: "This innocent piece of paper is most explosive bill that I have held in my hands for many years."

It was to be passed by a majority of six to one later in June 1980 and Dirk Mudge, the leader of the Democratic Turnhalle Alliance, which holds a majority of seats in the National Assembly, proclaimed jubilantly "We have abolished apartheid in SWA. I am sure there will have to be a change, a promotion of better understanding in South Africa."

Oddly, SWA/Namibia was not colonised or affected by any European power, not even when the Dutch first settled in the Cape in the 17th century or, later, when the British arrived in the 19th century, though the British did take for themselves and their sovereignty Walvis Bay, the country's main port. It was not until a German trader, F. A. E. Luderitz, arrived and bought some coastal areas from native tribesmen in the late 19th century and placed that land under the protection of the German Empire, that the German influence that is still so obvious first began.

In July 1915 German forces surrendered to a South African expeditionary force and from then until the end of World War 1, the South African Defence Force and a civilian administration jointly ran the country. In 1920 the Council of the League of Nations established a mandate for South West Africa.

Today it is a vast slab of medieval history and modern Africa. In an area four times the size of the United Kingdom (it is large enough for England and Wales, the Netherlands and Liberia to fit comfortably inside its borders) live a population of just under one million—an average of one person per sq km. The country has eight prisons, 11 ethnic groups who speak either the Bantu or the Khoesan languages, 18 railway stations covering a network of 5,450 miles and 36,000 miles of road surface.

For every 1,000 people there are 53.9 telephones and eight

beds in any one of the country's 74 hospitals. It has 124 general practitioners, 26 consultants and 16 dentists. It has blinding wealth in sections of the administrative, economic, military and medical capitals of Windhoek (pop: 77,300) and grinding poverty out in Bushmanland where, until recently, nomadic families survived much as they have since the Stone Ages.

The country is corseted with the huge and inhospitable Namib Desert, which occupies one fifth of its total land area in a long narrow strip up the Atlantic coast and, inland, the fearsome Kalahari Desert where less than 100 mm of rain falls each year.

The main industry is agriculture, closely followed by mining. Agriculture contributes about 17 percent to the gross domestic product and provides employment for more than half the labour force. SWA/Namibia lacks commodities such as iron ore and coal and power and water, but its domestic product more than doubled from R358.2 million (£200 million) in 1970 to R879 million seven years later. The country's per capita annual income of R661.5 (£367.50) was second in South Africa only to the Republic's R1,000 (£555).

It is also a country that is at war. In June 1971 the International Court of Justice concluded that South Africa was illegally occupying South West Africa. Gerrit Viljoen, the South African Administrator General for Namibia, has said: "For South Africa to maintain a presence in Namibia as long as we are tolerated is accepted here as being in our strategic, military and psychological interest but I do not think that South Africa would fight to remain in Namibia at all costs. If, through accepted democratic processes, Namibia should be put under a less friendly government, this would be against the interests of South Africa but we would have to accept it." A guerilla organisation has sprung up—SWAPO—and, in conjunction with UNITA forces in Angola, has struggled to kick the South Africans out.

This, more than anything else, was why Hall and his battalion were up in Caprivi. As well as his missionary work Hall was trying to train the Bushmen to be soldiers capable of matching the East German and Cuban guerillas who, Hall

The prime purpose of 31 battalion at the Caprivi Zipfel is to train recruits from the indigenous population, the Bushmen. The commanding officer's role is less that of a soldier and more that of 19th century missionary among the 700 bushmen troops, who account for 750 women dependents, 1,400 children and 250 other dependents. A typical day begins at 5.30am and includes practising attacking an armed enemy holding a gun. But the real strength of the Bushmen lies in their ability to track and utilise other more basic and natural skills, like making fire from two pieces of wood.

says, are stationed just over the border in Angola. At other border stations skirmishes broke out regularly. Just before our visit 15 guerrillas had been killed. Ten days after our visit, on the morning of 14 June, the day of the second Test, details of what was described as South Africa's biggest military success since the Second World War were announced: 200 guerrillas had been shot and killed by South African soldiers (16 South Africans were killed) on a raid into Angola.

We went off to see some recruits being trained. We drove off down a bumpy dusty track for two miles to a large earth training ground. There a group of 50 boys of no more than 16 or 17 were being instructed by three or four white NCO's. The recruits had been at Camp Omega for seven weeks, and had another four months to go before they could be sent off to join other battalions.

Their quarters were in nearby tents able to accommodate four or five of them. Soon their day, which had begun with reveille at 5.30, would end with a shower and then dinner of mashed potato, stew, Army biscuits and orange juice and coffee.

A young white NCO stripped to the waist and moved around as the recruits practised attacking an enemy who would be holding a gun in his hand. "The strengths of Bushmen are tracking" said Hall as he lit another cigarette. "They are brave, too, but it takes time to teach them how to use a rifle. They have a tendency to fire too high, as they would if they were shooting arrows. But they are brilliant at judging distance. They don't know how far something is away in yards or metres, but they judge it far better than we can."

Three recruits broke away from training and darted off into the long grass on the edge of the parade ground. They reappeared with two pieces of wood. In one they whittled a hole an inch or two deep, and laid it flat on the ground. Then they sharpened one end of the other piece so that it would fit into the hole. By rubbing their hands together with the vertical stick in between their palms they rotated the vertical stick so fast that smoke soon appeared. Four and a half minutes after they had begun, flames burst clear from the wood.

The importance South Africa places on defence can be gauged by the salary these soldiers will receive when they are fully trained. They may be practically illiterate but they'll still earn up to R170 (£94.40) each month and a further R4.50 (£2.50) each day if they are married. As a comparison, a maid in the Landdrost Hotel in Johannesburg earns a basic salary of R70 (£38.80) each month.

The next morning we watched the school children as they sat in their classes. In a small hut the teacher had written on the blackboard some mathematical questions: $4+5-?=6$. $9+3-?=7$ and $16-?+4=12$. The children buried their heads in their blue notebooks writing the answers as best they could.

In a clearing outside the huts they gathered to sing us some songs. A little girl in a green dress with a bow in her hair sang Ave Maria in a soft clear voice. "Totsiens" we shouted and waved.

"'Bamba' means goodbye to Bushmen," said Hall so we all shouted "Bamba."

Then we climbed back on board the planes. Hall stuck his head into the cabin. "I don't want to worry you but have you noticed how they do the pre-flight checks? They kick the wheels and count the wings."

The pilot started the engine, and soon we set off home. For 24 hours rugby had, for a change, seemed a long way away.

CHAPTER EIGHT

Three Lions in the turmoil of the tour

Clive Woodward barrelled in through the door of my hotel room, pulled up a chair, swung his sockless feet up on to the bed and gave a cheerful, slightly mischievous grin. He was happy. He should have been. He was about to play his first Test for the Lions.

"Some tea?" I asked. "I'd love a cup," he replied enthusiastically.

It was Friday before the second Test, and after another warm and sunny day dusk had settled over Bloemfontein. That morning the Lions had trained very gently on the Test pitch two miles from their hotel, and then many of them had gone to bed to rest in the afternoon. Woodward tossed and turned for two hours, and now he was due down at a team meeting at 6.30. Later there was dinner, followed by a film in the tea room. No, he said with a slight smile, he wasn't nervous. "That won't happen until I wake up in the morning and lie in bed thinking about the game."

In six weeks in South Africa, Woodward had become one of the stars of the tour. The Leicester player had been selected for the Lions as much as anything on the strength of his performance in the Calcutta Cup against Scotland, when his crazy-paving running had caused havoc among the Scots three-quarters. In South Africa he immediately took to the hard grounds, where his deceptively fast running and ability to sidestep were priceless virtues. He's a coltish-looking man, very slim and long-legged, which makes it surprising to discover that he is only 5′ 11″.

Woodward was born on 6 January 1956 in Ely, Cambridgeshire. His father was in the Royal Air Force, and Clive was sent away to school to make sure that his education did not suffer by his being dragged around as his parents moved from one Air Force base to another. He went to HMS Conway in North Wales. "It used to be a ship for training Merchant Navy Officers," Woodward explained as he drank his tea. "It sank in the fifties, and washed up in the Menai Straits. A number of shipping companies combined to build a school on board, but in the early seventies they decided they couldn't afford the upkeep and Cheshire County Council took it over."

Woodward remembers that there was considerable emphasis on outdoor sports at HMS Conway. There was the water of the Menai Straits for sailing and canoeing, and nearby Snowdonia for climbing. He played rugby for two terms and cricket and tennis in the summer. He was a natural stand-off at school and he carried on in this position when he played one season's first-class rugby for Harlequins. It was during this year that he was chosen to represent England Colts. Not until he went to Loughborough Colleges did he move out to the centre.

Now he works for Rank Xerox, selling photo-copiers in the heart of Robin Hood's England. He has a reputation for being a workaholic, the sort of man who takes a briefcase packed with documents everywhere he goes. "What, me?" he asked in genuine surprise as a smile spread slowly over his face. "A workaholic? I am fairly successful in my job and I work hard from 8.30 until 6, but I'm not a workaholic. Perhaps what they're thinking of is that twice each week, on Monday and Thursday when I go training at Leicester, I stay in the office late because there isn't time to go home."

There were two other marks of distinction about Woodward. He had twice broken the same leg in practically the same place—the tibia in his left leg—and he had twice had to postpone his wedding. His fiancée Helen was due to finish her degree at Loughborough University at the end of June 1980, and the first wedding date they set was August 2. Then Clive decided to go on Leicester's centenary tour of Fiji and Australia in August and though he later changed his mind about the club tour the wedding date was brought forward to July 12. "I could get married and then go off with Leicester, that was the plan," he explained. "But then I was picked for the Lions, and that's the day of the final Test, and so we had to move it again. We've fixed it now for a week later, July 19 and we can't change it again."

While he was in South Africa Helen, completed the purchase of a house at Uppingham—a house, incidentally, that Clive had never seen—where they would live after getting married. He would commute to Leicester, while Helen would be able to carry on teaching physical education and geography at Uppingham School.

In training in South Africa at the start of the tour, Woodward looked outstanding. He was forever looping exuberantly around his teammates to take an extra pass, always chasing an extra few yards to pick up a ball, and kick it or throw it. All the time he grinned with the sheer pleasure of it all. It was clear that he was young, on his first major tour, and loving every minute of it. And his passing was silkily smooth. He would gracefully swing his hips one way as he transferred the ball the other. Was he, one wondered, the most stylish passer since John Dawes?

And at his deceptively fast pace he moved elegantly and effortlessly, unlike, say, John Carleton and Peter Morgan, who bunched their shoulders and fought every inch of the way. When Woodward ran with the ball, he leaned forward slightly as if he was about to bend down. Opponents found it hard to tell whether he was going to move to their left or their right and, sometimes, to judge how fast he was going.

Woodward's first game for the Lions had been in their second match, against the South African Rugby Association team, the blacks, at the Border ground at East London. He was picked to play in the centre alongside Jim Renwick against the Leopards, as they were known, and within five minutes came the first surprise. The Lions won a penalty 35 yards out and most people thought that Renwick would take the kick. Instead Woodward came up, wiped the ball on his jersey, and then left-footed it clean between the posts.

"I take four steps back and one to the side," Woodward explained. "And then I concentrate solely on the quality of my run-up. I can tell whether the ball is going over before I hit it. I don't need to watch the ball. If my run's straight and good then I'll hit the ball okay. But if it's not, then I'm in trouble. That's what Ollie Campbell taught me. He taught me that kicking is all about getting the run-up correct, and he takes as many as 100 kicks each day just practising that."

Twice more in this half Woodward kicked penalties with his left foot giving him nine points by half-time. The Lions were leading 13–3. Within the space of 11 minutes after half-time he kicked eight more points. First he caught a miscued clearance kick by Ferdie Prinsloo, the stand-off, swivelled around from the touchline and, calm as you please, dropped a goal with his left foot from 30 yards. Then he converted tries by Elgan Rees and by captain-of-the-day Derek Quinnell. He had scored 16 points in the game and the Lions won 28–6.

Woodward's emergence as a kicker was a complete surprise, a bonus on a tour where good news was rare. At Leicester he was at best fourth choice behind England's full-back Dusty Hare, stand-off Les Cusworth and centre Paul Dodge—and possibly even, Woodward reckoned, behind Peter Wheeler, the club captain and hooker. In the early seventies Wheeler had been known to kick more than 100 points in a season.

After training sessions in South Africa, Woodward would take a couple of balls and practise his kicking. His shots went over time and again, and so for this second game of the tour it was decided that he should take the kicks from the right of the field and Renwick those from the left. A week later, in the famous Potchefstroom game, Woodward kicked four penalties and one conversion and missed two more penalties and one conversion. His tour aggregate from those two games was 10 successful place-kicks out of 13.

"He was a natural kicker," recalled Ollie Campbell. "He had such a lovely smooth style. Even when he miskicked, the ball was never viciously hooked or rolled along the ground. It was always very close. I was impressed, and I couldn't believe he was ranked so low as a kicker at Leicester.

"What he needs now is practice in matches," Campbell continued. "If he thinks he is going to kick only occasionally then he won't try very hard. On the other hand, if he could take the kicks from the right of the field and let Dusty take them from the left, then I think he would improve dramatically."

Another feature of Woodward's play was his versatility. In his first seven games for the Lions he played as centre and both left and right wing. He was a key man in the Wednesday side, almost ready for promotion. But there were worries about his defence and his distribution of the ball. Some players felt that Renwick distributed the ball better, and when the team was named for the first Test Woodward was not even among the replacements. Then in two games before the second Test he underlined his potential with commanding performances on the right wing against the Country XV and against Transvaal, when he scored two of the Lions' four tries as well as kicking a penalty and conversion.

These two tries were something special. For the first he came in off his right foot while running down a narrow corridor on the blind side of a scrum. He beat one man and scored. For his second try, which came in the second half, he had to work a bit harder. The Lions won a line-out and stand-off Gareth Davies ran flat across field on what is known as a "double dummy" move. He was pretending to pass first to his inside centre, Renwick, and then to the outside centre, Ray Gravell. In fact he didn't pass to either and, instead, threw the ball out to Woodward who was out on the right.

The Transvaal's left wing Gerrie Germishuys, who was so devastating in the Tests, allowed himself to be drawn infield leaving his full-back Pierre Wilkinson to take care of Woodward. Woodward had the job of getting past him to score.

It wasn't particularly difficult, for there was plenty of room to manoeuvre. In fact, he made it look easy. With a slight change of pace and swerve he rounded the Transvaal player as easily as a car rounds a traffic island. David Richards had been taken off moments earlier with a dislocated shoulder, to be replaced by Renwick, but he saw the try later on TV. "I must say, Clive had to work a bit for that one," said Richards. "It wasn't as easy as all that. He did very well to get it, I thought."

It was inevitable after these two performances that Woodward would be included in the Test team. As it happened, he was selected in the centre alongside Gravell.

"You can get a lot more bored playing wing," Woodward said as we talked on the eve of the second Test. "On the wing it can be very hard to get into the game. You can go for minutes on end without touching the ball. And in defence the centre just has to get his man, but for a wing there is the timing, knowing when to come in and when not to come in, when to stay out in other words. To play on the wing in a bad side would be awful."

Woodward was to face the Zimbabwean David Smith again in the Test, just as he had at Potchefstroom. "I don't rate Smith at all," Woodward continued. "He can't come in off his right foot. I know I missed him twice in the game at Potch, but if someone else gets him then I don't count it. I shall lie very wide on their ball tomorrow. There is no way he can run around me and if he tries to come inside me, then I'll get him."

There was a knock on the door. It was scrum-half Colin Patterson. Woodward got up to go. "You don't want me any more, do you?" he asked, slipping on his sandals before leaving.

Patterson was the smallest and lightest player in the team. In his stockinged feet the 25-year-old Ulsterman stood no more than 5ft 5in and weighed a constant 11 stone, which was exactly 12 inches shorter and almost 6½ stone lighter than the Lions' biggest foward Maurice Colclough. He is a cheerful, jaunty fellow with a distinctive Ulster burr, and often during games you would hear him shouting at Derek Quinnell "Keep going Derek, keep going" as the big No. 8 controlled a drive by the Lions forwards.

Like Woodward, Patterson had come on fast in South Africa where the speed of his pass was so noticeable. He had had to fight his way through, for in the first three Saturday games Welshman Terry Holmes was originally chosen ahead of him. But then midway through the third Saturday, in the game against the Free State at Bloemfontein, Holmes injured his shoulder so badly that Patterson became automatically the Lions' first choice.

"This Test could be the turning point of the tour," said Patterson. "We've got the confidence, we've started to run

Three Lions with one purpose—to win: Colin Patterson (above), with the ball, was the smallest and lightest player in the team, who eventually became the Lions' eighth major injury; Clive Woodward (right), who became in six weeks in South Africa one of the stars of the tour; and Woodward's Leicester captain, Peter Wheeler (below), who was an essential unit in the Lions forwards.

the ball at them instead of them running at us. There is no question that we have the ability to win tomorrow. What we have to do is to make them think, to change the pattern of the game as often as possible. You could hear Morné du Plessis, the South African captain, telling them how to play at times during the Cape Town Test.''

I asked Patterson which scrum-halves had impressed him so far? ''You can discount all the Wednesday players we have seen,'' he replied firmly. ''They're getting away with crooked put-ins. At the other end of the scale there is Divan Serfontein, the Springboks' scrum-half. I rate him very, very highly indeed though we haven't yet seen him under pressure, when the ball is wet and he is going backwards. He passes well with both hands, kicks well though I haven't seen him kick with his left foot, and he is very, very quick over the first five yards.

''I don't think he is faster than I am but he is certainly as fast. He got away from me once in the first Test and as I chased him I noticed I wasn't making much impression. And I reckon I'm just about the fastest in our team over 15 yards. John Carleton is quicker over 25 yards and Andy Irvine can really motor as well, but over 15 yards I would win any race, specially if we had to be lying down on our backs at the start.''

It was Patterson's first Lions tour and he was struck by some of its peculiarities. On this tour 30-plus men were thrown together for nearly 80 days. They were organised like children, yet lionised like Greek gods by men, women and children. The French temperament cannot cope with such unnatural strain, and tours by France are rarely more than a few weeks. Even among the more phlegmatic British players tiffs broke out in much the same way as newly-married couples can often end up screaming at each other across the kitchen table.

After the game against the Free State in Bloemfontein, Patterson and David Richards, the stand-off that day, became involved in a discussion in the bar of the team hotel. It was getting late and both had had a few drinks when, suddenly, it blew up into a major argument. They were, Patterson recalled later in some embarrassment, quite close to punching one another over something that had happened in the game that afternoon. Good sense prevailed; they backed off, and Patterson, still furious, went off to bed.

At the airport the next day as the Lions moved on to Cape Town, the little Irishman went up to Richards. "I gather we were entertaining the troops a bit last night," he said. Richards, just as embarrassed, nodded. The subject was never mentioned again.

Richards's father died just after David got to South Africa, and the player made a frantic trip home for the funeral before flying out to rejoin his teammates a few days later. His tour was to end sadly when he dislocated his shoulder in the Transvaal game, the ninth of the tour, just when it looked as though he was regaining his old form.

As for Patterson, he was just one of a band of Lions who had either made some considerable sacrifice to go on tour or had suffered as a result of it. Schoolteacher John Carleton had had to give up his job because the Labour-dominated Wigan education committee refused to give him leave of absence on political grounds. Gareth Williams, another teacher, was not being paid by his employers, the Gwent Education Authority, because they also disapproved of the tour. Ian Stephens had no job to go back to, and Ray Gravell hadn't even dared to ask for paid leave from the Manpower Services Commission in case it wasn't granted. Instead he took unpaid leave. And Patterson himself, who had been married only in February, had had to give up his job as a solicitor in Newtonards, Ulster, in order to make the tour at all.

His firm had made such a fuss when he toured Australia with Ireland the previous year that he knew he had no chance of getting 10 weeks paid leave in the summer of 1980. Accordingly he handed in his notice. Until he was injured on tour, his intention was to return to Ireland, pack his bags and fly out with his wife to Brisbane, Australia, where he could work and play rugby. He planned to stay there at least until Christmas.

Was it as a result of making such sacrifices, and of having to cope with the extraordinary run of injuries, that—little rifts apart—made the Lions of 1980 such an harmonious party? "The spirit is good," Patterson noted. "They're here to do a job and they know it. No-one is left out, I think that's why it is so good. There are no established players who stand in a row by themselves and the rest of the boys look at them and say 'He's in, he's in, he's in.' We've all got a chance."

After our talk, Patterson sprang to his feet and walked jauntily out of my room. The next and last Lion to come in was Peter Wheeler, Woodward's Leicester captain. Of my three visitors Wheeler was the oldest (he would be 32 at the end of November), the heaviest at nearly 14 stone and the only forward. He was also the only previous Lion of the three, having toured New Zealand with Phil Bennett's team in 1977.

He had been in a similar situation in New Zealand. The Lions lost the first Test in wet and windy Wellington and flew down to Christchurch knowing they had to win the second Test to keep the series alive. In a thrilling game that was marred by rough play they did it, 13–9.

"There's no tomorrow if we lose this time, is there?" Wheeler observed quietly, a cigarette burning slowly in his fingers. "I think we feel that we threw the game away in the first Test and we want to do something about it. Yes, I'm tense, we're all tense. You're bound to be tense in rugby because you can never be certain. The Springboks will be tense too, especially their forwards, because they'll be expecting another hiding like they got in the first Test. But I'm not so tense this time as I was before that second Test in 1977. That was my first Lions Test, this is my fifth, and I'm three years older. I can cope with it all much better now."

Wheeler was an essential unit in the Lions' forwards, who had been so impressive in the middle period of the Test at Newlands and again against Transvaal the following Saturday. The rolling maul was a technique that the Springboks couldn't match, and the more the Lions succeeded with it the more of an enigma it became to South Africans.

I wanted to know what Wheeler thought about the standard of refereeing in South Africa. He had a serious brush with Colonel Cassie Karstens, the referee in the Country match at Windhoek just after the first Test, and at the end of the game he refused to shake the ref's outstretched hand.

"I think the standard has been farcical," Wheeler replied.

"We have come up against the business of hookers being allowed to strike for the ball long before it is put in. At the first scrum at Windhoek they struck four times and then we were penalised for delaying the put-in.

"In New Zealand I felt that the reason why their scrummaging had declined was that they didn't contest the put-in, they didn't fight for the ball. Over here the front rows are not technically so good as in New Zealand, but the referees allow crooked put-ins. It's going to mean the total demise of the prop forward if they carry on like this. In one game Colin (Patterson) put the ball in straight the first time and then saw how much the referee allowed, so he put the rest in crooked.

"The referees I have seen out here have been below the standard of ours back home. Here they must wait six years to do a Lions tour so it all builds up in their minds. I honestly think that someone soon may settle not so much for being a good referee as for being a hero in his home town, and go for glory in one game and go over the top. If we get a bad referee in the Northern Transvaal game or the Western Province game then we're in trouble. I thought that Steve Strydom did okay in the first game, and Frans Muller in the Free State game was perhaps the best of the bunch so far."

Just three days before our talk the Lions had come across a referee they didn't like at all. Stoney Steenkamp was in charge of the game against Eastern Transvaal on a dusty pitch at Springs, an hour from Johannesburg. This game replaced the original fixture against Zimbabwe, and many of the Lions felt later that they would rather have gone to Zimbabwe.

Steenkamp's shrill tattoo on his whistle dominated the afternoon and was partly instrumental in keeping the score to 21–15 to the Lions. More to the point Steenkamp awarded 17 penalties to the home side in the second half and only three to the Lions. Overall he penalised the Lions three and a half times as often as the home side, 24–7. That kind of refereeing was unusual, yet it was to show up once more when the Lions played Northern Transvaal at Loftus Versfeld in Pretoria just before the third Test.

There, as the home side fought to recover from a 16–0 deficit at half time, referee Frik Burger gave 10 penalties to the Northerns in the second half and not one to the Lions.

We changed the conversation to captaincy. "Billy drives harder than Phil Bennett did," said Wheeler. "It's not meant in any derogatory way to either, but Billy's a workhorse of a man whereas Benny was more gifted. It's very hard therefore to refuse a man who works so hard himself when he says he wants one more effort and then one more."

Second Test Saturday dawned bright, clear and sunny. Patterson had forecast that he would know 15 minutes before the kick-off, from the mood in the changing room, whether or not the Lions would win. "I thought we'd do it," he said later. "The mood was right."

For a few minutes the two sides sparred with each other. A drop-shot by Naas Botha in the opening minute went wide, and a mortar-like up and under for Andy Irvine was gathered safely. But then came one of those mistakes that had cost the Lions so dearly in the first Test. Irvine, going for touch, mis-kicked and Germishuys gathered the ball near the touchline. The Lions streamed across field, the Springboks got there faster. Louw took a pass infield from the wing and passed to Willie du Plessis who passed back to Louw and the flanker scored in the corner.

Almost immediately the Lions took the lead. Patterson chipped a deft kick over a line-out 30 yards from the South Africans' line and Mordt, Pienaar and Serfontein all made a muddle of gathering it. O'Driscoll, meanwhile, and Patterson took the ball on and O'Driscoll stormed over in the corner. Gareth Davies's conversion curled in from the touchline. Botha's missed penalty, one minute later, was a blow for the Springboks but he made amends by kicking a relatively simple one from 35 yards midway through the half.

Now came the game's most controversial try, scored by the giant flank forward Theuns Stofberg, who was to play in the second row for Northern Transvaal against the Lions a week later. Ray Mordt was fiercely tackled by Bruce Hay out near the right touchline and fell to the ground. Hay turned to return to an onside position when Mordt suddenly picked himself off the floor, dashed for the line, and threw an inside pass to Stofberg who scored without a hand being laid on him.

The Second Test

The day dawned bright, clear and sunny and Colin Patterson thought the Lions would win. "The mood was right," he said. At half-time the Springboks led 16–9 but then penalty kicks by Davies and Irvine made it 16–15. "I thought then we would win," said Clive Woodward pictured (right) beating the Springboks' Naas Botha with Gravell and Hay in support. But it was not to be and the Lions lost 26–19 though attacking ceaselessly. Below (left) Peter Wheeler is stopped by a Springbok in front of a Lions phalanx consisting of Squire, Quinnell, Colclough and Beaumont; Quinnell himself is chased by the Springbok captain Morné du Plessis (centre); and John Carleton attempts the impossible task of trying to stop five Springboks on his own (right), as centre David Smith, with the ball, prepares to pass to prop forward Martiens le Roux (extreme right) supported by, left to right, Louw, du Plessis and Serfontein.

14

Surely Mordt had grounded the ball, the Lions thought, thus making it an offence for him to pick it up without first releasing it?

Patterson thought so, for he half stopped. Woodward, on the right wing, was too far away to see clearly, and Wheeler was just one forward who was streaming across. Referee Francis Palmade ruled that Mordt hadn't allowed the ball to touch the ground, and with Botha converting, the Springboks won themselves six points. An obstruction by Gravell on Pienaar gave Botha an easy three points and took them to 16–6. Then Davies kicked a penalty to make the half-time score 16–9, as it had been in Cape Town.

A revival by the Lions, as had happened in the first Test, was mounted straight after half-time. Davies kicked a penalty when Hay was obstructed and then after only 14 minutes Andy Irvine landed a 55 yards penalty to make it 16–15. "I thought then we would win," said Woodward later.

But some impetus was lost when Davies was injured and tore a medial ligament in his left leg. Ollie Campbell came on to replace him and immediately had a straightforward kick from some 30 yards when Morné du Plessis fell offside at a ruck. Campbell's attempt, which would have made it 18–16 to the Lions, slid wide of the left post.

The Lions attacked ceaselessly. Gravell charged upfield like some mad infantry commander, O'Driscoll and Squire barged on, but John Carleton chose to cut in from the right when he might have got over had he gone straight for the corner. He was stopped one yard short. This was the pivotal period of the game. If the Lions had scored now, as they should have done, they might have held on to win. But from two line-outs Botha put in long touch-finders and the Lions were forced back 60 yards.

Moments later the end came. Germishuys scored in the left corner, after Pienaar had kicked through from the right of the field, and then Pienaar himself scored after the ball had been hacked through from the Lions' 25. Two tries in as many minutes made it 26–15 to the Springboks and they were safe. Ray Gravell's try in injury time merely made the scoreline more respectable.

"We didn't play enough rugby among the backs," Woodward said later. "At 15–16 I still thought we could win, because we had the initiative and we were beginning to go well. Smithy was no problem to me. As far as I was concerned I had the better game. He stood wide and kept putting kicks through. If we pull out the stops we could beat them, but they are a very good side who don't make mistakes. And we do. That try by Pienaar was from an attack of ours and perhaps we should have scored from it. Instead they did and it won them the game."

Patterson was highly critical of his own mistakes, once, particularly, when he chose the wrong option in attack and kicked the ball to the right corner when he should have passed it and it ran over the dead-ball line. "Divan Serfontein exposed his weaknesses to me that he is not good enough under pressure and going backwards. When we got our first try all he had to do was to tap the ball into touch, and he missed it. He also miskicked twice, but one luckily bounced into touch. When we miskicked, the ball went straight into someone's hands.

"It was a strange game. We were in the driving seat near the end, and then they scored two tries in 90 seconds. If we can get the third Test then I think we can win the fourth. Our side is sound but misfiring. Theirs is a very sound all round side, but we haven't really put pressure on them yet."

I spoke to Peter Wheeler a day or so after the Test and some of his disappointment had gone. The Lions had spent the Sunday at the house of Choet Visser, the team's liaison officer, and there in peace and solitude they had come to grips with the reality that they had thrown away another Test match. "It was disappointing because we made the same mistakes as in the first Test, but with different people involved," said Wheeler. "We missed touch, we missed tackles, and we made Pienaar look good. Their kicking was far superior to ours. They are beatable but at the moment we are playing to their strengths. If we can't put them under pressure then we musn't run at them. I think that at the moment we are trying to run before we can walk."

CHAPTER NINE

Rabble rouser and patron saint

To many of the 4.5 million whites in South Africa he's an ogre, a wide-eyed rabble rouser, a black intellectual—in short, a man they can't quite understand and consequently feel uneasy about. Over the years they've taken away his passport and locked him in jail for civil disobedience, bugged his home and office, and done as much as they could to make his life a misery.

To many of the country's 22 million blacks he's their patron saint incarnate—who lives alongside many of them in Soweto, and is versatile enough to be invited on to television and radio, to write articles for newspapers and magazines. He is the most articulate standard-bearer of their cause in South Africa.

Of all the international figures in South Africa, the Anglican Bishop Desmond Tutu, a man of medium height with a cherubic face and hair flecked with grey at the temples, is one of the most entrancing. He is seldom out of the news. While the Lions were in South Africa, Tutu called Prime Minister Botha a liar and asked for a meeting with him. He marched illegally through the centre of Johannesburg and, consequently, was arrested and spent a night in jail. And he was unable to travel outside the country because his passport had been confiscated. In a life that has been pockmarked with controversy, it was an ordinary three months.

Bishop Tutu doesn't have the rolling, rising cadences of the late Martin Luther King, and one wouldn't expect him ever to captivate an audience as King did with that famous "I've had a dream" speech that sent shivers up and down the spine of even those who watched it on television.

He's irrepressible and informal, as likely as not to explain why he should be the next Pope ("There'd be no difficulty over celibacy, I'd overcome the racial problem, and I'd be the first Pope from the third world.") as he is to take off his shoe while talking and absent-mindedly scratch the sole of his foot. He has a gift for the florid metaphor.

Bishop Tutu is unique in his habit of wheezing and cackling like one of the Macbeth witches, and sometimes slapping himself on his knee as he doubles up at one of his own frequent jokes. "Do you mind if we use a tape recorder?" we asked. "No, not at all," he replied as a mischievous smile began to form around his mouth. "We're used to having several people interested in what we have to say."

In his overheated second floor office we talked first about the Lions tour. He wasn't surprised to learn that we had come across diverse opinions—blacks who applauded the Lions for visiting South Africa, and whites who felt the Lions should have stayed away. It's an axiom, he said, that on many issues in South Africa the whites and the blacks are on opposite sides. In broad principle he felt that whereas most whites were in seventh heaven when the Lions agreed to come "many blacks felt like execrating the Lions. I don't think you've helped us any. You've just made the other chaps feel a little better."

Tutu said he thought that boycotts did work. Why else, he asked reasonably enough, did the British Government work with the Americans to mount one against the Moscow Olympics? A sports boycott would have hurt the South Africans. "South Africans are rather schizophrenic in many ways. At one time they pretend we don't care what the world thinks of us, they will go it alone. But on the other hand they care about acceptance. It's almost pathetic the way they want to be accepted, and therefore the tour in that sense has been important for them. And of course it has been doubly so because they have beaten you hollow. They've really felt good, man, that they've paid back, more than paid back, the problem they got last time around."

If sport does mirror society, then it does so most noticeably at some sporting events in South Africa. When the black American boxer John Tate beat Gerrie Coetzee it was, for whites, recalls Tutu, as if there had been a death in the family, or they had lost a major war. On the other hand in Soweto that night horns blared, drums throbbed, and people were out on the streets whooping it up. "You'd have thought it was New Year's Eve," said Tutu.

Years ago Bishop Tutu earned a degree in divinity from London University, and afterwards worked as a curate, first at Golder's Green in north London and then at Bletchingley in Surrey. In a BBC TV programme, Heart of the Matter in June 1980, he talked with great affection of his time in England, and of Sunday mornings spent at London's Speakers' Corner, which he calls: "One of the most splendid monuments to a free society, where policemen are employed not to arrest cranks and critics but to protect them". England was the country where he came under the influence of Trevor Huddleston, and the country where he learned tolerance, that there are some nice white people as well as those who lack only horns and a tail. "This has been very important for my ministry in South Africa," he says.

Yet there are subjects that strain even his tolerance. As a black in South Africa and therefore a member of an oppressed majority, he finds many of the government laws to be offensive. He has demanded abolition of the pass laws, and as a personal protest he refuses to carry his own passbook, thereby deliberately breaking the law. He wants an end to detention without trial and an end to the forced transfer of blacks from one part of the country to another "as if they were bags of potatoes, just to satisfy some ideological pipedream".

His firmest belief is that shortly in South Africa there is going to be a massive confrontation between whites and blacks. In optimistic moments he longs for power-sharing, as has happened in neighbouring Zimbabwe, though naturally the blacks would have a majority. He is genuinely puzzled that his concept of brotherly love cannot be understood all over the country.

Bishop Tutu is Secretary General of the South African Council of Churches, which includes 20 member churches but not the Dutch Reform and the Catholic. And he likes to point out that in his office in Johannesburg the staff is multi-

Bishop Desmond Tutu: "If it's a choice between freedom and Nazism, then you go to war. But when it comes to the question of black liberation, then you suddenly wake up to find that western Christendom has suddenly become pacifist. That concerns me very much."

racial, with a black as its head, and whites working under him without problems. "When, oh when, will our white brothers come to feel that nobody really intends to drive them into the sea?" he asks.

But you feel he can sense in his heart of hearts that it won't be solved amicably. He believed, he said, that the confrontation would come within five or ten years, and as the natural climax to the industrial unrest and student disturbances that marked South Africa while Beaumont's Lions were there. "The whites may try and make accommodation for us. They keep shifting the furniture around, but the room remains the same. The international community has to continue to apply pressure on the government—economic, diplomatic and political pressure.

"If that fails, and if our campaign for so-called disobedience or for obeying God rather than Man fails, then we are for the high jump because then I think what former Prime Minister Vorster used to call 'the ghastly alternative' will be upon us. It could be bloodier than anything we have seen in Africa yet. Of course, we who are in the church will say 'To goodness we hope we can resolve this thing be sitting around a table'. But we do not want concessions thrown to us like crumbs. We want to be at the table to decide the menu together. Otherwise," and he paused, frowned, and shrugged his shoulders before continuing, "otherwise I think we've just got to accept that we'll have a bloodbath."

It seemed incongruous, not to say morally questionable, that this gentle man, who wore his bishop's cross over a sweater and claimed himself to be a man of peace, should be advocating violence. "Surely you oppose urban terrorism?" he was asked.

He threw his head back and cackled. "Why do you say 'surely'? I'm opposed to violence, yes. I keep saying I find Westerners an extraordinary group of people because during the Second World War most of the heroes in occupied Europe were the underground, and today one of our outstanding modern martyrs is Dietrich Bonhofer, who was involved in a plot to assassinate Hitler.

"Our churches have blessed participation in what they

consider to be just wars. For example, if it's a choice between freedom and Nazism, then you go to war. But when it comes to the question of black liberation, then you suddenly wake up to find that western Christendom has suddenly become pacifist. That concerns me very much. People talk about violence as if it is something that is being introduced into South Africa for the first time, something that is being brought in by the liberation movement. That is not true. South Africa is already a violent situation. Detention without trial is an example of it. Population removal schemes—they are a violence that are being done to people."

It is not possible to live in Soweto, as Tutu does, and not be aware of violence. In that sprawling township 10 miles south west of Johannesburg, which contains 102,000 houses for nearly two million people (many of them there illegally) in an area of 85 square miles of polluted urban sprawl, there is a woman raped every eight hours and a person killed violently every nine.

Tutu's obvious saintliness doesn't protect him. He used to jog around the streets of Soweto early in the morning, often when it was still dark, until his wife persuaded him that it would be safer to run around the track at nearby Orlando Stadium instead. She still worries that after working late he might get mugged as he walks to his car parked in a garage some way from his office. But he is cheerfully philosophical and realistic. "God is looking after me, and when I've done my part somebody else will take my place. Obviously you take reasonable precautions. There may be cranks around. But I think that if I am doing God's work, then he jolly well will have to be looking after me. We aren't indispensable. When he reckons I have done my part he will raise somebody else, so I don't keep looking over my shoulder."

His house, surrounded by a white wall and well lit at night, is only a few hundred yards from Ngakene Street where Winnie Mandela lives. Her husband Nelson Mandela is locked in solitary confinement while serving a life sentence on Robben Island, a notorious prison a few miles offshore from Cape Town. 8115 Ngakane Street, Orlando West, is a corner house with a trim lawn. Newspapers were stuck in the door when we passed and milk bottles stood on the step. The blinds were drawn.

Mandela, who was leader of the banned organisation, the African National Congress, is the man Bishop Tutu predicts will become Prime Minister of the new South Africa, the free South Africa that will come within five or ten years. Bishop Tutu slapped his knee and said forcefully: "Look man, there is no question in my mind, there is no doubt at all that we are going to be free. We will take you along, you whites, and let you share the freedom. Okay, some of us are not going to see the day freedom dawns and we tell our people that there are going to be casualties in the struggle. Our people know this. Some of their children are in exile, some are in jail.

"But we tell them you really are going to have a new kind of South Africa where you are going to be free. The only decision that whites can make, can still make, is how that freedom is going to come. It's going to happen. That we are not debating. It's only the how and the where and the when that we are still talking about."

CHAPTER TEN

Taking the medicine from Doc Craven

Doc Craven was in his 70th year when Beaumont's Lions were in South Africa. He still had the eyes of an iconoclast and liked nothing better than to be in the centre of the action having a good scrap, relishing both the trappings of power and the to and fro of an argument. He loved making speeches, rolling on the balls of his feet, hands clasped behind his back while acolytes laugh and applaud. This doughty campaigner has, in his time, taken on the titans in South Africa, the Nationalist Government, the Broederbond—South Africa's all-powerful secret society—and the Church, as well as the verkrampte, the unenlightened, in his own South African Rugby Board.

Now he was in the midst of his most difficult fight—to make South African rugby once again acceptable in world sport. "I have only one ambition left," he told British journalists "and that is to see the youth of my country welcomed as I was in countries all over the world."

The Springboks had not toured, except to France 1974, since the winter of 1969/70 and it took 10 years of sporting isolation by the rest of the world before the SARB was persuaded to approve and send a multi-racial team abroad. Following the visit to Britain of the South African Barbarians in 1979, the Lions played five out of their 18 matches against teams containing whites and non-whites. Craven felt proud of these improvements. "Change brought the Lions here," he admitted. "You were right and we were wrong." But, like many other South Africans, Craven naively thought that these few token changes would bring them peals of praise.

Far from it. Apartheid was still rampant in South African rugby in 1980. The inclusion of non-white players in rugby teams for 80 minutes on a Saturday afternoon does not change

Doc Craven at home, and on the attack: "I am proud to be South African. I've lived for this country. It's the o one I know, though my grandfather came from England; and you are not going to do damage to my country. Do look for stories in South Africa that you could find in England. You don't have to come to South Africa to f stinking ghettoes. You don't have to come to South Africa to find riots. You've got them in your own country. W pick on us?"

their lives for the rest of the week. They are still ruled by a bagful of controversial laws as to where they may live, work and whom they may marry.

Craven is a nice man and a firm friend, a reassuring figure in tweedy jacket and sturdy shoes. Among rugby men in South Africa he is a verligte, an enlightened man. But he couldn't understand why some reporters wanted to write about aspects of South African life that had nothing to do with rugby. This, and the outburst against the "loaded midweek teams", caused running battles with visiting journalists who accompanied the Lions. And then, when he did appreciate these problems, he created others by talking so clumsily and tactlessly that he offended many of the very people he was trying to reconcile. There were times in South Africa when Craven seemed completely to have lost his once-deft touch.

It all began with the resentment felt by the Lions management and players at the way that the South Africans had bolstered some of the invitation sides. The Lions knew that certain matches would be extremely hard. The game against Northern Transvaal has always been regarded as the fifth Test, and the Junior Springboks would to all intents and purposes be the South African second team. "Junior" in this context means any player who has not represented his country. It has no bearing on age. But the overt and repeated cramming of high-class, usually white, players into midweek matches, revealed an urge by the South Africans to beat the Lions that went beyond normal practice. Excluding Tests, Wynand Claassen, a No 8 from Natal, played in three of the first ten matches, and Hempies du Toit, a strong tight-head prop, in two and was due to make a third appearance against the Lions for Western Province.

One day Millar lost his temper and raged about being "conned into accepting a tour plan which was not what it seemed." He was, if anything, even more angry a few days later when he heard rumours that the South African Barbarians team to play the Lions in Durban in July would be selected by the SARB and not by the Barbarians' selectors. Millar, himself a Barbarians selector in the UK, was livid.

"This is completely contrary to the spirit of the selection of a Barbarians side, and I intend to bring it to the notice of the Barbarians committee at home," he said furiously. In the end good sense prevailed. The team, containing the electrifying Argentinian stand-off Hugo Porta and a catholic and welcoming smattering of white and non-white players, was acclaimed when it was announced.

It's an indictment of Craven that he couldn't understand the Lions' dissatisfaction and their resentment at what seemed to be a win-at-all-costs approach by the South African selectors. Was it because Craven's own loyalty to the Lions was unquestioned? "Good God, do you know what we think of the Lions?" Craven demanded as we sat in his office at Stellenbosch one morning in June. "The Lions made South African rugby when they came here in 1891. They came here when we were ruffians and barbarians. Five years later they came again. And when the war clouds were still hanging over South Africa, from the Anglo–Boer war, they came in 1903. Some of the soldiers who remained behind played for South Africa and got Springbok colours. Three of the 1896 players got VCs in battles against my people. It didn't worry us. The tradition that comes from 1891 we will not part with for anything in the world. You simply can't imagine South African rugby without the Lions.

"I've come to look upon rugby as a game that belongs not to us, or to you," continued Craven. "A man like Billy Beaumont belongs to South Africa as much as to Britain. His name is indelibly written in the annals of South African rugby history."

Craven had also been involved in other incidents that had disappointed players and journalists. In an emotional speech after the first Test he talked of his country being united in victory. Many people were shocked and bewildered. During the week preceding the first Test hundreds had been arrested and detained by the police in civil unrest all over South Africa. Two coloured youths were shot dead when police opened fire without warning in a desolate area of Cape Town. How could this country be united, we thought to ourselves? Later in his speech, Craven made it worse by attacking all the British press over some inflammatory comments that had been made by just one journalist. He was so unctuous towards his own team that one Lion walked out in silent protest, and others were still complaining about it days later.

In those early weeks in South Africa I felt that Craven hovered spiritually and physically over visiting journalists, like some sort of touring headmaster complete with mortarboard and cane. Sometimes he would reach down and pat one of us on the head. At other times he lashed out with his cane at one who had dared to criticise his country.

The rift between us deepened when Craven tactlessly returned to the attack in Bloemfontein in his speech after the second Test. He made an oblique apology for his earlier remarks but then chose to speak out again about South Africa's critics, using the Biblical term stone-throwers to describe them.

Surely he regretted those outbursts, I asked him, forgetting how fierce a South African can be when he is cornered. "No," he replied firmly. "I tried to differentiate between enemies and friends. I said our enemies both here and overseas. As far as I was concerned, if the shoe fitted then it fitted, and if it did not then ignore it. That's what I meant when I talked about stone-throwers and the like."

He suddenly leaped forward and jabbed his right forefinger into the air. He looked angry. "Look, you are not going to touch my country. I am proud to be a South African. I've lived for this country. It's the only one I know, though my grandfather came from England, and you are not going to do damage to my country.

"Don't look for stories in South Africa that you could find in England. You don't have to come to South Africa to find stinking ghettoes. You don't have to come to South Africa to find riots. You've got them in your own country. Why pick on us?"

In South Africa there were significant similarities between two of the country's principal characters: Craven and Prime Minister P. W. Botha, who both come from the more liberal Cape. Botha was trying to honour his election pledges to dismantle apartheid, yet finding that his great rival was the reactionary Transvaaler Dr Andreis Treurnicht, and similarly, Craven's coat-tails were being sat upon by the hardliners from the Transvaal and the Orange Free State. As he made changes, so the others resisted. The end result was compromise, camouflaged as change. After apartheid, neo-apartheid; after segregated rugby, neo-multi-racial rugby.

Over the years Craven dominated South African rugby by being dogmatic, dictatorial and didactic. I crossed swords with him several times. "You, you're the person who based his whole story on what a waiter told you," he said to me one day. "Let me tell you that if I were your professor I would fail you straight away, because for every statement you make you have to show your bibliography. What's the bibliography for your story? A waiter in an hotel. Everyone knows that waiters will tell you what they think you want to hear. That way they'll get bigger tips."

The question now was whether Craven could win his last battle. He talked optimistically of changes coming in South Africa, changes that could sweep the apartheid laws aside. "I've seen the Promised Land," he told us fervently. "I'm luckier than Moses; I've been to the Promised Land. I see it coming here in two years." When that happens what better time could there be for Craven, already president of the SARB for 25 years, to retire?

We talked for a few more minutes before it was time to go. "I'm sorry you won't stay and have some lunch," he said, pushing back his chair and standing up. "We have some lovely wine here, you know, and I was hoping to introduce you to some of it." We walked out of his office down the wooden-floored corridor and into a room with a number of oil paintings hanging on the walls. In 1700 the Cape Dutch style farmhouse, where we were standing, had been owned by one Hanneis Marais, whose portrait dominated the room. He gave a donation of R180,000 (£100,000) with which the University of Stellenbosch was founded.

Craven opened a window and climbed out over the low sill. "Come and look at this," he said over his shoulder. He walked to the middle of a lawn and looked up at the mountains that surrounded the university. "That's the Peak mountain, that's that's the Stellenbosch, and that's Simonsberg," he said, pointing. "Look, you can see Napoleon's head with his arms on his chest if you look carefully." Rocky outcrops on the side of the mountain did indeed make up the outline of that famous head, and further down the mountainside you could see the Emperor's arms, folded on his chest, and further down still, his feet.

As we travelled back to the airport I remembered what someone close to the Lions had said about Craven. "He's an old man, he's going slightly deaf," said this perceptive observer. "He has fought longer and harder than anyone else to get multi-racial rugby into South Africa, and no-one else could have achieved what he has done. So my attitude is to forgive him these indiscretions, which he didn't mean, and which he didn't realise would be so offensive. Not everybody realises quite how much he has done for South Africa. It may be that the true worth of Doc Craven will only be realised when he is dead."

The Lions were to come across Craven again in Port Elizabeth at the third Test. Meanwhile, they had two relaxing days in Durban, there being no midweek match before the Test, and trained hard in Kings Park on the morning of Wednesday, 25 June. The team to play in the Test was almost the same as that which had defeated Northern Transvaal the previous Saturday.

In the backs, Paul Dodge won his first Test cap after two solid performances in four days, against the Junior Springboks when he scored a try, and Northern Transvaal. To accommodate him his Leicester teammate, Clive Woodward, was moved out from the centre to the right wing. Scrum-half Colin Patterson had missed the game at Loftus Versfeld because of 'flu but now that he had recovered he just gained the vote over his Irish rival John Robbie. Injuries and loss of form had caused such problems among the Lions backs that Patterson was the only back playing in the third Test who had also been originally selected for the first Test a month earlier.

In the forwards Jeff Squire was moved from the flank to No 8, replacing Derek Quinnell, enabling Colm Tucker to make his first appearance in a Test. He had been outstanding against Naas Botha in the Northern Transvaal game, and his inclusion gave the Lions some more pace in the back row.

The flight from Durban to Port Elizabeth was delayed by two hours. I ordered tea and biscuits in the airport restaurant and sat down at a table with the all-Welsh trio of Gareth Williams, Elgan Rees and Peter Morgan. Williams, who had taken unpaid leave from his post as a physical education teacher at Maesteg Comprehensive in order to join the tour, said: "I'm going to have to change my job when I get back. I can't afford not to. I've lost £700 or so in two months out here on this trip and it could take me five years to get that back again. I can't expect my wife and son not to have a holiday for five years."

Peter Morgan said: "I've just bought three one-arm bandits, and when I get back I've got to find somewhere to put them in." He was 21, the youngest man in the team but described by Peter Wheeler as "the oldest 21-year-old I've ever met." A year earlier Morgan had been a drayman with a brewery in Haverfordwest. That hadn't worked out, and now he was working as a sales representative in West Wales for Fiat Alliss, manufacturers of earth-moving equipment. Morgan was witty and businesslike, not at all overawed by being on his first Lions tour. He was nicknamed Fagin because of his financial shrewdness, and his old looks when he took his teeth out before games.

"What's it like being a reporter on a tour?" he asked. "Do they cover, like, your expenses, what you spend? And when you get home will you get time off, like, or will it be straight back to work?"

"I tell you what," said Williams, who at 24 was only slightly more worldly-wise than his younger countryman. "You want to work on a Sunday paper. It's easy, mun. You only work one day each week. It's just like being a vicar."

After breakfast on the Friday morning Beaumont and Murphy held an impromptu press conference, as they had before the two previous Tests. Again they felt confident. "We've had it a little easier this time," said Murphy, who was wearing his red Lions tracksuit trousers and a green tee shirt, and had stretched out on a bed. "We've had 29 players to choose from. We're well prepared and there haven't been any disruptions in the side. It has been a hard physical tour and the players are under greater pressure than any other Lions tour. They wouldn't have survived if they didn't have great spirit. I've been on two Lions tours myself and read about four or five others, and I think the spirit and feeling around this tour is an example of what you want from a Lions tour.

"I think that the South Africans have remembered 1974 more than we have," Murphy continued. "They have prepared well this time and I think they have picked men who represent what South Africa stands for—a tremendous will-to-win. I must say that on the field they have shown a lot of character."

Beaumont intended to tell his team that they simply couldn't afford to make as many mistakes again as they had in the first two Tests. "We've all watched the films of those Tests with horror and dismay at how much we gave them," said the captain. "When was the pivotal moment in the second Test? After those series of drives up to the right hand corner in the second half. We put them under real pressure then for several minutes but we took the wrong options two or three times and that was when we lost the game. It wasn't when Ollie Campbell missed the penalty just after he had come on."

At 11.30 that morning the South African team had their photo-call in their hotel. It was an interesting ritual. In the first floor lounge three rows of chairs were set against a wall, and three arc lamps stood nearby. Two dozen photographers moved around anxiously lining up their cameras. Slowly the players filed out from a room and took up their appointed places. They were wearing precisely what they would wear for the game the next day and the studs of their boots thudded dully on the floor.

Morné du Plessis was one of the first to settle, and he sat quite still, his ankles crossed, while his teammates took their places around him. The first photograph was of the team and coach Nelie Smith, the former Springbok scrum-half and captain, and manager Butch Lochner. The moment the arc lights were switched on the cameras began to click and whir. This continued for five minutes until it was time to take another photograph, this one including the selectors, team doctor, and team liaison officers as well. Lochner seemed mesmerised by the camera. He chewed gum steadily and even when a Welshman who was watching it all with interest shouted out "Cheese! You're bloody winning", Lochner only managed a tiny, thin smile and his eyes barely moved from the cameras.

Before Naas Botha went off to change, I asked him what he thought was going to happen in the Test. "The second Test was hard but this is going to be even harder," he replied. "I don't know whether we will win. I think this is the Lions' best side, and I'm surprised it has taken them so long to find that out. Colm Tucker is a good player. He played very well against us last Saturday." Doc Craven, who had successfully forecast South Africa's victories in the first two Tests, was pessimistic. "We could lose this one," he said as he watched the South Africans training on Friday. "The Lions have had some good wins recently."

The weather turned out to favour the Lions. A strong south-westerly wind blew up from the Cape and with it came torrential rain. "Wonderful," Beaumont thought to himself as he heard it drumming on the window of his room. "I hope it snows." The weather was so bad that by kick-off time spectators were flocking away from the ground in their hundreds. Some of them were going home to watch on television in more comfortable surroundings.

What had been the traditional script in the Test series so far was changed when the Lions went ahead through a penalty by Campbell in the second minute. For the next 20 minutes South Africa were allowed to make only occasional attacks into the Lions half as they struggled against the wind and rain and it was not until Botha landed a straight, though long penalty from nearly 50 yards that the Lions stranglehold was broken—though not for long. After a scrum on the South African line scrum-half Divan Serfontein tried to hack the ball clear, was half-tackled by John O'Driscoll, and thus miskicked the ball. It popped into Bruce Hay's anxious hands and the left-wing was unstoppable from 10 yards. The score was only 7–3 to the Lions, but they had the look of victors.

The rain was stopping and starting and occasionally the sun even peeped out from behind dirty grey clouds scudding overhead as the second half opened—and it began with a huge punch-up. The tiny French referee, Jean-Pierre Bonnet, fluttered like a bird as he tried to stop the big men from swapping punches. Then came a warning for the Lions. Botha landed a 40-yard dropped goal, his first of the series, and he was growing in confidence. For that matter, however, so were Lions Jeff Squire, who had another beautiful game at No 8, Maurice Colclough, Beaumont and the curly-haired Irishman Colm Tucker. And Campbell, despite having a streak of congealed blood down his left cheek, was making a silk purse out of some pig's ears of passes from Patterson. After 10 minutes van Heerden was caught venturing offside at a line-out, and Campbell's second penalty, this one from 22 yards, gave the Lions a lead of 10–6.

If ever a team should have won a match, then it was the Lions now. For a time the Springboks seemed not to know which way to turn. They were being pulverised by the Lions forwards, where Beaumont was outplaying Moaner van Heerden, back after missing the second Test through injury, and the Lions forwards' scrummaging and mauling were magnificent. Unhappily for the Lions this possession was being squandered by the backs. Dodge knocked on during a sally down the blind side of a scrum five yards from the South African line. Patterson chose to have a dab at scoring a try himself when he should have passed to his right, and then Irvine entered the line at speed only, like Dodge moments before him, to knock-on with the line gaping before him. By any standards, and even allowing for the foul conditions and the wet ball, the Lions backs should have scored from one of these opportunities.

Even so, no-one sensed any trouble when moments later Botha put in a long shallow kick that right-wing Woodward just side-footed into touch in his own 25 before turning round and walking back 10 yards. But as the Lions forwards, and most of the Springboks' slogged across the field for the line-

The Third Test

Before the match, the Lions captain Bill Beaumont told his team that they could not afford to make as many mistakes as they had in the first two Tests. And in the game they dominated the line-outs, rucks and mauls, tied up the loose ball, and led for 70 minutes. This was against Springboks, who included one of South Africa's line-out heroes, Louis Moolman (above), winning the ball from Jeff Squire; and Moaner van Heerden, gathering the ball (below) supported by Theuns Stofberg. For a time, indeed, the Springboks did not know which way to turn, and one such moment is epitomised in the action, caught right, when Beaumont, taking the ball from scrum-half Patterson, charged forward like a human tank. The Lions, the better side, nevertheless lost 12–10.

out, South Africa's left-wing Gerrie Germishuys quickly spotted an opportunity. He threw the ball to teammate Theuns Stofberg, the big second row turned flanker, who was the first Springbok forward to arrive, and the two of them interpassed—and as Woodward came in to tackle Stofberg, Germishuys was able to dive over triumphantly in the corner for his third try of the series. Botha's conversion from the left touchline, a pressure kick if ever there was one, was judged to perfection, so the Springboks, who had been behind since the second minute, now led 12–10, a lead they scarcely deserved.

It scarcely need be said that the Lions tried everything in the last 10 minutes. And when Ray Mordt late-tackled Irvine, Campbell's penalty from five yards inside the left touchline flew straight and only just past the right upright. Then came a flurry of attacks: by Gravell down the middle, by Dodge going right and by Hay, chasing a kick to his left. But each time, Pienaar or Serfontein or Botha kicked the ball miles upfield to waste time. Two minutes of injury time had passed when the last line-out came five yards from the South African line. But this time Moolman won the ball, Botha booted it away from danger, and referee Bonnet's whistle went.

So South Africa had won the game and the series with a try executed with the speed of a cat burglar, the skill of a surgeon. In three Tests they had outscored the Lions by 10 tries to four and, in doing so, had upset all the canons of modern rugby which state that forward dominance wins matches. Beaumont's Lions were brave and showed huge resources of character but the backs just weren't good enough.

As the Lions huddled in their beachfront hotel on Saturday night with the rain rattling on the windows, they could scarcely believe their ill luck. They had dominated the line-outs, rucks and mauls, and tied up the loose ball. They had avoided making any wild clearance kicks that Germishuys or Pienaar could run back at them and, like good little boys, they had made their tackles. Despite squandering at least three copper-bottomed scoring chances they had led for 70 minutes. Yet they, the better side, had lost. "It's like a bad dream," said Noel Murphy. "I'm desperately sorry for the boys."

CHAPTER ELEVEN

Emergency Ward —an Irish injection

TUESDAY morning, 8 July, when the Lions were in the diamond town of Kimberley, was another brilliantly clear though somewhat chilly morning, typical of the winter days on the high veld. Soon the sun would come out and lift the temperature to the mid-sixties. It had last rained at the end of June when the Lions were in Port Elizabeth for the third Test, and the last wet day before that had been Monday, 26 May.

This particular day, the 66th since the original party of Lions had left London, Tony Ward awoke promptly at eight in his room on the third floor of the Kimberley Hotel. In the other bed Elgan Rees was still asleep. Soon the alarm-call Rees had ordered would waken him with a start. Ward looked sleepily around the room and couldn't help noticing that it wasn't the usual jumble of books, tracksuit, and other kit.

The room had two beds, three armchairs covered in a yellow mock-velvet material, a bathroom off to the right as one entered, and a cupboard set into the wall opposite the bathroom. There was a vanity mirror and a writing table along another wall, and the room's telephone was on the table by the side of Ward's bed.

It was a room typical of those in most of the 12 different hotels the Lions had stayed in up to that time. The smallest hotel had been the Elgro in Potchefstroom, the largest the Elangeni in Durban, which had 20 floors, 800 bedrooms, six lifts and at least four restaurants. Most of the hotels, such as the identikit Holiday Inns, were of three- or four-star quality, and the two-star Elgro and the five-star Landdrost in Johannesburg, and Beverley Hills in Durban were the two exceptions to the general rule.

No matter what the standard of their hotels, the Lions,

wherever they stayed, had to be alert to prevent thefts from their rooms. Most players nevertheless lost small items such as ties and sweaters, but Colin Patterson had a £200 camera and a lens worth £100 stolen from his room in Port Elizabeth. During the fourth Test, held in Pretoria, someone was to sneak into the Lions' changing room and steal John Carleton's blazer and with it nearly 200 rand (about £110). The blazer was returned the next day. The final straw came when Peter Wheeler and fellow hooker Alan Phillips found two South Africans rummaging through their bags during the reception after the fourth Test. "We just wanted some souvenirs" they said, not very shamefacedly, as the two Lions advanced on them.

Ward was lucky. He hadn't lost anything prior to the game at Kimberley and, in fact, he was to see the tour out without losing more than a tie, which disappeared from his room on the last morning. Like many of the players he made a point of keeping all his valuables in the hotel's safe. In Kimberley he stowed away his camera and some presents he had bought a few weeks earlier while at Bloemfontein and, in common with his teammates, he always kept the key of his room in his pocket rather than leaving it at reception.

That Tuesday morning he awoke with a sense of foreboding. "It's match day," he realised, and immediately he started worrying and thinking about the game. "I may be a confident person on the field but off it I am a pessimist. I worry about everything. I think of everything that can possibly go wrong during a game, and at times like this you say silly things to yourself.

"You ask yourself 'Is it really worth it and why the hell do I do it?' Bill (Beaumont) has said that to me two or three times on tour as he goes around the rooms on the morning of a match. I know it's worth it, definitely, but it is pressure and it does make me feel nervous. Personally I feel that if I hadn't got the added chore of place-kicking then I wouldn't feel the pressure as much. Maybe I'm wrong, I don't know."

This particular Tuesday the Lions were to play the last midweek match of their tour. It was at the de Beers Stadium in Kimberley, ten minutes drive from the hotel, against the fiery local team, Griqualand West, known as Griquas, a team who played in the second division of the Currie Cup. Although it was the Lions' eighth midweek game it was only the second they had played against a recognised, regular team. Their six other midweek games, played on Tuesdays and Wednesdays, were against such sides as a South African Invitation XV at Potchefstroom or the South African Country XV at Windhoek. Then there were the games against the non-white unions—the South African Rugby Association at East London and the South African Rugby Football Federation at Stellenbosch.

What added interest to the game at Kimberley was that if the Lions beat Griquas they would be only the second team from Britain to be undefeated in non-Test games in South Africa. After their 3-0 drubbing in the Tests, they wanted this record. As Ward lay on his back, staring at the ceiling and worrying about the game, he realised that he was much more tense than he had been the week before, when the Lions played the South African Barbarians at Kings Park, Durban.

He got up quickly, shaved and dressed in a white tee shirt and shorts, and slipped on his red Lions tracksuit trousers. Then he walked down to breakfast in the team's dining room where he ate cereal, eggs, bacon and tomatoes and two slices of thickly-buttered toast. It would be almost his last food until dinner. He went for a quick haircut at the barber's salon on the ground floor of the hotel, and then returned to his room and climbed back into bed to rest.

On the table by his bedside was a pile of books, among them The Electric Horseman, The Memory of Eva Ruyker, and Kramer v Kramer. He chose the one on the top, Peter Benchley's The Island, and started to read it. Soon, however, his mind began to wander and he rang reception and asked if they would put a video cassette on the television. The Bermuda Triangle had been shown the night before but both he and Rees had been so tired they had fallen asleep while trying to watch it.

For the next two hours Ward didn't move from his bed. The chirpy Irishman Colin Patterson, who was playing scrum-half that afternoon, kept coming in to talk about moves the two of them could try during the game. Patterson was edgy too, anxious to retain his place in the Test team.

He had played in the Tests at Cape Town, Bloemfontein and Port Elizabeth but then he was dropped for the Lions' penultimate Saturday game, against Western Province in Cape Town. His place was taken by John Robbie, another Irishman, who had scarcely put a foot wrong in the four games he had played since, like Ward, he had joined the Lions as a replacement. He was the fourth, and his arrival had meant that all four half-backs now on the playing strength were Irish.

"Colin must have come into my room at least four times during the morning," said Ward. "He kept going on about trying out this move from here, and then that from that situation he'd want me to do something else. He was so keyed up for the game. He was desperate to get back into the Test team. He really wanted to prove a point. When you're knocked down you always want to bounce back. Colin is a very confident person—scrum-halves usually are, unlike stand offs—but I knew he was edgy."

At 12.45 Ward swung his legs out of bed and went downstairs for lunch, which he always eats three hours before kick-off (it was a 4 o'clock match). There is great ceremony about what rugby players eat immediately before they play. The 1977 Lions captain in New Zealand, Phil Bennett, preferred only an egg nog before a game. Trevor Evans, the former Wales flanker, liked steak and chips, while Naas Botha, the South African stand off, eats scrambled eggs, bacon and drinks two or three Cokes. Ward, deprived of his usual plaice he had on match days in Britain, settled for Kingklip, a fish that tastes like plaice, with a slice of lemon and a cup of tea.

By 1.15 he was back in bed, able to rest for another hour. "I reckon the really hard work is done from 12 to three when you think about the game and get yourself in the right frame of mind, so that hopefully when you run on to the field it's just a matter of enjoying yourself." At 2.15 he got up and started to dress, this time in his blue No 1 blazer with the larger Lions badge on the breast pocket (the Lions No 2 he 25-year-old Irishman ony Ward, a brilliant kicker, els "the pressure" on the orning of a match. In imberley before the last idweek match of the tour, ter a breakfast of cereal, eggs, con, tomatoes and toast, he d his hair cut and then went ck to bed to rest. He rose ter to eat some fish and have a p of tea, after which he went ck to bed again. Ward was e of the Lions' first placements. Included in the am for the first Test, he cked an astonishing 18 points all and was the hero of the itish Isles side.

blazer was black and had a smaller badge), his grey flannels and black shoes and a white shirt and Lions tie.

By now he had got all the official Lions clothing: two blazers, one pair of grey flannels and one pair of black and white check trousers that the Lions complained made them look like Rupert Bear. Their clothing also included three shirts (one red, one white and one pink), a blue V-neck sweater two Lions ties and one Lions bow tie, and a red holdall stamped with BIRUT, as well as one Lions track suit.

The clothing had all been sent on to him about two weeks after he arrived in South Africa on 23 May. He had been flown out to cover while Campbell received treatment for his hamstring and Gareth Davies's left shoulder was given time to mend. Ward arrived when the Lions were in Bloemfontein and he did not expect to stay very long. "I wasn't on stand-by at home and I had been playing a lot of sevens and doing a lot of travelling. In the three weekends before I came over here and I had been to Bermuda, Paris and Amsterdam. I wouldn't have done that if I thought I might be later be called out to South Africa."

When Ward was in Amsterdam he had heard rumours that he might be needed by the Lions but he thought no more about it until Monday, 19 May, eight days later. That morning he happened to be at the vets with his dog and while he was there he received a call from the manager of his sports shop in Limerick saying that reporters from British newspapers had been trying to contact him.

That night, at home, Ward had a phone call from Ronnie Dawson, one of Ireland's representatives on the International Board. Dawson wanted him to go to South Africa to become a Lion and to go as soon as possible. Ward was thrilled, but he had to speak to his wife and put his business in order first.

His wife Maura, who was studying to be a PE teacher at a teacher-training college in Limerick, happened to be away on an outdoor-pursuits course in Cork and it wasn't until Tuesday morning that Ward managed to contact her. They agreed that she should travel to Limerick that evening so that the two of them could go to Dublin on Wednesday.

Ward had opened his own sports shop in Limerick a couple

of years earlier and he spent the Wednesday before he left for London en route to South Africa signing cheques, taking stock in the shop, chasing up outstanding orders, and paying a quick visit to the bank manager.

Early on Thursday morning 22 May, he flew out of Dublin to London where he was met by John Lawrence, the secretary of the Four Home Unions Tours committee. The two of them travelled in to Barkers of Kensington where Ward was measured for his Lions clothes and they returned to Heathrow airport just in time for Ward to catch the 6.15 flight to Johannesburg that night.

As he checked in at Heathrow's Terminal Three he did not know that former Springbok, Jan Pickard, had already tipped off South African Airlines that Ward was travelling, and had arranged that he be given four seats in a row so that he could curl up and sleep on the 15-hour flight.

Ward duly joined the Lions on the Friday morning, 23 May the day before the team played the Orange Free State. He looked tired and a little bewildered, but within an hour or two he was out training. It was a dramatic return to international rugby. In 1979 he had been elected Player of the Year by Rugby World magazine. In nine internationals he had kicked 77 points and, incidentally, he had scored in all nine games. Then, when Ireland toured Australia in the summer of 1979, he was dropped in favour of Ollie Campbell and he didn't regain his place during the 1979/80 championship, when Campbell scored 46 points to beat the record of 38 Ward shared with Roger Hosen, Phil Bennett and Steve Fenwick.

While Campbell and Davies had both been injured the Lions limped along with David Richards at stand-off, where he plays for his club Swansea. Richards's versatility was a priceless gift for the Lions but he hadn't quite got the authority of a natural stand-off. It was clear that the Welshman was better as a centre. So once Ward, who was a natural stand-off, arrived in South Africa, he was immediately picked for the game against the Proteas, the team from the South African Rugby Football Federation, at Stellenbosch. If he proved his fitness in that game, which was played on a

Tuesday, he would be selected for the first Test four days later.

Ward survived the rough-and-tumble of the extremely ill-tempered game in Stellenbosch, in which Fran Cotton went off with his heart trouble and in which the Lions failed to reach 20 points for the first time on tour. He kicked one conversion and, with his last two shots, two penalties, but before that he had missed an agonising six other kicks. "Kicking is in the mind," says Ward. "It all depends how well you kick that first one. If the first one goes over then you are so confident that you could kick all the rest. This was just one of those days." Later, on the eve of the fourth Test, he and Campbell went to Loftus Versfeld for some kicking practice, and Ward, who was not playing, could do no wrong. When his 11th successful kick out of eleven attempts sailed through the posts he decided to stop.

Having lasted out the Stellenbosch game Ward was duly included in the Lions' team for the first Test at historic Newlands, Cape Town. There he was heroic. He was the Lions' baggy-trousered hero, kicking an astonishing 18 points in all. Three times he landed penalties in the first half, one bouncing in off an upright, to keep the Lions only seven points behind the Springboks who had already scored three tries. He kicked two more penalties after half-time and when he spotted an opening in front of him he dropped a goal with his left foot, a goal that actually took the Lions into the lead.

There were only two blemishes on his performance, the more culpable when with less than ten minutes remaining his kick across field was caught on the full by the speedy left wing Germishuys, who eventually was to go on to achieve the notable distinction of scoring tries against the Lions in each of the first three Tests. Here Germishuys raced across field in a slanting run, and after passing to Pienaar, the full-back passed it on quickly to Rob Louw and then to right wing Ray Mordt before it came back infield for Germishuys to take it again and race 20 yards for a brilliant try.

"I felt bad when Germishuys scored," Ward said later, "but not as bad as when I missed touch in the first half and they scored from that. The kick to Germishuys was not a good kick, but we should have stopped him." Two minutes after Germishuys's try Ward made amends when he kicked his fifth penalty to level the scores and, incidentally, to nose past Tom Kiernan's previous Lions record of 17 points in a Test match at Pretoria in 1968.

The Lions' Cape Town hero did not remain a hero for long. There is no sentimentality in rugby. For the next four games Ward was kept on the touchline as first Davies and then Campbell returned after injury. Ward was not to play again until 18 days later, against the Junior Springboks in Johannesburg, four days after the Lions had been beaten in the second Test. On the lush grass of the famous Wanderers ground the Lions ran in three tries in the second half against the "Juniors" and Clive Woodward converted the one by right wing Elgan Rees. Ward ended the game having failed to score after attempting one penalty and one conversion.

He was back in form by his fourth game, against the South African Barbarians at Kings Park, Durban, despite having had to be rescued by a lifeguard while out swimming the prevous day. "It was no joke, I'll be honest with you," said Ward. "Myself, Woody (Clive Woodward), John O'Driscoll and Colm Tucker were swimming and I was about 15 to 20 yards out, no problem.

"I just dived under the water and the next thing, when I came up, I was about 40 yards out from the beach. I heard something over the loudspeaker and it was obvious that those who were far out were to swim in. I panicked and started to try to do so, but I couldn't, no matter how hard I tried. John O'Driscoll was only about ten yards from me and slightly further in but he didn't realise that I was in trouble.

"The lifeguard swam out to me with one of those round buoys with a handle on each side and a piece of rope about ten yards long. He flung the rope to me and I held on to it, and he dragged me in with one hand while swimming with the other hand. I lost the rope twice coming in. I tell you I could easily have gone. We've been joking about it since but it scared me. It's the first time it has ever happened. I am not a weak swimmer, but I'm not a strong swimmer either, and I couldn't handle that."

The next day, obviously recovered, Ward kicked two conversions, three penalties and scored a try against the Barbarians. His total of 17 points was his second highest from any one game and his overall total of 43 points made him one of the Lions' highest scorers so far even though he had played only four games and had scored in only three. And now in Kimberley he was as nervous as a kitten as he joined his teammates in Beaumont's room for a quick team meeting just before the Griquas game.

There had also been a meeting the night before at which Syd Millar, Murphy and Beaumont had all stressed the importance of winning the game against Griquas, and Murphy had emphasized some basic tactics. But the main team talk was to be given now by Derek Quinnell, the captain of the day. "This is the last time I shall ever wear a Lions jersey," said the big Welsh forward as he spoke to his men in Beaumont's room. "It's the last time some of you will wear it too. I want to make sure that we go out with a win."

On the way to the ground the Lions sang their team song, "Flower of Scotland", before they got off the bus. They had a shock when they went into the changing room because there were still four or five players there from a curtain-raiser, the floor was littered with beer cans and someone had to be called to clean it up. Finally, the Lions were able to put their kit down before they walked out to examine the burned, grassless pitch. Said Ward: "As a stand-off you're meant to have a look at the sun and find out which way the wind is blowing, but it's going to be no different doing it then than when you go on to the field, and so I don't bother. We had the wind at our backs in the first half and the sun was no particular problem."

It was a nervous game that began in spectacular fashion with Bruce Hay barging into a three-quarter movement, and Ian Stephens and John Beattie linking, for Beattie to go over. It was only the third minute and it looked as though the Lions would run up a big score. "Woody and I were talking just after the game," recalled Ward "and we both agreed how often it is that when one side score in the first minutes it is inevitably a hard game thereafter."

And so it proved this time. Oosthuisen scored a rampaging

try in the corner for Griquas after a fierce attack and Patterson, in making a tackle fell heavily and tore badly the ligaments of his right knee. Ambulance men pulled at his leg as he lay on the ground and the pain was so intense that he cursed and shouted at them to leave him alone. "He was shouting like a stuck pig," said one player later.

It was three minutes before Patterson was carried off the field on a stretcher and John Robbie, who had done his warming up while Patterson was being examined, was immediately able to take his place. Robbie had a brief word with Ward, telling his stand-off to come a little nearer to start with until he had got his accuracy. They had played together twice on tour before this game.

"John and Colin are both excellent passers of a ball," said Ward. "Because Colin has a smaller physique he probably gets the ball away quicker, whereas John is that bit taller and has to wind up slightly. Terry Holmes is big too and when he is passing from left to right he has to dive-pass or else pivot-pass if he has time. I'd say that of the three Colin is the fastest passer from both sides, left to right and right to left."

At half-time the Lions trailed 7–9, the fourth time on tour, outside Test matches, that they had been behind at the interval. If they were to win and achieve that record they wanted so badly, they had to improve in the second half. They needed to slow the game down and play it at their pace and to their tactics. "We had put pressure on ourselves because we knew we had to win," recalled Ward. "It was a very loose game, very ragged and negative. Griquas didn't want to play constructive football at all. They preferred just to kick the ball, to hack it anywhere, and when they kicked it ahead we were at sixes and sevens."

Derek Quinnell spoke firmly to his men at half-time. "We've got 40 minutes to lift ourselves from humiliating defeat," he said. "Come on!"

Ward recalls: "I was conscious that we might lose, but somehow I didn't think that we would. Forty minutes is a long time. It wasn't good, though, that I was even conscious that we might lose. We were all internationals and they're not. We had to keep saying that to ourselves."

In the second half the Lions faced the wind and pulled their game together. They fell three more points behind when Gawie Visagie, a brilliant scrum half, kicked his second penalty but were saved by their youngest player, Peter Morgan, who first dropped a goal and then, after Robbie had scored a try, also scored a try between the posts.

A dropped goal by Robbie from an indirect free-kick gave the Lions 16 points in as many minutes in the second half. Now they led 23–12. But then in a final flurry Visagie kicked his third penalty for Griquas, this one from 35 yards, and in injury time his chip over a scrum led to a try by Koch. The final score was 23–19 to the Lions.

There was an air of muted excitement in the changing room. While Ward sipped a drink of orange from a paper cup, Murphy and Beaumont went to the door to talk to a knot of journalists anxious to find out about Patterson's knee. "It's a shocker all right," said Murphy, clearly distressed. "I'd say it's the worst I've ever seen. You can move his leg like a fiddle."

There were other injuries as well. Elgan Rees had a crack on his jaw, Peter Morgan had taken a bang on his left knee and need physiotherapy, while Ward, when tackled near the end of the game, had landed heavily on his right shoulder and, at the same time, banged his right knee. His shoulder stiffened up and his knee became more sore. For 20 minutes after the game he had had to have ice put on his knee to curb the swelling and bruising and by the time he was ready for a shower the water had gone cold. Ward, Phil Orr and Quinnell returned to their hotel to have showers and change.

The rest of the team attended the reception which was held in the town hall, an Edwardian style building in the centre of Kimberley. They arrived at six o'clock and walked into the main room where tables were laid with sandwiches, crisps, peanuts, vol au vents. White-jacketed waiters bustled around serving drinks and a hundred or so people stood around in little knots.

Soon the speeches began, by the Mayor, by the home team captain Piet van Zyl, by Lions manager Syd Millar and by Beaumont, who as tradition demands of the touring captain, was expected to speak at every after-match function, whether he played or not. In fact Beaumont did not do so after only one of the 18 matches and that was when Cotton was taken to hospital after the game at Stellenbosch. Beaumont was so worried that he went with his fellow Lancastrian, and then the captain's speech was left to Derek Quinnell.

At Kimberley, Beaumont was laconic and full of praise for Griquas. "There were a few moments when I was a worried man today," he said. "I'm sure that if you play like this more often you won't stay in the second division of the Currie Cup very much longer." As tradition demands, a presentation of a Lions tie and badge was made to the referee, Dr Louis Wessels of Northern Transvaal, and to the two touch-judges.

Back at the hotel Ward dumped his kit in his room and went down to the foyer to join Robbie and Campbell to visit Patterson in hospital. They stayed for a half hour, found that the scrum-half was as chirpy as ever, and then returned to the hotel for dinner.

By now Ward was exhausted. The four o'clock kick-off had made it an even longer day than usual and he was so tired his appetite had gone. He picked unenthusiastically at his steak and chips. By half past ten he was in bed. His knee throbbed badly and was swelling up so John O'Driscoll, the flanker, in his other capacity as a doctor, came to give him some pain killing and anti-inflammatory tablets and sleeping pills. And he put some strapping on Ward's knee as well. By the next morning the swelling had gone down and Ward was named as a reserve in the team to play in the fourth and final Test on the Saturday.

CHAPTER TWELVE

Great Gatsbys Gathered in Song

In defeat as in victory, rugby players sing. On the Saturday night after their defeat in the third Test, in Port Elizabeth, many of the Lions gathered in a room overlooking the rain-lashed ocean and sprawled on beds and chairs, sat on the floor, or leaned against a wall. It was a condition that everyone entering the room had to have a centre parting in his hair and his collar turned up. Failure to do so meant a penalty, and Bruce Hay imposed it with pleasure. "Down in one," he would say holding out a full glass. "Hey! down in one!"

"The Great Gatsby look is all the rage," said Ollie Campbell, peering at himself in the bathroom mirror, tugging at his collar, and smoothing down a plaster that covered the four stitches inserted in his left cheek after the Test.

Derek Quinnell sat on the edge of the bed, quietly smoking a cigarette. Jim Renwick, playing the guitar, and John Carleton both wore camel-coloured flat caps and led the singing. Alan Tomes quiffed his hair back, wiggled his hips, and did his version of Jailhouse Rock. Ray Gravell went through a half dozen verses of the Ballad of Big John.

From time to time a waiter brought in bottles of rum. Gravell grasped each and anxiously peered at the label. "No, no, haven't you got any Captain Morgan? I must have Captain Morgan rum. This stuff is gut-rot. Honest, it's awful."

For two hours they sang their hearts out as teammates and friends drifted in and out of the room. Bill Beaumont, the captain, lay on a bed smoking and singing quietly. His face was puffed, one eye blackened. His head ached from where he had been kicked almost into unconsciousness just after the start of the second half. He looked, and probably felt, disconsolate.

As the Lions trooped off to bed that night a familiar face peeped out from the switchboard cubbyhole. "What time would you like a call sir?" asked Phil Orr, the burly Irish prop. "Seven fifteen? Very good. We'll look after you, don't worry."

The innermost soul of the 1980 Lions was bared for those few hours, and in adversity they showed dignity and control. They had lost the Test series, were three down and one to play, and now faced the possibility of being the first Lions side ever to be whitewashed in Test matches in South Africa. But where earlier Lions teams might have smashed down doors, set off fire alarms, and hosed colleagues out of bed, the 1980 Lions proved themselves the most self-controlled, best managed and best disciplined party to have left Britain for years.

They were one of the best led sides too, for in South Africa Beaumont matured from a workmanlike player into an outstanding captain. He worked harder than any other player and cheerfully accepted the round of social engagements. Until even his patience wore out, he accepted every phone call that came for him, and sometimes they came at ten-minute intervals. He, more than any other Lion, always had time to stop for a chat with the supporters around the team's hotel, regardless of whether or not he knew them. *They* knew *him*, and to Beaumont that was as important as if it had been the other way around.

Another characteristic of his that shone through brightly in South Africa was his feeling for others. One day he heard that the young son of a British journalist had broken his elbow and was in hospital. He was genuinely concerned and dug around in his suitcase and produced three prized Lions badges and an autographed team sheet. "Poor kid," he said. "Here, give him these."

Beaumont thrived on the pastoral work he had to do with his team, and though he didn't ever play in a midweek game he nevertheless made a point of spending an hour or so talking to the captain of the day. "He has been terrific," said Derek Quinnell, who captained the Lions' midweek side five times, more than any other player. "If he has a fault then it's perhaps that he spent *too much* time with me, but that's his enthusiasm coming out. You can't blame him for that."

Being a tour captain also means leading in little things too, and not once in dozens of coach journeys was Beaumont late on the team's bus. During delays at airports the captain used to act as quiz master. "Which Englishman scored 3,500 runs in 1959 and also played rugby for England?" he asked as we whiled time away at Johannesburg airport one day. That was easy. Mike Smith was the answer. "Which First Division football manager once sang professionally with Joe Loss's orchestra?" Beaumont looked around waiting for an answer that never came. "Terry Venables" he said finally.

He paused for a moment to think up another question. "Which team have played rugby in ten countries over the last two years and had their club disbanded in 1979?" No one knew the answer to this. Beaumont grinned, making the most of his moment of triumph. Then he blurted out, almost apologetically, and to a chorus of boos: "HMS Ark Royal RFC."

On the Sunday after the Test defeat, Beaumont and Tony Ward joined a group of journalists and tried to visit New Brighton, a black township on the outskirts of Port Elizabeth. As the cars swept in convoy up to the township they noticed that police Land Rovers were blocking the road. "This is a riot area," said an armed policeman wearing the familiar khaki uniform. "You must turn back." To those who had been into the township before, all seemed quiet and normal. But to make sure the visitors saw nothing, a police Land Rover shepherded them out of the township and back on to the main road to their hotel.

The same day Noel Murphy took Paul Dodge and three Welshmen from the midweek side, Peter Morgan, Elgan Rees and Gareth Williams, for a drive up the windswept coast. They stopped for tea and scones at a roadside cafe and then returned to their hotel in time for dinner.

On the Monday the Lions flew back to Durban, to the five-star Beverley Hills hotel perched on a cliff above the Indian Ocean. The rehabilitation that was now underway included a period of deep self-examination. Since the storming triumphs of the Lions in New Zealand in 1971, and of Willie-John McBride's men in South Africa three years later, the Lions had lost six of their last seven Tests to New Zealand and South Africa.

On the Tuesday, after a hard training session at Kings Park where the Lions were to play the South African Barbarians, Beaumont wallowed contentedly in his bath and considered this doleful record. "Pete Wheeler and I were just saying how we've played in six Tests and won more ball than our opponents and dominated them completely and yet we've lost five of them," said the captain as he poured shampoo on to his hair. "I think that we were good enough to take the series. On Saturday we had three chances and we could have been 18 points up if we had taken them all. But we didn't take any." He gave a sad grin, as much as to say, "So it's our own sweet fault, isn't it?"

He was racing to get ready for a lunch in Durban where he was standing in for Syd Millar, who had had to cry off at short notice that morning. "I could do without this actually, but I suppose I've got to go," he muttered as he bustled around his room dressing himself in his blue blazer, grey flannels and Lions tie, and struggling with his cufflinks. "Still, the Springboks don't deserve to be 3–0 up. I would put any money you like on it that if they were to tour Britain next year they won't win all their games."

In his eight games up to and including the third Test, Beaumont's play had improved steadily. He was more combative at line-outs, more fiery in the loose. His tactical direction, his one weakness, had been less obvious. Scotsman John Beattie said admiringly, "There are big men who play small, and small men who play big. Bill's one of the second group. If only he had a couple more inches."

Ray Gravell christened his captain Bobo. "Bobo's been fantastic," said the exuberant Welshman. "He's a great leader and a great bloke. Imagine me, a Welsh nationalist, saying that about an English donkey, a second row forward. Well, I tell you, I wouldn't have said that before the tour."

Gravell had a particular role among the Lions of 1980. An occasional visitor into the party could be forgiven for thinking that the bearded Welshman was a self-confident extrovert. "Bobo," he would shout in a mock plummy English accent across the most crowded room. "Well played old chap. Terribly good show. Top hole, what."

In reality Gravell was nervous and unsure of himself. After every game he played he would keep asking journalists: "I did all right, didn't I? I did all right?" Tony Ward remembers one training session when he, Gareth Davies and Ollie Campbell were practising their kicking and Gravell was fetching the balls for them. In between kicks he would ask ceaselessly: "How did I look in training today? Did I look sharp?"

You would have to scour Wales to find a more overt Welshman than the 14-stone, broad-shouldered centre. He cries during the Welsh national anthem and on tour he kept joking that the number of English-owned holiday cottages being burned in the Welsh borders had mysteriously dropped while he was in South Africa. "Wait until July 14th when I get home," he liked to say.

A memory many Lions will have is of Gravell pacing the changing room before a game, singing Myfanwy or Cwm Rhondda or Calon Lan while pulling on his red Lions shirt and pausing from time to time to be sick in the lavatory. "He's the most generous bloke you'll ever meet," says Peter Morgan of his Llanelli clubmate. "When the Lions played the Invitation XV at Potchefstroom Hennie Shields came out of the hotel after the game as if it was Christmas. Gravs had given him everything. Honest, he'd let you have the shirt from his back if you wanted it."

During the three days in Durban the least pleasant task that Beaumont had was that of raising his team's morale after the Test which had lost them the series and cast them as failures, regardless of whatever else they might do. The captain was blunt and forthright. "He said we must stick two fingers in the air to the Springboks and make sure that we win the next four games," recalled one Lion, somewhat dazed at the simplicity of his captain's advice.

The Lions were helped in their rehabilitation by their surroundings. In warm sunshine they went water-skiing

One of the most popular tourists, and the most superstitious, was the Irishman Rodney O'Donnell. Naturally, on Friday 13 June, his teammates had a lot of good-natured fun with him. When O'Donnell tentatively stuck his head out of the door of his room that day he found the corridor barricaded with every conceivable booby trap. A ladder supported by chairs was overhanging the doorway, the floor leading to the lift and the top of the stairs had been plastered with tape making dozens of straight lines, which O'Donnell will go to almost any lengths to avoid, and floor was moreover sprinkled with salt. The number 13 could been seen everywhere. O'Donnell recoiled with horror and jumped—carefully—back into bed. Later, one of the tour's many casualties, he injured himself while making a tackle during the game against the Junior Springboks and the following day underwent an operation for a dislocated neck which involved wiring the sixth and seventh vertebrae. In this case O'Donnell was a lucky man. Another fraction of an inch and he could have been paralysed.

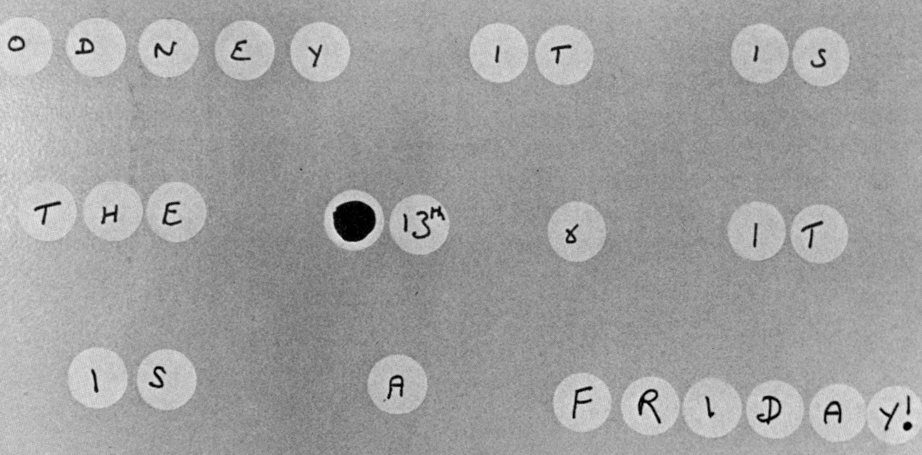

(Beaumont is good enough to mono-ski) and they lounged like lords by the hotel pool. Even Tony Ward's equilibrium was unharmed when he had to be rescued by a lifeguard after getting into difficulties in the heavy waves just offshore. The next day he scored 17 points against the South African Barbarians.

To cheer them up even more, the superstitious Irishman Rodney O'Donnell, one of the most popular tourists, was fit to rejoin them briefly. He had been in hospital in Johannesburg after dislocating his neck and going within a whisker of being paralysed in the game against the Junior Springboks two weeks earlier. "Wouldn't you know it," said O'Donnell, who was wearing an elaborate neckbrace. "I get hurt tackling No 13, I was 13 days in hospital, and this damn contraption has 13 holes in it."

O'Donnell's superstitiousness had been a talking point among the Lions since they had gathered in London. An obvious sign was the way he always threw the ball back over the bar after fielding a successful penalty or conversion, and he would go to almost any lengths not to walk on lines. He was even reported to be avoiding them as he arrived at the hospital in Johannesburg with his dislocated neck. The Irish journalist Ned van Esbeck observed: "I tell you, there's more of a ritual when Rodney comes out of his house in Dublin, walks down the garden path and gets into his car than there is in the Tridentine Mass."

Less well known was O'Donnell's ritual for getting into bed. First every picture in the room had to be straight, the telephone resting squarely on its cradle, the lights out, the bed covers turned back. Then, O'Donnell would charge at his bed like a high jumper, approaching it at a trot in a curving run. At the last minute he would leap backwards into the air, doing a Fosbury Flop, and, if he had judged it correctly, he would land on the bed hitting the bottom sheet without first touching the top sheet or blanket. Once safely in bed he thrashed his feet around half a dozen times and once that was done he could go to sleep. If, however, anything went wrong, he had to start the whole procedure all over again.

And of course, he had the usual nervousness about numbers.

Arriving at the Landdrost Hotel in Johannesburg he screamed when he noticed the number on his room key. It was 418. "I can't have this one," he explained anxiously to Syd Millar. "The numbers add up to 13."

Coach Murphy was in trouble after O'Donnell's accident. Normally the full back wore size 32 waistband shorts, and although three and two add up to five that is not, apparently, an unlucky number. Seven is, however, and O'Donnell didn't like it when in the changing room before the Junior Springboks game Murphy handed him a pair of shorts with a size 34 waistband. "He thinks I hexed him," Murphy said later.

The Lions had had a lot of fun with O'Donnell on Friday, 13 June. When the freckle-faced Irishman gingerly stuck his head out of the door of his room he found the corridor barricaded with every conceivable booby trap. A ladder supported on chairs was overhanging the doorway. The floor leading to the lift and the top of the stairs had been plastered with sellotape, making dozens and dozens of straight lines, and salt had been sprinkled all over the floor. In case O'Donnell should somehow manage to get past these omens and reach the lift, then every button was renumbered 13.

He recoiled with horror when he saw what had been done and he jumped—carefully—back into bed. "I'm not coming out," he shouted as teammates gathered outside his door. "There's no way I'm going through that door. If you want me out of here on Friday the 13th you can carry me out." In the end that's what happened. Just before noon O'Donnell was borne downstairs like some ancient Pharaoh.

The afternoon when O'Donnell rejoined the Lions at Durban I cornered Noel Murphy; we drew up a pair of deckchairs on the lawn overlooking the sea, and talked. He was in shorts, barefoot, and clearly enjoying the sun and relaxation. How did it feel now the series had been lost, I asked?

"I have a feeling of frustration at our cruel luck," Murphy replied. "I have a feeling of 'what more did we have to do to win?' We have given away perhaps 36 points in three Tests. The forwards know they have done very very well. Sometimes they've won better ball than I've ever seen in my life. The backs know in their heart of hearts that they could have done better. It's easy to say that I should have spent more time on the backs and less time on the forwards, but I don't agree. I had to get the platform right and, after all, when you're talking about backs you're talking about inherent skills, about running, kicking and passing. I don't think that any words of mine would help them do any better. What can you tell a wing or centre? He has got to have flair."

The decline of the Lions backs had been one of the bad features of the tour. It was partly due to the injuries suffered first by Ollie Campbell in training and then, midway through the first half of the first game, by Gareth Davies. From the time of that opening game against Eastern Province at Port Elizabeth on 10 May, until nearly a month later, the Lions had to manage with David Richards or Tony Ward at stand-off, except for the game against Natal when Campbell played even though he wasn't fit. Richards was not a natural international stand-off and Ward arrived late and hadn't played international rugby in the domestic season, and neither player could quite impose himself on the game. Consequently the Lions backs lacked authority.

In five games the Lions lost three half-backs. Their plans were so disrupted that in the eighth game of the tour, which was against the South African Country XV at Windhoek, the Lions fielded their seventh different half-back combination, including mid-match substitutions: Gareth Davies, in his first game back after injury, and new arrival John Robbie. The previous partnerships were: Eastern Province—Holmes and Davies, who was replaced by Morgan; SARA—Patterson and Richards; Natal—Holmes and Campbell; SA Invitation XV—Patterson and Richards; OFS—Holmes, replaced by Patterson, and Richards: SARFF—Patterson and Ward; first Test—Patterson and Ward.

Murphy pointed out that this crop of injuries meant considerable disruption to plans, and that certain players had suffered. He cited the case of Peter Morgan, the talented utility back from Llanelli who had appeared in only five games out of the 14 in the 8½ weeks up to then. "When we asked someone to play out of position, then we had to give that person a chance in his rightful position later on," explained Murphy. "Poor Peter suffered because after Dai Richards had played stand-off so often (in three of the six consecutive games he appeared in between the 14 and 31 of May) we had to give Richards a chance in the centre. He did very well for us at stand-off, but when he had settled down at centre he showed us what he could really do, in the first half of the Transvaal game for instance—and then he dislocated his shoulder."

It was indeed unfortunate for the team that Mike Slemen should have had to return home after the first Test, for in his five games he had scored five tries, as well as one conversion and one dropped goal. Even so it was a damning indictment of the Lions' backs, and therefore of Murphy their coach, that Slemen's five tries should make him the team's highest try-scorer to the end of the tour, six weeks after he had gone home.

"I'm bound to say I'm disappointed," Murphy continued. "I feel we should have had better results but for six or seven weeks we had a crisis every day of the week. I'm very sorry for Bill, Syd and myself because I am convinced we were a better side. But we lost three Tests by 13 points and that is very, very close. I don't know whether I failed the boys. When a side fails every one has a certain amount of responsibility."

Murphy looked out to sea. "I think you'll see in a few years how good this team could have been. Watch and see how the young players come on. Watch Clive Woodward and David Richards. Remember how good Gareth Davies looked at times, and yet he was not available to us because of injuries for so much of the time. That game at Windhoek was played on a difficult pitch and on a windy day, yet I think you could see there what a difference it made to us to have a proper stand-off who could impose his will on the game."

On Wednesday against the Barbarians the Lions did loosen up a little. There was less dashing back to the forwards by the inside-centre to set up a ruck, and Andy Irvine's breathtaking pace in counter-attack and when joining the three-quarters far out was shown off to better advantage. It was a light-hearted match in which both sides scored three tries and Tony Ward's fine kicking, which brought him 13 points, helped to edge the Lions home 25–14.

The next day O'Donnell flew back to London and the Lions flew down to Cape Town for their 16th game of the tour. There had been a number of pressure games along the way—the Invitation XV at Potchefstroom, Transvaal at Johannesburg, then both the Junior Springboks and Northern Transvaal in four hectic days after the defeat in the second Test. All these had been important games. So too, had the frolic against the Barbarians.

Yet it was essential that the Lions didn't slip up now, against Western Province, the joint Currie Cup holders, in their penultimate Saturday game of the tour. "Don't worry, we'll win 19–10," forecast Beaumont at dinner on the Thursday night after the team had arrived from Durban and settled back into the Holiday Inn in Cape Town.

He was spectacularly wrong. The team the Lions anticipated would also play in the fourth Test the following week made mincemeat of a Province side that had been weakened by the late withdrawal of their captain Morné du Plessis and stand-off Robbie Blair. Helped by some pinpoint kicking by Ollie Campbell, who missed only one of eight kicks at goal and totalled 22 points, the Lions raced to victory by 37–6, their highest on tour. How paradoxical that they should do it against one of the strongest provincial sides in South Africa.

Yet even in their most handsome victory the Lions' main weakness was glaringly obvious. Despite enormous forward superiority—again—they could score only three tries. One was a soft one that came after an interception 40 yards out by Bruce Hay on the left wing, and another try, this time by Irvine, was the result of smart work when the Province three-quarters made a hash of things in midfield. The only real worry the Lions had as they moved on was that Andy Irvine's hamstring nagged him again slightly and he left the field midway through the second half after scoring a try. He flew to Johannesburg the next day for treatment.

As the Lions left Cape Town, Morné du Plessis ruminated: "It would be silly to say I feel sorry for what has happened to them in the Tests. But I do feel sympathy for them. The Tests could have gone either way believe me." He paused as much as to say 'You don't believe me, do you?' Then he added forcefully: "You'd better believe me. I know how close they were. I was there. Despite everything I think the Lions go into the last Test as slight favourites."

Beaumont had won many hearts for his captaincy and his friendliness, and the rest of the team were very popular in South Africa as well. As a result there were a good many who thought that victory at Loftus Versfeld, Pretoria, where they so revere their rugby heroes that there is a statue to The Unknown Rugby Player, would be no more than Beaumont's Lions deserved.

CHAPTER THIRTEEN

Day by day by day a chapter of accidents

The 1980 British Lions were more severely hit by injuries than any other Lions team in history. When Colin Patterson tore the ligaments in his right knee in the last game but one he became the eighth player for whom it was necessary to fly out a replacement. In all previous Lions tours there had been only 15 replacements.

Many of the ailments that are inevitable on a ten-week rugby tour containing 18 matches were dealt with by Dr Jack Matthews, the former Wales and British Lions centre, who was the team's doctor, or by flanker John O'Driscoll, a doctor at London's Westminster Hospital. But many players had to be taken to hospital for more serious injuries. The Rosebank Clinic in northern Johannesburg handled so many of the Lions at various times during the tour that Ray Gravell suggested there were more autograph hunters outside the Clinic than there were lurking around the team's hotels.

Here is a day by day catalogue of the accidents and injuries of the tour.

Friday, 2 May: Andy Irvine arrived in London in time for the noon deadline feeling pessimistic about his chances of making the tour. The previous night when he had been out running the hamstring in his right leg had gone, causing him to pull up. By midday on Friday it had swollen up so he was unable to join the rest of the party. Welshman Elgan Rees was drafted into the team instead and became, officially, the first replacement—even before the team had left London.

Sunday, 4 May: Big Scotsman John Beattie missed the tour's first training session because of a sore throat, a relic of the 18-hour flight from London. The remaining 29 players probably envied him as they sweated through an hour-long session under 80-degree sunshine—all this at 6,000 ft.

Monday, 5 May: Ollie Campbell came off the training pitch complaining of a niggling hamstring in his right leg. Matthews's first diagnosis was cramp. Campbell jogged by himself around the field. "Easy, Ollie," shouted a worried-looking Millar. Campbell later went back to the hotel and had physiotherapy treatment at a gymnasium in the hotel's grounds. By the end of the second session of the day blisters caused by new woollen stockings or new boots had erupted on the feet of Allan Martin, Fran Cotton, Jim Renwick, Clive Woodward, Colm Tucker, Phil Blakeway, Bill Beaumont and John Carleton. Many of the forwards took their boots off and continued to train in their stockinged feet.

Tuesday, 6 May: Campbell rejoined his teammates at training and survived the day's two sessions. Ray Gravell's nose had turned beetroot red, and he walked around the hotel stroking it gently. And some of the forwards shed their boots for training again.

Wednesday, 7 May: David Richards heard that his father, who had been ill, had died back in Wales. He flew from Johannesburg for the funeral.

Thursday, 8 May: In the Lions' seventh training session in four days Graham Price left the field with what he called a dead leg. "It happens to me quite often," he said. Derek Quinnell did not practise because of stiffness in a calf muscle. And Campbell was favouring his right leg in training.

Friday, 9 May: Campbell dropped out of the team to play in the opening game against Eastern Province with what was described as a slightly strained right leg. Millar said, "If this had been a Test match we would have kept him in the side, but at this stage of the tour it seems sensible to let him rest his leg." Campbell may have aggravated his injury in a kicking session on Wednesday with former Springbok Gerald Bosch.

Saturday, 10 May: Within 50 seconds of the start of the game, flanker Stuart Lane twisted to try to tackle Gavin Cowley, the Eastern Province stand-off, and damaged the lateral ligament in his right knee so badly that he did not play again on tour. He hadn't even touched the ball. A year earlier, when on tour in South Africa with Cardiff, he damaged the same leg and didn't play again until December. In the 25th minute of the match against Eastern Province Gareth Davies slipped past one man and set up a try for left wing Mike Slemen. As Davies did so, he was sandwich-tackled and landed on his left shoulder, straining the joint at the end of his left collarbone. He converted the try but was then helped off in considerable pain. Davies's predecessors as Lions stand-offs had not been treated kindly in South Africa. Richard Sharp broke his cheekbone in 1962 and six years later Barry John's collarbone was broken. In 1974 Alan Old's knee ligaments were severed in a late tackle. To round off today's chapter of accidents, Allan Martin gashed his hand on some glass in the changing-room.

Sunday, 11 May: Medical diagnosis confirmed that Lane's leg injury was serious, and he will have to return home. Millar immediately telephoned to London to check on replacements. Davies will be available for selection again within "two to three weeks," said the manager, though this meant he would not be considered for the first Test at the end of the month.

Monday, 12 May: Only 26 Lions trained this morning. Lane and Davies of course were two of the absentees, and the other two were Richards, though he rejoined the team in the late afternoon after attending his father's funeral on Saturday, and Campbell, who did some light jogging by himself. His injury was now admitted to be a hamstring. He went to hospital with Lane, and an orthopaedic surgeon said he had slightly torn the hamstring. Davies must keep his left arm in a sling for 10 days and, meantime, was to be given a static bicycle to exercise his legs. Lane had been advised not to fly home for at least 10 days. His right leg was encased in bandage but not plaster, and he hobbled around on crutches.

Wednesday, 14 May: Prop Phil Blakeway injured his ribs and left the field near the end of the game against the South African Rugby Association's team, the Leopards. Cotton replaced him. It was announced that Bridgend flanker Gareth Williams will replace Lane. He heard the news while in Seattle on the Wales B tour of North America, and he returned home to Wales immediately.

Thursday, 15 May: Campbell took a full part in training for the first time in eight days, but didn't look fit. He did not once kick with his right leg. Nevertheless in a kill-or-cure move he was named for the game against Natal on Saturday, and, said Millar, will also take the goal-kicks.

Friday, 16 May: Campbell ran more freely today and fully tested his right leg, which had enabled him to score 74 points for Ireland in his seven internationals. There was an air of cautious optimism about. Had he beaten his bogey?

Saturday, 17 May: Gareth Williams arrived to join the Lions after being delayed at Las Palmas. Campbell survived the Natal game, his first for seven weeks, though occasionally he was seen to be holding his leg after kicking for touch, and Martin and Slemen also took some kicks at goal. Campbell did land two penalties and one conversion, however. It was almost 80 degrees in Kings Park and the players may have lost three or four pounds each in the course of the afternoon.

Monday, 19 May: Blakeway, who some years ago played with a broken neck, is suffering from the ribs he broke in February, when playing for England against France, and which he re-injured last Wednesday. Today he went for another medical, hoping it would reveal nothing too serious. No such luck. It was bad enough for Millar to ask for a replacement, though he wouldn't reveal who. And at training in Durban this morning Campbell's hamstring injury flared up again. With Davies still injured the Lions now had no internationally recognised stand-off, so Millar telephoned London and asked for Irishman Tony Ward to fly out as quickly as possible. A change in the tour's agreement allowed Millar to send for reinforcements without forfeiting the services of injured players (see Chapter 6). Slemen retired early from training to rest the knock he had received in Saturday's game.

Tuesday, 20 May: Blakeway's replacement was named today as the uncapped Welshman Ian Stephens of Bridgend who, like his clubmate Gareth Williams, was on Wales B's five-match tour of North America. He left Vancouver today and will fly from London to Johannesburg on Friday evening. Today Campbell left the team to go to Johannesburg, where he will have intensive treatment and exercise at the Rosebank Clinic. Davies, who did some light training with the Lions in the morning with his left arm in a sling, travelled with Campbell to the same clinic. Millar said there were no plans for Campbell to go home, and he should be able to play again in 10 days. Cotton stopped training today because he was having difficulty breathing.

Thursday, 22 May: Casualties from that memorable game at Potchefstroom yesterday included Clive Woodward, with a strained shoulder muscle, and Elgan Rees, who had strained a knee ligament, while Cotton, who didn't play, went to bed suffering from inflamed varicose veins in his left leg, an old complaint. This left the team so bare of front-row players that Stephens, though due to arrive only on the morning of the match against Orange Free State will, nevertheless, have to sit on the replacements' bench that afternoon. But there was some good news, too. Davies is expected to have recovered fully and be able to start training, early next week.

Friday, 23 May: Ward arrived, looking fit but tired. Cotton was still in bed in Potchefstroom.

Saturday, 24 May: Terry Holmes injured his left shoulder just before the end of the game against Orange Free State today, and was replaced by Colin Patterson. So victories in each of the five games so far have been achieved at the cost of at least one injury, and now the Lions have only one fit scrum-half for Tuesday's game against the Proteas (the South African Rugby Football Federation's side, the coloureds). The first Test is a week away. Cotton arrived at Bloemfontein from Potchefstroom with Blakeway.

Monday, 26 May: Millar confirmed today that the Irish scrum-half John Robbie, at present in Zimbabwe playing for the Goshawks, an all-star touring party, will fly to join the Lions tomorrow. Now we have four Irish half-backs. Meanwhile left-wing Slemen practised his passing in torrential rain. He was expecting to be named as reserve scrum-half against the Proteas. Gareth Davies trained with the team, and passed the ball with no obvious signs of distress, but it was very doubtful that he could be considered for the Test at

Newlands on Saturday. There was a slight scare about Ward. He withdrew from some of the sprints saying he felt some pain in his left hamstring. The pain passed, however, to everyone's relief. Holmes appeared with his left arm in a sling and was not expected to be able to play for at least two weeks, ruling him out of the second Test in Bloemfontein on 14 June.

Tuesday, 27 May: Robbie, after playing in a Goshawks match in Bulawayo yesterday, arrived in Cape Town and, like Stephens in the previous game, immediately sat on the replacements' bench against the Proteas. After half an hour Fran Cotton, who had looked pale when he ran out on to the field, was led off, clutching his chest. First thoughts were that he had had a heart attack (see Chapter 6) and he was rushed to hospital. Clive Williams replaced him. Patterson complained that he had stud marks up his back where he had been deliberately kicked, Rodney O'Donnell was hit when he was on the ground and later said he had strained a shoulder muscle, and Ward was kicked on the leg after being tackled early on.

Wednesday, 28 May: Phil Orr, the burly Irish loose-head prop, was named as the replacement for Cotton. He will be the fifth replacement flown out since the Lions left London after Gareth Williams, Ian Stephens, Tony Ward and John Robbie, a total that already exceeded any other major tour and there were still 12 of the 18 matches to go. A decision about Rees still had to be made. He has been in Johannesburg, at the sports clinic, since injuring his leg at Potchefstroom a week earlier. He was also suffering from flu. His absence meant that the Lions had only two specialist wings—John Carleton and Slemen.

Thursday, 29 May: Ward, picked as stand-off for the first Test on Saturday, could not train today because of a badly bruised right thigh, a reaction from Tuesday's hard game at Stellenbosch. It was confirmed that Cotton had not had a heart attack. He was expected to be released from Groote Schuur Hospital the next day, and has been told he must rest for several weeks.

Friday, 30 May: Ward's leg had recovered sufficiently for him to try to have a half hour's kicking practice with fellow

Players laid low during the most severely injury-hit tour in Lions' history included: Top left—David Richards, who in the match against Transvaal fell and dislocated his shoulder, his tour thus at an end. Top right—John Carleton, who injured his ribs when he was buried under a pile of bodies after making a tackle. A diagnosis later said he had sprung a rib and damaged a rib cartilage. Bottom left—Terry Holmes who injured his left shoulder just before the end of the game against Orange Free State. Bottom right—Team captain Bill Beaumont, who damaged his left knee in the match against Orange Free State and later in the second Test, the day after which he had to have a glassful of blood drained from his knee.

Irishman Campbell at the University of Cape Town, but students opposed to the tour barracked them and after a few minutes they left the field. Cotton returned to the team hotel at lunch time.

Saturday, 31 May: Soon after half-time in the Test, Carleton injured his ribs when he was buried under a pile of bodies after making a tackle. "A knee went into my chest in the tackle and forced my bottom ribs upwards," he said. A diagnosis later said he had sprung a rib and damaged a rib cartilage, which could keep him out for three weeks.

Sunday, 1 June: Quinnell bruised a shoulder in yesterday's Test, and Ward's bruised right thigh, for which he needed pain-killing injections, to see him through, will keep him out for a week. On the other hand, Campbell should be fit to play within a few days. He has not played for a fortnight and, in all, had appeared in only one of the seven games. Millar said he would make a decision about Rees on Thursday after speaking to an orthopaedic surgeon. Tentative enquiries have been made about the availability of England wing Peter Squires. Meanwhile, Slemen announced he was returning home because his pregnant wife Eileen had entered hospital in Liverpool with a chest complaint, and their baby son had also been ill. That left the Lions without a single fit wing so Millar requested that Irvine, an original choice for the tour as wing, be given a fitness test at home. Millar was hoping the Scot had now recovered from the hamstring strain that prevented him travelling out with the Lions in May. Assuming Irvine passed the test, Millar said he would arrive in Johannesburg on Wednesday. Alan Phillips went down with conjunctivitis and will stay in Cape Town rather than travel to Windhoek, but hopes to be fit for Wednesday's game there.

Monday, 2 June: Slemen, Blakeway and Lane flew to London together today while the Lions flew to Windhoek for their eighth game. At training today Campbell's calf muscle gave way. Talk about the luck of the Irish! It was thought, though, that he could play on Saturday against Transvaal if necessary, while Davies reported fit enough to play in Wednesday's game.

Tuesday, 3 June: Millar confirmed that Irvine will arrive in South Africa tomorrow. The Lions team named for tomorrow's game against the South African Country Districts included the two most recent replacements—scrum-half Robbie and loose-head prop Orr. With no regular wings available the Lions chose utility player Peter Morgan on the left and Woodward on the right. Training was light-hearted today. Holmes, who had previously had his left arm in a sling, ran and passed the ball gently while Campbell kicked with his right foot. Carleton jogged around the dusty pitch and then said, defiantly, "Next Tuesday's game is make or break for me. I'm going to play in it to test my ribs. If I survive I shall be able to stay on tour. If I don't then it will be time to make way for a replacement."

Wednesday, 4 June: Davies survived his first game for nearly a month, and only his third since 1 March. Phillips's conjunctivitis hadn't cleared and Wheeler played instead. Hay, captain for the day, bruised a hip.

Thursday, 5 June: Irvine was waiting for the Lions when they arrived in Johannesburg from Windhoek. Team selection for Saturday's game against Transvaal was delayed while Millar and Murphy examined reports on the fitness of Rees, and gave Campbell another day's grace. Jeff Squire was suffering from a strained hamstring and was doubtful for Saturday's game.

Friday, 6 June: A cloud seemed to have been lifted from over the Lions' heads today and their training at the Wanderers ground was impressive and purposeful. Irvine was named as full-back for the Transvaal game and Campbell as a replacement. Millar said this morning that Rees was able to run flat out and had been side-stepping, though his knee was heavily bandaged. He would be available for Tuesday's game against Eastern Transvaal, as would stand-off Ward. Holmes would be playing within one week, Millar said. And a delighted Noel Murphy proclaimed: "Everybody is back in contention. For the first time in weeks we have a lot of players to choose from. Our morale is high."

Saturday, 7 June: Murphy's euphoria didn't last long. He wasn't too concerned when Clive Williams went down with flu and his place against Transvaal was taken at the last minute by Orr, but he was very disappointed that midway through the second half, when the backs had started to hum for almost the first time on tour, Richards fell in trying to catch a precision kick by Davies, dislocated his right shoulder, and was carried off on a stretcher. It was the end of his tour. Seven seemed to be his unlucky number. He was the party's seventh serious casualty, playing on the seventh day of the month, and it was seven days after he had played his seventh international. "I told Gareth it was a bad kick," Richards said later, with a hint of a smile. "It wasn't very accurate and it was too far." Davies laughed. "Nonsense," he said. "If you'd been a bit faster and run straighter you'd have been all right." By the end of the game a muscle, but not the hamstring, in Irvine's right leg was niggling him again and there were doubts about his fitness for the Test in a week. It was a game that juxtaposed triumph and tragedy, for the Lions won scoring six tries to one.

Sunday, 8 June: Millar went through the by now familiar ritual of ringing London for a replacement player today. He must have known the telephone numbers by heart. Richards's replacement was to be Paul Dodge, the 10-times capped Leicester and England centre, becoming the seventh replacement in the five weeks so far. He will leave England tomorrow. Even at leisure the Lions seemed jinxed. In a charity cricket match in a Johannesburg suburb today, Robbie twisted his right ankle when he accidentally stepped into a hole for a water spray. His ankle swelled up and turned black and blue. Three of the injured players were named in the team to play Eastern Transvaal—Carleton, Campbell and Holmes. Irvine spent part of the day at the Rosebank Clinic having physiotherapy.

Monday, 9 June: Beattie left training early and spent most of the rest of the day in bed with a heavy chest cold. He seemed certain to have to drop out of tomorrow's game. Robbie was named among the replacements, which was optimistic. His ankle was still swollen. Irvine missed training because of his hamstring niggle.

Tuesday, 10 June: Poor Holmes! Eastern Transvaal

kicked off, the ball was palmed back to him and as he went to tap it into touch he twisted his right knee. Moments later Martin left the field for his right hand to be bandaged. Holmes got slower and slower and midway through the half he came off the field, limping badly, and with tears in his eyes. He knew his tour had ended. He had strained ligaments in his right knee. Patterson replaced him (Robbie's leg was still too sore and stiff) and had strict orders to stay out of trouble. Beattie had recovered from his chest cold and played at No 8 as selected. More good news was that Campbell came through the game well, kicking 17 points, and that the courage of Carleton was rewarded when he scored the only try and lasted the game even after deliberately making some fierce infield charges which ended with him being heavily tackled. "It had to be make or break," said a pleased-looking Carleton after the game. "There was no point in my staying out there on the wing, sheltering. I had a lot to prove, to myself and to the management. I strapped the ribs up very heavily and felt a bit sore for the first ten minutes, but after that I felt okay."

Wednesday, 11 June: Robbie, Wheeler and Irvine all returned from physiotherapy in time to hear the announcement of the Test team. That afternoon the bar-stool on which Alan Phillips was sitting collapsed with a crash, dumping Phillips on his bottom on the floor. It was a genuine accident, but with the Lions' luck it's surprising that Phillips didn't break a vertebra.

Thursday, 12 June: It was announced today that Holmes was to return home after the Test at the week-end with Richards and Cotton, in the second batch of three injured players to leave the tour. This meant that Robbie now became a fully-fledged Lion. Previously there had been the possibility that he would leave the tour once Holmes had recovered from his shoulder injury. In training at the Free State stadium Irvine was rubbing his right leg. Had he really recovered?

Saturday, 14 June: Just before half-time in the second Test, as the Lions trailed 9–16, came the very rare sight of Beaumont needing treatment. He'd had a knock on his left knee. A worse blow came midway through the second half when Davies, in being tackled by Naas Botha, tore the medial ligaments of his left leg. "I don't know how it happened," he said. "I had my rubber studs in, so I shouldn't have got my boots stuck. I'm looking forward to seeing it on television to try to see what happened." Like Holmes in the previous match, his tour had ended. On his first Lions tour he had played for only 253 minutes in four games.

Monday, 16 June: Beaumont, his knee heavily bandaged, went to the clinic in Johannesburg where he had a glassful of blood drained from his knee. Cotton, Holmes and Richards were joined by Davies on their flight home. In training Colm Tucker, one of the few players almost to avoid a mention in this injury list so far, twisted his right ankle. "I thought my tour was over," he said tonight. Rees was chosen to play only his fourth game of the tour, and his first since 21 May. He will play right wing against the Junior Springboks on Wednesday. Irvine was selected as left wing. Dodge, the seventh tour replacement, was to make his Lions debut.

Tuesday, 17 June: Tucker limped around the hotel, out of Wednesday's team. Stephens returned to the hotel after training in a game park, complaining of his stomach being in a whirl. "My guts ache something rotten," he said. "I took some medicine and that made me feel better." Beaumont's knee injury was also better. There was no damage to any ligaments. He should definitely be fit for the third Test at Port Elizabeth in 11 days time.

Wednesday, 18 June: Orr gashed the back of his left thigh soon after the start of the game against the Junior Springboks and Clive Williams replaced him. Orr went to hospital and had five stitches put into his leg. The second half had been going for only three minutes when O'Donnell badly injured himself in tackling Danie Gerber, the Junior Springboks' centre. At first it was said to be a pinched nerve in O'Donnell's neck, but it looked more serious than that. He was put on a stretcher and taken to the side of the pitch. But then he climbed off the stretcher, holding his neck, and walking slowly and gingerly to the changing room from where he was taken to hospital.

Thursday, 19 June: O'Donnell was operated on today for a dislocated neck. The operation was to wire the sixth and seventh vertebrae. Yet he's a lucky man—another fraction of an inch and he could have been paralysed. Quinnell had a slight cold and a slight groin strain (a recurrence of the injury that kept him out of the Wales team last season) which ruled him out of Saturday's game against Northern Transvaal. Gravell spent part of the day in bed with a tummy upset and Price had a sore arm, but Beaumont's knee had improved so fast he declared himself fit for Saturday. Tucker's ankle had also mended, so he was ready to play on Saturday as well. Millar asked for Fergus Slattery, the Ireland flanker to replace O'Donnell. Hay and Irvine can play full-back and a fast flanker is badly needed.

Friday, 20 June: Patterson retired to bed with a temperature of 102 and Robbie was named to take his place tomorrow against Northern Transvaal. Ward injured an Achilles tendon in training, and Morgan took his place among Saturday's replacements. We heard that Slattery could not join the tour because of business commitments.

Saturday, 21 June: A still-not-fit Patterson had to be ready to act as Robbie's replacement against Northern Transvaal and sat in the stand wrapped in blankets. Fortunately he was not needed. That's one of the first bits of luck the Lions have had for weeks. And there's not another match till the third Test next Saturday, which gives the Lions a few days' grace.

Thursday, 26 June: At the Lions training at the Boet Erasmus stadium in Port Elizabeth there was an injury but for once it wasn't to a Lion. A woman fell down on the terracing and broke an ankle. John O'Driscoll was the first to help her. The Lions heard in the evening that Fran Cotton had been briefly admitted to hospital in Boston, Lincolnshire, where he was on holiday, suffering from a high temperature and complaining of feeling unwell.

Saturday, 28 June: Within minutes of the start of the third Test Campbell got a knock on his cheek. Later he had to have four stitches. Beaumont had a bang on his head but was all right. Irvine had trouble with his Achilles tendon in his right leg, caused by trying to protect his right hamstring.

Tuesday, 1 July: O'Donnell, wearing a neckbrace,

rejoined the Lions at their beachside hotel in Durban and said he may never play rugby again. "I'm lucky to be alive. You only get one life and I came bloody close to losing that." Now he had to wait eight weeks to see whether the graft from his hip to the sixth and seventh vertebrae had fused. "I thought I was paralysed after I had made the tackle. I owe a lot to referee Steve Strydom, who said he heard a click and told people not to move me. John O'Driscoll came off the field to attend to me and told me not to allow them to put me in any position that was uncomfortable. He also told me to keep squeezing my hand." Meanwhile the Lions discovered a new hazard, the sea. That afternoon Ward got into difficulties in the surf offshore, and was rescued by a lifeguard.

Wednesday, 2 July: Irvine again strained his hamstring against the South African Barbarians, his sixth match since arriving on 10 June. Flanker Gareth Williams slightly tore his hamstring in the first 10 minutes. Forwards have hamstrings too.

Thursday, 3 July: Irvine didn't train. O'Donnell flew back to London.

Friday, 4 July: Irvine didn't train, not because of his hamstring but because of a slightly bruised Achilles tendon. But he will be fit for tomorrow's game against Western Province.

Saturday, 5 July: Quinnell dropped out of the replacements with a shoulder injury. His groin still hasn't fully recovered either. Irvine came off the field midway through the second half having aggravated the same hamstring in his right leg that had caused him to be dropped from the team in May. He was replaced by Woodward on the left wing, and Hay moved to full-back.

Sunday, 6 July: Irvine flew to the clinic in Johannesburg for treatment on his hamstring and his Achilles tendon.

Monday, 7 July: Wheeler and Colclough trained only gently in Kimberley and Price, nursing a cut foot, packed down in scrums as a flank forward. Gareth Williams, who hadn't eaten for several days because of a stomach upset, asked for a fitness test. "Okay," said Murphy, "it's mind over matter, Gar. I don't mind and you don't matter."

Williams passed the test and will play against Griqualand West in the Lions' last provincial game.

Tuesday, 8 July: Patterson became the tour's last major casualty. In the sixth minute he badly tore the coaxial and medial ligaments in his right knee as he tried to tackle Gawie Visagie, his opposite number. He was in agony as referee Louis Wessels, a doctor, waggled his knee from side to side to try to find out what had happened. It took three minutes to get Patterson off the field, and O'Driscoll went with him to hospital and decided that it would be better for him to have the necessary operation in Johannesburg on Wednesday. He was bandaged from hip to ankle, sworn off food and drink, and put to bed. Meanwhile Ward banged his right shoulder and right knee when he fell heavily near the end of the game (see Chapter 11). Morgan hurt his left knee in a tackle, and Rees got a crack on his jaw. To cover for Robbie in Saturday's fourth Test, England's scrum-half Steve Smith was called out. He will arrive on Thursday.

Wednesday, 9 July: Patterson rejoined the team mid-morning, chirpy as ever, though hungry. By 4.30 he was in the clinic in Johannesburg and by 4.35 the operation on his knee had begun. He woke up yelling from the pain—he had been sick and thrown up the pain-killing tablets he had been given—but when he was given an injection he was able to doze off fitfully. The pain was excruciating. "I honestly wished I could have passed on, it was so bad," he said later. He had a huge, heavy plaster on his right leg, and it was discoloured by blood seeping to the surface. Meanwhile, back with the team in Pretoria, Ward, Morgan and Renwick went for physiotherapy to a blind physio.

Thursday, 10 July: Patterson alternated between fitful sleep and wakefulness. His leg was throbbing unmercifully. Cards, letters and telegrams were piled by his bedside. In a bed across the ward was a young South African rugby player who had had a similar operation a few hours earlier. The doctor said that Patterson's injury was the worst he had ever seen, except after car accidents. The injured ligaments were repaired with carbon fibre. Back in Pretoria, Smith arrived too late for training.

Friday, 11 July: Patterson had slept from 9.30 the previous night until reveille at 5.30 am, and though pale and still weak felt much better. He was given the choice of leaving the clinic on Saturday or Sunday and, sensibly, chose Sunday. Learning how to use crutches, he managed at his first attempt to cross the ward but was so tired as a result that he fell back into bed and promptly went to sleep once more.

Saturday, 12 July: Before the Test Irvine had a pain-killing injection to help him cope with his Achilles tendon problem in his right leg. Then, to cap it all, he tore his left hamstring during the game.

Sunday, 13 July: Patterson returned to London on the same flight as the Lions. He sat just behind the first-class section, with his leg wrapped in blankets and propped up on boxes. Tony Ward, Liverpool footballer Steve Heighway, and Dave Sexton, manager of Manchester United, all helped to amuse him during the long overnight flight from Johannesburg.

Monday, 14 July: At London Airport Patterson was whisked off to the medical centre, where his luggage soon caught up with him and then he was put on board the Belfast shuttle. At Belfast airport he gave two BBC interviews while waiting for his wife Gail to come and pick him up.

CHAPTER FOURTEEN

A charismatic Springbok brought down at last

On the Thursday morning before the third Test, six Eastern Province women hockey players playfully captured the Springbok rugby captain Morné du Plessis from the team's hotel in Port Elizabeth and held him to ransom for 20,000 cents, around £120. "Abide by these instructions and your captain will be unharmed," said the ransom note. "To put your mind at rest, he is at present involved in a loose scrum with 13 lithe EP hockey players."

If those hockey players thought that du Plessis was worth only that sort of money to South African rugby, then someone had badly miscalculated. It was a miserly assessment of the value of a man who throughout the Lions tour proved himself a more than adequate player, a good captain and a generous opponent, a man who had a rare and instinctive feel for saying the right thing at the right time. Bill Beaumont didn't get particularly close to his rival captain, perhaps because their jobs were too similar, but by the end of the tour he had formed a considerable respect for the South African.

If breeding stood for anything then Morné du Plessis was destined to be an outstanding sportsman from the day he was born in Krugersdorp, Transvaal, on 21 October 1949. His relatives had adorned South Africa's sports fields with distinction. His father Felix led the Springboks to that famous 4–0 whitewash over Fred Allen's All Blacks of 1949 (despite being dropped for the fourth Test); his mother Pat captained South Africa at hockey; an uncle of Felix du Plessis was a Springbok in the twenties; an uncle of Morné's, Horace Smethurst, led the 1947 Springbok soccer team to Australia; and another uncle, Eric Smethurst, also played soccer for South Africa.

With understandable paternal pride, Felix du Plessis

wanted his son to become an outstanding sportsman, and when Morné was still a schoolboy, and an exceptional cricketer, his name was mentioned to Dr Craven at Stellenbosch. In due course du Plessis arrived at the famous university, where he studied industrial psychology, and he was billeted in Craven's hostel.

It was the start of a close friendship. It was Craven who switched the gangling youth from the second to the back row on the eve of Morné's first senior game for the university. "Doc had been away and when he returned he asked to see the team," du Plessis told the *Rand Daily Mail's* rugby writer Dan Retief in 1980. "Doc took a look at me and said 'No way. This guy can't play lock. He is a loose forward.' So they changed the team, I went to flank and eventually made my debut for Western Province in that position."

He was converted to No 8 on the Springbok tour of Australia in 1971, in place of Tommy Bedford who had been badly injured. It was not a permanent change, for from time to time du Plessis was still liable to be switched to the side of the scrum. When the Lions crushed the Springboks 28–9 in the second Test in 1974, Dugald MacDonald, a Western Province teammate, was at No 8 and du Plessis on the flank. Only on tour in France later that year did Morné settle at No 8.

His career as captain showed fewer fluctuations. He was both captain of the university and also of the Western Province under-20 side, while at Stellenbosch. "Morné stood out from the others," Stellenbosch's under–20 coach Jannie Krige told Retief. "There was a certain authority in the way he adapted to different playing conditions. You know some players are phenomenal when they are under 20, but then they level off. The advancement of Morné as a rugby player has been a steady process of improvement."

By the time the French arrived in South Africa in June 1975 for a two Test series, du Plessis had been named the 35th Springbok captain. He thus became the first son of a Springbok captain to emulate his father.

One of the most interesting aspects of the rather complex character of this tall Capetownian is that although he was born to leadership, once he had it he became restlessly uncomfortable. He is by nature a shy person. He has a slightly diffident manner and a tendency to hang his head, which may be nothing more than a habit acquired to make himself seem less tall than he really is—he is 6ft 5in. He says he is not confident of himself as a player and he is unsure enough of himself to worry quite considerably if he has to make a speech. Morné du Plessis is more at home on the fringes of a group than in the centre commanding attention.

"I believe circumstances create leaders," he says. "The person who has the best qualities for the situation is the man who comes to the fore. Quite often, he may not be the right guy, and I'm not talking about leadership in sport only. I'm talking about leadership in any situation in life. The situation often forces a guy into leadership which he is not suited for. Personally I don't have much belief in the born leader syndrome. I am absolutely certain that good leaders are made."

Then what did he think were his own leadership qualities? He was slightly embarrassed at the question, and typically he searched around, uncomfortably hedging his answer. "You have got to have confidence in your ability to influence a group of people to move in the direction you want. I would say that this is something that maybe I have. But I don't know that I could do it with all people. I might not be able to do it with 15 different guys."

"I believe the guys who played for us in the Test series created a situation where they let me lead them. I believe . . . " His voice trailed off. "Hell, it's a difficult question. It's like asking me 'what do I think of myself?' I can tell you my weaknesses but my strengths, well that's different. Maybe it's because I'm not confident about them. Maybe I should have a good look at myself. Maybe I haven't had a good enough look at myself."

Before the fourth Test du Plessis had captained South Africa in the last 12 of his 19 internationals, and they had lost only one—the second Test against Andy Leslie's All Blacks in 1976. He had also captained Western Province on 95 of his 104 appearances. Yet he had never silenced the critics who disapproved of his style of play. North of the Orange River, in the dour, Afrikaner provinces of the Transvaal and the Orange Free State, they had christened him the scrummage inspector because of his reluctance to graft away in rucks and mauls, and his preference to get out among the three-quarters. The Lions agreed with that view.

Beaumont was not the only Lion who couldn't understand the extent of the reputation that surrounded du Plessis. "He's a very loose player, not at all a European-style No 8," said the British captain. "He's always out on the fringes, always wanting to take drop-outs, to kick for touch. I suppose if the Springboks want to keep it loose then he suits their kind of game, but there is no way he is the best in the world. The New Zealander Murray Mexted is a better player for my money." And Jeff Squire, who played opposite du Plessis in the last two Tests, said: "I think he's over-rated. I don't think he's much of a tactician frankly. He's got three inches on me and he never calls the ball to himself at the back of the line-out. He's also very loose."

But du Plessis won considerable respect from the Lions for the way he leaped to their side during a row before the second Test. On the morning of the game the Springbok manager, Butch Lochner, was quoted in *The Citizen*, a Johannesburg morning paper, as saying that "the 'Boks had proved to the world in three Tests this year that they played their rugby hard and clean. The Lions, on the other hand, do the opposite." At the after-match reception an angry Millar publicly attacked Lochner, without naming him. The situation was tense and unpleasant when du Plessis got up to speak but he handled it with the flair of a born diplomat. "I hope we will learn a lesson from Syd Millar and Bill Beaumont," said the South African captain, "and if we can be as gracious in winning as they have been in losing then we will have achieved something. I hope that I will not be misquoted when I say that I hope the unfortunate statement that appeared in the press this morning will be withdrawn, because we owe the Lions so much."

Beaumont said later: "I don't know that I could have said something like that about an England selector. Morné did very well there."

For extending this unexpected hand of comradeship, du Plessis was rewarded by being invited into the Lions' team room late that night to join in the singing. A visitor putting his head around the door in the early hours of the morning recalls with pleasure the sight of the Springbok captain in his green blazer edged with gold and his fawn trousers standing alongside Syd Millar, and both having happy grins on their faces as they waited for the opening bars of the next song to be sung by choirmaster Fran Cotton.

There were other occasions when du Plessis showed maturity and graciousness of a higher than usual level. For example: He was blatantly punched in the eye by Derek Quinnell in the opening minutes of the first Test, but he didn't retaliate even though his temperament used to be so fiery that he had laid out a rival during a Springbok trial, and as recently as 1977 had been sent off after a clash with another forward in an important final at Newlands. Another example: After victory in the third Test, du Plessis, having been carried shoulder high from the field, had enough feeling for the Lions to acknowledge that: "At half-time I had started preparing a losing speech. We know that we came through a game today where Lady Luck played a great part."

Thirty one on 21 October 1980, du Plessis was just about at the end of his international career. Nowadays his time is taken up more and more by his work as a director of the sports-shoe side of a shoe company, which has its offices down by a railway line in suburban Cape Town. The pressures on him now are two-fold: those of rugby and business. He describes himself as a hard but not long worker. To maintain his equanimity, he rarely discloses his home telephone number, which is ex-directory, and at work a honey-voiced secretary screens all his calls. His wife Jenny is not seen much around the rugby circuit.

It's obvious from the enthusiasm with which he talks about the shoe business that he is successful and happy. He flies to the Adidas factory in West Germany twice each year, and says he should travel much more in South Africa. "You have to get out into the field to see what is going on," he says. "A marketing man's job is outside. I can't do enough of it because

I've got other interests, like rugby." But for how much longer? South Africa had better start looking for a new captain.

Up in Pretoria the Lions had settled into the Burgers Park hotel for the fourth and final Test. Their team showed only two changes from the third Test team—Robbie had to replace the injured Patterson, and Carleton regained from Woodward the place on the right wing where he had played in the first two Tests.

The last days of a rugby tour are always devoted to buying presents and to packing, and the Lions were no exception. They had only a brief 45-minute workout at Loftus Versfeld on the Thursday before fanning out to the curio and African art shops of Pretoria and Johannesburg. "If we haven't got it right by now then we never will," said Beaumont after perhaps the 50th training session of the tour. There had been a plan for helicopters to whisk the Lions to Sun City, a huge entertainment complex an hour's flight from Johannesburg, but this was ruled out as the players flocked instead to the shops.

On the Friday, Beaumont walked around the hotel with a zebra skin under one arm. Allan Martin was just one of a group who covetously eyed some butterfly wing pictures in the hotel's curio shop. "I'm just going down town and I want to compare prices," he said. "If you buy from me I'll give you a 10 per cent discount," said the lady behind the counter, who turned out to be a white refugee from Zimbabwe. Noel Murphy breezed in laden with a huge box for one of his children, and started to finger the key rings and the gem bracelets.

That afternoon Clive Woodward, Peter Wheeler and Andy Irvine spent some time with golfer Gary Player at his home in Johannesburg. "He has a heavily weighted club that he swings to strengthen his forearms," Woodward said that evening. "You know, he's so strong that he can hold it horizontally between his thumb and index finger."

In the clinic in Johannesburg Colin Patterson was slowly recovering from his knee operation. They had whitewashed the huge plaster that encased his right knee from hip to toe to cover the dark stains where the blood had seeped through. He'd had painkilling injections the previous night, and slept like a top from 9.30 until reveille at 5.30 the next morning. His bedside table was ringed with cards and at lunchtime he received a call from his wife in Belfast. He was looking forward to joining his teammates on the flight home on Sunday. "I suppose I'll have to borrow some trousers from a prop forward," he said. "There's no way I can fit my leg and this plaster into any trousers of my own."

The last curtain-raiser before the Test was a specially arranged match between the South African Barbarians and a Junior Springbok side that contained the two coloureds, Errol Tobias and Charles Williams, the first two non-whites ever to wear the dark blue shirts of the Springboks' second team. Morgan, Rees, Renwick and forwards Orr, Gareth Williams, Beattie, and Martin were all selected to play for the Barbarians, with the brilliant Argentinian stand-off Hugo Porta and the captivating Frenchman Jean-Pierre Rives. But they were overrun as the Junior Springboks, prompted by Tobias, ran in seven tries and won 43–14. Gawie Visagie, who had been so devastating against the Lions at Kimberley the previous Tuesday, kicked three penalties and five conversions. The Barbarians' tries all came from Lions—by Beattie, Renwick and Morgan. After this match there was a five-minute display from hundreds of schoolchildren carrying gaily-coloured balloons.

As the Lions and Springboks ran on to the pitch after the spectacular was over, one or other side stood to make history. No Lions side had ever before won a fourth Test in South Africa, not even Willie-John McBride's who had drawn their last game in 1974. And the South Africans had never whitewashed a Lions side 4–0.

Beaumont's team started as they had in the third Test. In the first half they could have scored 15 points if Campbell had landed more than one of four shots at penalties. Their forward supremacy was astonishing. They won the line-outs by three to one, taking all of the first six, as well as winning the rucks and mauls.

All the scoring in the first half came just before half-time.

The Fourth Test

In this match, one or other side stood to make history. No Lions team had ever won a fourth Test in South Africa; and the South Africans had never whitewashed a Lions side 4–0. On the Thursday before the clash, the Lions had only a brief 45-minutes workout. "If we haven't got it right by now then we never will," said Beaumont. In the event, the Lions did have it superbly right. Their forward supremacy was astonishing. In the first half line-outs, where Beaumont is shown challenging for the ball (immediately left) with the Springboks' Louis Moolman, they won by three to one, as well as winning the rucks and mauls. And when South Africa led 13–7, the Lions showed their true character. The forwards drove down the right and scrum-half John Robbie (below) quickly moved the ball to the openside. After O'Driscoll had swallow-dived over the line and Campbell had converted, the scoring was at an end, and though the Springboks fought back during the last 20 minutes, the Lions won 17–13. Both Beaumont and the Springboks' captain Morné du Plessis (left) were carried shoulder-high from the field. Of the Lions du Plessis had said after the second Test: "If we can be as gracious in winning as they have been in losing then we will have achieved something."

A penalty by Campbell was cancelled out by one from 30 yards by Botha, his only successful kick of the afternoon. Then Clive Williams burrowed through a maul on the South Africans' line to score in the corner after Irvine, Campbell and O'Driscoll had interpassed in a 40-yard run. The scoreline of 7–3 to the Lions was grossly flattering to South Africa but the Lions had only themselves to blame. Time and again the Springboks were saved by errors among the Lions backs. Heroic as the Lions forwards had been in their Saturday matches—and many were saying they were the best from any country ever to visit South Africa—the backs had been desperate at times, knocking on, dropping the ball, clearing it too slowly, taking the wrong options. Whatever happened to the brilliant backplay by British Lions of yesteryear?

The old familiar story of the Lions' forward superiority being overcome by sparks of brilliance from the Springboks' three-quarters seemed about to be repeated just after half-time when Willie du Plessis, no relation to Morné, burst through from 30 yards for a try that levelled the score. Then in the space of six minutes Pienaar kicked two penalties, one a monster from two yards inside his own half. He had taken over the kicking from Botha, who was so off-form that when he missed a drop at goal he was booed by the crowd. So after Pienaar's kicks, South Africa led by 13–7.

This was precisely when the Lions showed their true character, scoring two tries in three minutes, just as fast as two tries had been scored against them in the second Test. The forwards drove down the right and Robbie quickly moved the ball to the openside. Hay, Irvine and Gravell all made ground and as Gravell was stopped five yards from the goal-line, Irvine swooped acrobatically, picked the ball up and touched it down in the corner. Campbell missed the difficult conversion from the corner, leaving South Africa still 13–11 ahead.

A moment later South African hearts jumped into their mouths as Irvine broke clear 30 yards out, and with Carleton unmarked outside him a score seemed certain. But Pienaar laid Irvine low just five yards from the line with a magnificent ankle tackle. As it happened it didn't matter for scarcely had play got going again than Gravell, who had his fieriest and best game of the tour, burst through and when he was finally stopped close to the posts the ball rolled invitingly clear. For once it was a Lion, O'Driscoll, who was first to it, and he picked it up and swallow-dived over the line all in one movement for his second try of the series. This time Campbell converted. The South Africans, wounded and angry at their inability to penetrate the Lions' defence, were bound to fight back. And they did in the last 20 minutes, often helped by bad kicks by the Lions. The big flanker Stofberg once knocked on just when he looked clear of all the Lions' defenders.

Twice Irvine took drop shots at goal in the last minutes and right at the end Hay had to make a fine catch, while running backwards, from a high kick by Botha. But unlike previous Tests, the Lions played the last quarter in South Africa's half, often in their 25. This time they were determined there would be no mistakes—and there weren't.

This against-the-odds victory was straight out of the pages of the Boys' Own Paper. As Beaumont was carried shoulder high from the pitch, there were tears in the eyes of his team-mates who had learned to admire the sad-faced Lancastrian, and in the eyes of team coach Noel Murphy. The Lions had outplayed the Springboks even more convincingly than they had in all but the scoring in the third Test at wet and windy Port Elizabeth. This time they outscored them by three tries to one, and they had defied history and the odds by becoming the first Lions side ever to win a fourth Test in South Africa.

So though they had lost the series by three Tests to one and been outscored by 11 tries to seven, the Lions had at last given an accurate demonstration of their ability. And once again they had showed that unquenchable spirit that was so striking to those who had observed them on their 10-week trek.

In their 18 matches the Lions had scored 47 tries, 21 conversions, 45 penalty goals and 12 drop goals. Their forwards had been magnificent but their backs, badly affected by injuries, had been bitterly disappointing. By the start of the second Test, three key backs had already been lost—Slemen, Richards and Holmes—and after half-time in that Test they were to lose a fourth, Gareth Davies. A revealing statistic is that 15 backs were used in the four Tests and only nine forwards.

A quiet and thoughtful Peter Wheeler observed after the game: "I began my Lions career with a Test victory and I've ended it with one. A lot of the boys out there today put on the old red shirt for the last time. I'm happy for them. I'm also happy for Ollie Campbell. He is the best kicker of a ball from the ground I have ever seen, and it would have been tragic for him if we'd lost the Test because he hadn't kicked his goals."

Said Gareth Williams: "I'm happy for Billy. He has been a great captain and he deserved this one." A girl came up to Williams and asked him for a souvenir. "Sorry love," he said, rummaging through his pockets, "I haven't got anything. I've given them all away."

Beaumont and du Plessis stood quite close to one another, each deep in conversation. Beaumont was telling a journalist that the way the Lions had used their backs in this game made him think that perhaps that was the way they should have played all through the series. He didn't seem elated. Nearby, du Plessis looked poker-faced. "It was a strange game," said the South Africa captain, "not like any of the others in the series. It was unreal at the start with all those kids on the field and the balloons and things. And then we were stuck in our own 25 for so long. We could never get going. We've played six Tests since April, and there may be five or six more this year. I think there were some of us who felt we couldn't lose. Perhaps it was a good thing we did."

Match Reports

MATCH I

EASTERN PROVINCE 16pts, BRITISH ISLES 28pts
Saturday, 10 May. Boet Erasmus Stadium, Port Elizabeth.
Weather: Bright sunshine, clear sky, temperature in mid-seventies, slight wind.
Crowd: 25,000, not quite capacity.
Half time: E. Province 10, Lions 21.

EASTERN PROVINCE, Currie Cup semi-finalists in 1979, gave the Lions a torrid welcome. Within 50 seconds Lane was helped off with cartilage damage to right knee without having touched the ball. Quinnell replaced him. Inside another 25 minutes Davies, having kicked two penalty goals, a dropped goal and set up a try for Slemen, went off with shoulder trouble. He was replaced by Renwick, with Morgan moving to stand-off. Pretorius and Cowley kicked penalty goals for Province and then Lotz and Potgieter were injured and replaced. In the 29th minute Heunis scored in the corner to reduce the Lions' lead to 15–10 but after three minutes of first-half injury time Holmes darted over after a five-yard scrum, and Renwick converted. Rees scampered over in the second minute of the second half, and within another two minutes Campher barged past Morgan for a try. The only remaining score was a 45-yard penalty goal by Renwick in 71st minute.

Eastern Province: H. Pretorius; C. Heunis, R. Lotz, D. Campher, H. Potgieter; C. Cowley, M. O'Shea; No 8: N. Snyman; Second Row: T. van der Merwe (Capt.), S. Burger, P. Human, A. Johnson; Front Row: J. Ferreira, K. Delport, D. Olivier. *Replacements:* C. van Zyl for Lotz (28 min), I. Kankowski for Potgieter (28 min).
Tries: Heunis, Campher.
Conversion: Cowley.
Penalties: Pretorius, Cowley.

British Isles: Hay; Rees, Gravell, Morgan, Slemen; Davies, Holmes; No 8: Beattie; Second Row: Lane, Martin, Beaumont (Capt.), Squire; Front Row: Price, Wheeler, Cotton. *Replacements:* Quinnell for Lane (5 min), Renwick for Davies (27 min).
Tries: Slemen, Holmes, Rees.
Conversions: Davies, Renwick.
Penalties: Davies (2), Renwick.
Drop: Davies.
Referee: Steve Strydom (Orange FS)

● This equals Lions' highest score against Eastern Province, whom they beat 28–14 in 1974. The 1955 Lions had lost 20–0 and the 1924 Lions lost 14–6 to Eastern Province.

TOUR TALLY	P1 W1		T	C	P	D	Pts.
		For	3	2	3	1	28
		Agst.	2	1	2	0	16

Note: The teams are listed throughout in numerical and descending order from 15 to 1. Therefore the first wing mentioned after the full back is the right wing and the last player's name is that of the loose-head prop.

SA RUGBY ASSOCIATION INVITATION TEAM 6pts, BRITISH ISLES 28pts
Wednesday, 14 May. Border RU Ground, East London.
Weather: Bright, clear sky, temperature in low seventies, windless.
Crowd: 10,000, two thirds of capacity.
Half-time: SARA 3, Lions 13.

WOODWARD emerged as Lions' surprise kicker, scoring 16 points without missing once, and captain-for-day Quinnell scored two bulldozing tries to help enhance otherwise lacklustre game. SARA team superceding Leopards beaten 56–10 in 1974, had six white forwards and two white backs, and included six of the 1979 SA Barbarian tourists to Britain. Thys Burger, Northern Transvaal flanker, outstanding for SARA and full-back Solomon Mhlaba also impressive. Woodward kicked penalties from 35 and 38 yards in first 13 minutes and Quinnell's first try followed penalty five yards out. Renwick hit post with conversion. Third penalty by Woodward suggested a really big margin but instead Northern Transvaal's Ferdie Prinsloo, understudy to renowned Naas Botha, kicked penalties for SARA either side of half-time. Referee Jimmy Smith-Belton made some puzzling decisions, but Woodward got Lions going again with dropped goal and converted late tries by Rees, after blindside chip by Patterson, and Quinnell, barging over from scrum, which made scoreline more respectable.

SARA Invitation XV: S. Mhlaba; T. Nkonki, H. Mhlaba, C. Ebersohn, S. Bridgeman; F. Prinsloo, W. Speelman; No 8: T. Burger; Second Row: T. McGee, F. Weits, A. Poro, M. Cushe (Capt.); Front Row: C. Badenhorst, E. Malan, H. van Aswegen.
Penalties: Prinsloo (2).

Referee: J. Smith-Belton (E Province).

British Isles: O'Donnell; Carleton, Renwick, Woodward, Rees; Richards, Patterson; No 8: Quinnell (Capt.); Second Row: O'Driscoll, Tomes, Colclough, Tucker; Front Row: Blakeway, Phillips, C. Williams.
Replacement: Cotton for Blakeway (72 min).
Tries: Quinnell (2), Rees.
Conversions: Woodward (2).
Penalties: Woodward (3).
Drop: Woodward.

● New fixture. Woodward, probably Leicester club's fourth-choice kicker, had scored only four points with boot in 1979–80 domestic season. Quinnell first forward to score two tries in Lions match since Terry Cobner in first fixture in New Zealand in 1977, a 41–13 win over Wairarapa-Bush, and first in South Africa since Gordon Brown in 20–16 victory over Quaggas on 27 June, 1974.

TOUR TALLY	P2 W2		T	C	P	D	Pts
		For	6	4	6	2	56
		Agst	2	1	4	–	22

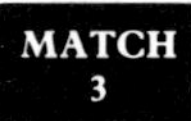

NATAL 15pts, BRITISH ISLES 21pts
Saturday, 17 May. Kings Park, Durban.
Weather: Bright, clear sky, temperature in eighties, windless.
Crowd: 40,000, capacity.
Half-time: Natal 3, Lions 6.

NATAL levelled the score three times, the third five minutes from the end with a fine try, but this spurred the Lions to a courageous final burst. The Lions picked almost their anticipated Test pack, which dominated Natal's lighter and less experienced forwards, except in the loose where Claassen, Watt and Loane often produced moments of panic. Slemen soon dropped a goal from 25 yards, and in the 16th minute Campbell, playing his first game, kicked a penalty from 15 yards, but Brown equalised with 28-yard and 48-yard penalties, either side of half-time. Campbell quickly restored Lions' lead with shaky but successful penalty from 45 yards, and Brown equalised again with 58th-minute penalty. After a frantic period the Lions eased the pressure and Holmes battered over following two five-yard scrums for Campbell to convert. With only five minutes left Natal's forwards peeled away from a line-out close in, Mortassagne burrowed through ensuing maul for a try, and Brown levelled score yet again, with his fourth successful kick out of six. But in injury time Campbell snaked through Natal's defences, running for practically the first time; a ruck formed 20 yards from Natal line; and Holmes and Gravell on the blind side flicked the ball to Carleton, who crossed and ran round for Slemen to convert. An incidental statistic—for once the Lions suffered no serious injuries.

Natal: T. Cocks; L. Sharp, D. Hoffman, R. Haarhoff, C. Brown; P. Smith, P. Manning; No 8: W. Claassen (Capt.); Second Row: W. Watt, H. van Heerden, A. Botha, M. Loane; Front Row: B. de Klerk, D. Speirs, M. Mortassagne.
Try: Mortassagne.
Conversion: Brown.
Penalties: Brown (3).

British Isles: O'Donnell; Carleton, Gravell, Richards, Slemen; Campbell, Holmes; No 8: Beattie; Second Row: Squire, Martin, Beaumont (Capt.), Tucker; Front Row: Price, Wheeler, Cotton.
Tries: Holmes, Carleton.
Conversions: Campbell, Slemen.
Penalties: Campbell (2).
Drop: Slemen.
Referee: S. W. Malan (North-West Cape).

● Lions maintained unbeaten record against Natal, their only check having been 3–3 draw in 1924. Brown became first South African to total double figures against Lions since C. F. Luther kicked four penalties for Northern Transvaal, beaten 16–12 by 1974 Lions on 6 July.

TOUR TALLY	P3	W3		T	C	P	D	Pts
			For	8	6	8	3	77
			Agst	3	2	7	–	37

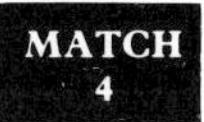

SA INVITATION XV 19pts, BRITISH ISLES 22pts
Wednesday, 21 May. Olen Park, Potchefstroom.
Weather: Overcast, little wind, temperature in high sixties.
Crowd: 23,000, capacity.
Half-time: Invitation XV 12, Lions 10.

A PERFORMANCE of character by the Lions, who finally won by Slemen's historic "team" try after they had trailed for first time on tour and in fact been behind on four occasions. It was their second victory in the last five minutes in five days. Invitation XV had eight men bidding for Springbok places, though one, huge prop Flip van der Merwe, was outplayed by Price in the scrums. Woodward kicked two 50-yard penalty goals in the eighth and 32nd minutes and Blair replied with three in 10th, 24th and 30th. In the 35th minute Woodward slipped past Shields, Hay joined the line and put Slemen over for try, but six minutes later Blair kicked his fourth penalty. At half-time Springbok flanker Theuns Stoffberg replaced Meyers who had injured ribs. Two minutes into second half Woodward kicked his third penalty, but within three minutes Serfontein darted 40 yards upfield for Invitation XV, and though van Heerden was crushingly tackled by Hay, Smith crossed in corner after two rucks. Woodward and Blair exchanged further penalties, leaving Invitation XV 19–16 ahead, until the Lions won with the finest try most of 23,000 crowd will ever see. From line-out they ran and ran, and Slemen was over 1 min 36 sec later after the ball had been through 32 pairs of hands. Four South Africans were on their knees, exhausted, as Woodward converted.

S.A. Invitation XV: T. K. D. Cocks (Natal); S. T. Konki (SARA), D. J. Smith (Zimbabwe), H. Shields (SA Fed.), N. Davids (Western Prov); R. Blair (Western Prov), D. Serfontein (Western Prov); No 8: W. Claassenn (Natal) (Capt.); Second Row: T. Burger (N. Transvaal), J. L. van Heerden (Transvaal), J. de V. Visser (Western Prov), J. J. Meyers (Western Prov); Front Row: M. Le Roux (Orange Free State), W. J. H. Kahts (N. Transvaal), P. R. Van der Merwe (Western Prov).
Replacement: T. Stofberg (N. Transvaal) for Meyers, half-time.
Try: Smith.
Penalties: Blair (5).

British Isles: Hay; Rees, Woodward, Renwick, Slemen; Richards, Patterson; No 8: Quinnell (Capt.); Second Row: G. Williams, Tomes, Colclough, O'Driscoll; Front Row: Price, Phillips, C. Williams.
Tries: Slemen (2).
Conversion: Woodward.
Penalties: Woodward (4).

Referee: G. Bezuidenhout (Transvaal).

● New fixture. Invitation XV's 19pts and Blair's 15 team and individual records against Lions so far on tour (total not exceeded by South Africans since Lions lost second Test 25–20 in 1968, while Blair matched Gerald Bosch's three penalty goals and two dropped goals for Transvaal, beaten 23–15 by 1974 Lions on 15 June). First game of tour in which Lions did not drop a goal, Slemen scored for third successive match.

TOUR TALLY	P4	W4		T	C	P	D	Pts
			For	10	7	12	3	99
			Agst.	4	2	12	–	56

LIONS' LEADING SCORERS:
Tries: 3—Slemen; 2—Holmes, Quinnell, Rees. *Points:* 30—Woodward, 17—Slemen, 11—Davies.

ORANGE FREE STATE 17pts, BRITISH ISLES 21pts
Saturday, 24 May. Free State Stadium, Bloemfontein.
Weather: Overcast, wind blowing down the pitch, temperature in mid-sixties.
Crowd: 24,000, 60,000 capacity.
Half-time: Orange Free State 7, Lions 0.

THE LIONS should have won more convincingly after having played into wind in the first half, but they made silly mistakes and gave away a soft try, while Renwick missed eight goal-kicks. State scored a beautiful try in 28th minute when they won a ruck after a penalty by Renwick rebounded. They worked right-wing du Toit clear, and though he was stopped after 30 yards by a crunching tackle by Morgan, the ball was moved infield and left-wing

Jeffery raced 60 yards to score. Springbok full-back Gysie Pienaar added a 40-yard penalty just before half-time after Ras had left the field with a groin injury following a dubious tackle by Gravell. Holmes (second minute) and Slemen (seventh and 15th) scored tries in the second half, Renwick converting the first, but Wolmarans replied with try in 22nd. Holmes went off with suspected dislocated shoulder in 27th minute and Renwick landed his only penalty. Wheeler nipped round the front of a line-out for the Lions' fourth try but one minute later Richards got in a muddle trying to run from his own 25, Gerber pounced to score for State, and Pienaar converted.

Orange Free State: G. Pienaar; J. du Toit, D. Gerber, J. Rainsford, D. Jeffery; de W. Ras, B. Wolmarans (Capt.); No 8: G. Sonnekus; Second Row: J. Wessels, R. Visagie, J. Kritzinger, E. Jansen; Front row: M. le Roux, K. Fenwick, D. Pretorius. Replacement: R. Froneman for Ras (half-time).
Tries: Jeffery, Wolmarans, Gerber.
Conversion: Pienaar.
Penalty: Pienaar.

British Isles: Morgan; Carleton, Gravell, Renwick, Slemen; Richards, Holmes; No 8: Squire; Second Row: G. Williams, Colclough, Beaumont (Capt.), O'Driscoll; Front Row: Price, Wheeler, C. Williams. *Replacement:* Patterson for Holmes (69 min).
Tries: Holmes, Slemen (2), Wheeler.
Conversion: Renwick.
Penalty: Renwick.
Referee: F. Muller (Eastern Province).

● Lions' highest score against Orange Free State since 31 points in 1955, and State's highest ever score against Lions, though they had beaten the Lions 6–3 in 1924 and drawn 14–14 in 1962. First side this tour to score three tries against Lions, the previous South African side to have done so being Eastern Province, beaten 28–14, in fourth match in 1974. Slemen maintained record of scoring on all four appearances so far, Holmes on all three, Wheeler the first Lions forward to score since Quinnell in second match.

TOUR TALLY	P5	W5		T	C	P	D	Pts
			For	14	8	13	3	120
			Agst.	7	3	13	–	73

MATCH 6

SARF FEDERATION (PROTEAS) INVITATION XV 6pts, BRITISH ISLES 15pts
Tuesday, 27 May. Danie Craven Stadium, Stellenbosch.
Weather: Clear, warm, cloudless, temperature in high sixties.
Crowd: 15,000, capacity 20,000.
Half-time: Proteas XV 3, Lions 9.

FOUR days before the first Test the Lions gave one of their worst performances and lost Cotton with his heart trouble. The SARFF side, the Proteas, were bolstered by the Western Province white front five forwards, who won three tight-heads to none but were later accused of violent and excessively dirty play. Syd Millar said later, "There were some incidents that I hope I won't see repeated on a rugby field." Ward, making his debut for Lions, missed five penalty attempts in the first half but kicked two out of three in second, and converted seventh-minute try awarded to Carleton after the referee consulted the touch-judge. O'Donnell dropped goal from 40 yards three minutes later. Tobias kicked 45-yard penalty in the 18th minute. In the second half fighting broke out between the hookers, the captains were spoken to, and Ward sandwiched penalties from nearly 50 and 30 yards round a 50-yarder from Tobias.

SARFF: R. Louw; J. Noble, Charles Williams, M. Shields, F. Davids; E. Tobias, A. Lategan; No 8: P. Williams (Capt.); Second Row: W. Williams, H. Bekker, J de V. Visser, K. Paarwater; Front Row: H. du Toit, R. Cockrell, H. van Aswegen.
Penalties: Tobias (2).

British Isles: O'Donnell; Carleton, Richards, Woodward, Morgan; Ward, Patterson; No 8: Quinnell (Capt.); Second Row: Tucker, Tomes, Martin, Beattie; Front Row; Stephens, Phillips, Cotton. *Replacement:* Clive Williams for Cotton (33 min).
Try: Carleton.
Conversion: Ward.
Penalties: Ward (2).
Drop: O'Donnell.

Referee: Dr J. Gouws (Eastern Transvaal).

● New fixture, and the first match on tour in which the Lions did not reach 20 points. They now total as many penalty goals as tries. First time Woodward played without scoring—Leicester fourth-choice kicker handing over to Ward, former Home Championship record-sharer. O'Donnell became fourth Lion to drop a goal on this tour.

TOUR TALLY	P6	W6		T	C	P	D	Pts
			For	15	9	15	4	135
			Agst.	7	3	15	–	81

MATCH 7
FIRST TEST

SOUTH AFRICA 26pts, BRITISH ISLES 22pts
Saturday, 31 May. Newlands, Cape Town.
Weather: Clear, warm and sunny, temperature in high sixties.
Crowd: 50,000, capacity.
Half-time: South Africa 16, British Isles 9.

ON Republic Day the Springboks ran riot and scored five tries in a Test for the first time for 18 years. They led by 10 points at one stage, were then rattled to their eye-teeth by a magnificent counter-rally in which the Lions took the lead, lost it, and then levelled the score with seven minutes remaining. A fine try by the Springboks in injury time gave them their first victory over the British Isles in a Test since 1968. Louw, who had a magnificent game, scored the first try for South Africa in the 22nd minute and Botha converted. Ward, his right thigh heavily bandaged because of a haematoma, replied with a penalty three minutes later. In the 29th minute centre Willie du Plessis scored a try that Botha converted and two minutes later Ward kicked another penalty. South Africa's third try in 10 minutes was scored by van Heerden, and Ward, inevitably, kicked another penalty in reply just before half-time to make it 16–9.

The second half belonged to the Lions' forwards. Ward kicked his fourth penalty in the 20th minute just after Carleton had injured his ribs and Gravell had replaced him, and three minutes later, with the Lions' forwards rampant, Price barged over after a line-out (South African throw) for a try that levelled the score 16–16. Four minutes later a quickly-taken dropped goal by Ward, using his less-favoured left foot, put the Lions into the lead. They had scored 10 points in seven minutes. Their lead was brief for in the 31st minute Germishuys rounded off a movement he had begun on the left by scoring out near the right and Botha converted. Two minutes later

Ward levelled the score at 22–22 with his fifth successful penalty, his five penalties and dropped goal giving him an individual points-scoring record in Tests in South Africa with 18. Morally, however, South Africa were the victors and in the first minute of injury time they rounded off a memorable Test when Serfontein nipped over from a maul on the Lions' line.

SOUTH AFRICA: G. Pienaar (Orange FS); **R. Mordt** (Zimbabwe), **D. Smith** (Zimbabwe), **W. du Plessis** (W. Province), **G. Germishuys** (Transvaal); **H. E. Botha** (N. Transvaal), **D. Serfontein** (W. Province); No 8: **M. du Plessis** (W. Province, Capt.); Second Row: **T. Stofberg** (N. Transvaal), **L. Moolman** (N. Transvaal), **J. L. van Heerden** (Transvaal), **R. Louw** (W. Province); Front Row: **M. le Roux** (Orange FS), **W. Kahts** (N. Transvaal), **R. Prentis** (Transvaal).
Tries: Louw, W. du Plessis, van Heerden, Germishuys, Serfontein.
Conversions: Botha (3).

BRITISH ISLES: O'Donnell; Carleton, Richards, Renwick, Slemen; Ward, Patterson; No 8: **Quinnell;** Second Row: **O'Driscoll, Beaumont** (Capt.), **Colclough, Squire;** Front Row: **Price, Wheeler, C. Williams.** *Replacement:* **Gravell** for Carleton (59 min).
Try: Price.
Penalties: Ward (5).
Drop: Ward.

REFEREE: F. Palmade (France).

● Lions' first defeat in South Africa for 29 matches, the last having been in 1968, final Test. And it was the first time they had conceded five tries in South Africa since 1962, Final Test, and highest score against since 34–14 defeat—same points aggregate as here—in that same 1962 match. Ward's 18 points surpassed Lions' Test record, 17 made up of conversion and five penalties by Tom Kiernan in 25–20 defeat in First Test in 1968, though exceeded in 1974 non-Test tour matches by Alan Old (37 points v South West Districts), J. J. Williams (24 points—six tries—v S. Western Districts), Phil Bennett (23 points v Western Transvaal) and Andy Irvine (22 v Rhodesia, 20 v SARA Leopards, and 19 v Griqualand West). Richards made sixth successive appearance. Slemen's last match on tour, and the only one in which he did not score.

TOUR TALLY	P7	W6	L1		T	C	P	D	Pts
				For	16	9	20	5	157
				Agst.	12	6	15	–	105

LIONS' LEADING SCORERS:
Tries: 5—Slemen; 3—Holmes; 2—Carleton, Rees, Quinnell.
Points: 30—Woodward; 26—Ward; 25—Slemen; 12—Holmes.
Most appearances:
6—Richards; 5—Carleton, Patterson, Price, Quinnell, Renwick, Slemen, C. Williams.

SA COUNTRY XV 7pts, BRITISH ISLES 27pts
Wednesday, 4 June. South West Stadium, Windhoek.
Weather: Clear, warm, cloudless, temperature in high sixties, wind across field.
Crowd: 9,000, three-quarters capacity.
Half-time: Country XV 3, Lions 16.

A MARGINALLY better performance by the Lions. Davies returned to bring poise and control to the backs, and Hay—acting captain—provided considerable punch from full-back. There were two new 1980 Lions—Robbie, who looked accomplished and sharp, and the 1977 Lion Orr who had arrived the weekend before to replace Cotton. Shields was playing his third game against the Lions. Country XV started with the wind from left to right and in the third minute Tobias kicked a penalty from 15 yards. Davies soon kicked an equaliser, another penalty in the 13th minute when Shields fell offside, and midway through the half converted a push-over try credited to Beattie. Renwick darted over for a try in the third minute of first-half injury time. Davies landed another penalty in the 10th minute of the second half, and in the 26th Woodward, playing on the right wing, raced over from 20 yeards. Then the Country XV broke out of defence, led by Mhlaba, and Els was nearly over between the posts. There was a scrum, and a chip to the corner ended in a frantic chase between Charles Williams and Hay which the referee ruled that Williams had won. In the 34th minute Hay joined the line, Gravell punched his way through, and when he was stopped on the line Gareth Williams wrestled the ball clear to score.

South Africa Country XV: S. Mhlaba (SARU); E. Durrheim (E. Transvaal), H. Shields (W. Province Fed.), J. Els (E. Transvaal), B. Venter (SWA); E. Tobias (W. Province Fed.), F. Venter (N. Natal); No 8: H. Schrader (SWA); Second Row: M. Cushe (SARU), R. Meier (SWD), A. Botha (NOK), W. Wolfaardt (SWA); Front Row: N. van Rensburg (SWD, Capt.), J. Volschenk (E. Transvaal), D. Mather (SWA). *Replacement:* Charles Williams (W. Province) for B. Venter (17 min).
Try: Charles Williams.
Penalty: Tobias.

British Isles: Hay (Capt.); Woodward, Gravell, Renwick, Morgan; Davies, Robbie; No 8: Beattie; Second Row: G. Williams, Martin, Tomes, Tucker; Front Row: Stephens, Wheeler, Orr.
Tries: Beattie, Renwick, Woodward, G. Williams.
Conversion: Davies.
Penalties: Davies (3).

Referee: Col. N. Carstens (N. Transvaal)

● New fixture. Woodward's first try of tour marked his first appearance on right wing, and Davies totalled 11 points for second time in two appearances. Tobias became first opponent to score in two matches against Lions.

TOUR TALLY					T	C	P	D	Pts
	P8	W7	L1	For	20	10	23	5	184
				Agst.	13	6	16	–	112

MATCH 9

TRANSVAAL 12pts, BRITISH ISLES 32pts
Saturday, 7 June. Wanderers Ground, Johannesburg.
Weather: Overcast, warm and a watery sun, temperature in high sixties.
Crowd: 35,000, capacity.
Half-time: Transvaal 9, Lions 19.

IRVINE's first appearance dramatically lifted the Lions' backs to new authority. Woodward was stunning on the right wing and Davies brilliant at stand-off, making two tries and scoring one himself. At last the backs capitalised on the forwards' sturdy work. Richards scored a ninth-minute try after inter-passing, and three minutes later he knocked over Wilkinson, who was attempting to catch a high ball from Davies, and Price was there to score. Barnard replied with a penalty from in front in the 17th minute, but three drives by the Lions' forwards cleared the way for Woodward to cross in the corner in the 21st, and in the 25th minute Davies sneaked in after a muddle between Fourie and Wilkinson. In the 36th minute Pypers broke away in midfield, Maritz ran through from 30 yards, and Barnard converted, and in first-half injury time Woodward kicked a 30 yard penalty. Scoring slowed down in the second half after Irvine, who had hit a post with three shots out of four, had exchanged penalties with Barnard. Richards fell and dislocated his right shoulder after 21 minutes, a tragedy for he was just returning to his best form. Two minutes later Woodward scored his second try of the game and converted it, and seven minutes later Patterson scampered through from 30 yards.

Transvaal: P. Wilkinson; J. Fourie, W. Hollander, D. Maritz, G. Germishuys; L. Barnard, J. Minnaar; No 8: D. MacDonald; Second Row: T. Bosch, L. van Vuuren, K. de Klerk, C. Pypers (Capt.); Front Row: J. Strauss, C. Venter, R. Prentis.
Try: Maritz.
Conversion: Barnard.
Penalties: Barnard (2).
Referee: Capt. F. Burger (Western Province).

British Isles: Irvine; Woodward, Gravell, Richards, Hay; Davies, Patterson; No 8: Quinnell; Second Row: O'Driscoll, Beaumont (Capt.), Colclough, Squire; Front Row: Price, Wheeler, Orr. *Replacement:* Renwick for Richards (61 min).
Tries: Richards, Price, Woodward (2), Davies, Patterson.
Conversion: Woodward.
Penalties: Woodward, Irvine.

● Lions highest score of tour so far against a state who had beaten them 14–6 in 1968 and 13–6 in 1910. The six tries, which meant they again totalled more tries than penalty goals, were two more than in any previous match on tour and most for Lions in South Africa since 1974 team's 10 against SARA Leopards on 9 July. Davies and Patterson became seventh half-back partnership starting in nine matches, Davies playing with his third scrum-half in three appearances and maintaining his record of scoring every time. Woodward reached 47 points for tour, and Price became first Lions forward to score in two matches.

TOUR TALLY	P9	W8	L1		T	C	P	D	Pts
				For	26	11	25	5	216
				Agst.	14	7	18	–	124

EASTERN TRANSVAAL 15pts, BRITISH ISLES 21pts
Wednesday, 10 June. Pam Brink Stadium, Springs.
Weather: Clear, sunny and hot, temperature in seventies.
Crowd: 20,000, two-thirds capacity.
Half-time: E. Transvaal 6, Lions 12.

A ROTTEN match, best forgotten, with only one try among 36 points and Holmes tearing ligaments in his right knee midway through the first half. At least Campbell marked his return with 17 points. Referee Stoney Steenkamp seemed to favour the home side and gave them 17 penalties in the second half, compared with three for the Lions, and 24 to seven overall. Syd Millar said darkly afterwards: "I prefer not to talk about the referee". Eastern Transvaal did not have the skill to play with the ball they won, and the Lions could not win enough ball to play rugby. The only try came in the fifth minute when Beattie went to the blindside of a scrum, Holmes kicked through, Carleton cut inside to score, and Campbell converted. Three minutes later Geere dropped a goal for Eastern Transvaal, and the rest of the scoring was a series of penalties by Campbell and Geere, punctuated by a late dropped goal by Campbell, with Eastern Transvaal never closer than six points to the Lions.

Eastern Transvaal: D. van Rensburg; L. Lubbe, J. Els, E. Durrheim, C. van Zyl; P. Geere, P. Grobler; No 8: W. Boshoff (Capt.); Second Row: M. van Eeden, K. Wentzel, K. van Wyk, K. Fourie; Front Row: J. Volschenk, T. Kloppers, T. Botha.
Penalties: Geere (4).
Drop: Geere.

Referee: J. Steenkamp (Orange FS)

British Isles; O'Donnell; Carleton, Renwick, Morgan, Hay (Capt.); Campbell, Holmes; No 8: Beattie; Second Row: G. Williams, Martin, Tomes, Tucker; Front Row: Stephens, Phillips, C. Williams. *Replacement:* Patterson for Holmes (27 min).
Try: Carleton.
Conversions: Campbell.
Penalties: Campbell (4).
Drop: Campbell.

● Only a substitute fixture for cancelled Zimbabwe match, though the Lions lost 19–16 to Eastern Transvaal in 1962 and could only draw 17–17 in 1955, before winning 33–10 and 37–9 on last two tours. Campbell became sixth Lion to drop a goal on tour, Geere's for Eastern Transvaal being the first by an opposition player. Lions again total more penalty goals than tries.

TOUR TALLY	P10	W9	L1		T	C	P	D	Pts
				For	27	12	29	6	237
				Agst.	14	7	22	1	139

SOUTH AFRICA 26pts, BRITISH ISLES 19pts
Saturday, 14 June. Free State Stadium, Bloemfontein.
Weather: Clear, hot and sunny, temperature in high sixties.
Crowd: 60,000, capacity.
Half-time: South Africa 16, British Isles 9.

ANOTHER exciting Test, and it bore uncanny resemblances to the first Test at Newlands, Cape Town. Again the Springboks led by 10 points at one time, again the half-time score was 16–9, again the Lions climbed back with a strong second-half revival and again the Springboks scored two late tries. The Lions made five changes, all in the backs, from their first Test team—Irvine for O'Donnell, Hay for the absent Slemen on the left wing, Gravell and Woodward at centre for Renwick and the injured Richards, and Davies at stand-off instead of Ward. South Africa had Kevin de Klerk for the injured Moaner van Heerden in the second row in their only change.

Again Louw scored the first try, this time in the 13th minute after a clearance-kick by Irvine had landed in Germishuys' arms, and he interpassed with Louw and Morné du Plessis. Three minutes later Patterson chipped over the Springbok forwards, Mordt, Pienaar and Serfontein got in a muddle, Patterson helped again with a fierce tackle and O'Driscoll, who had a fine game, snatched the ball and touched down. Davies's conversion curled in from the touchline. One minute later Botha missed a kickable penalty, but he was successful in the 25th minute with a penalty when Woodward and Gravell obstructed Smith. In the 32nd minute Mordt got off the ground after a tackle by Hay—referee Palmade ruled he hadn't let the ball touch the ground—and threw a pass infield that was collected by Willie du Plessis, who gave it to Stofberg who ran over from 20 yards. Botha's conversion made it 13–6 and three minutes later he kicked a penalty from 40 yards. Davies kicked a penalty for the Lions in the 38th minute, and one minute later Beaumont injured his left leg, though he played on.

After half-time came the revival. Davies landed his second penalty within five minutes and in the 14th minute Irvine landed a monstrous 55 yard goal to make it 16–15. But in the 24th minute Davies limped off with a twisted knee, and Campbell, who replaced him, immediately missed a chance of putting the Lions ahead with a penalty from 30 yards. South Africa regained control when Pienaar deftly measured a crossfield chip-kick for Germishuys to score, and Pienaar himself got another try when Morné du Plessis kicked a loose ball through and Carleton was robbed after making a brave fall. Botha converted. Louw was carried off with bruised kidneys, black eyes and a cut lip and was replaced in injury time by Thys Burger, just before Gravell broke through and scored in the corner for the Lions. Campbell missed the conversion.

SOUTH AFRICA: G. Pienaar (Orange FS); **R. Mordt** (Zimbabwe), **D. Smith** (Zimbabwe), **W. du Plessis** (W. Province), **G. Germishuys** (Transvaal); **H. E. Botha** (N. Transvaal), **D. Serfontein** (W. Province); No 8: **M. du Plessis** (W. Province, Capt.); Second Row: **T. Stofberg** (N. Transvaal), **L. Moolman** (N. Transvaal), **K. de Klerk** (Transvaal), **R. Louw** (W. Province); Front Row: **M. le Roux** (Orange FS), **W. Kahts** (N. Transvaal), **R. Prentis** (Transvaal). *Replacement:* **T. Burger** (N. Transvaal) for Louw (81 min).
Tries: Louw, Stofberg, Germishuys, Pienaar.
Conversions: Botha (2).
Penalties: Botha (2).

BRITISH ISLES: Irvine; Carleton, Gravell, Woodward, Hay; Davies, Patterson; No 8: **Quinnell;** Second Row: **O'Driscoll, Colclough, Beaumont** (Capt.), **Squire;** Front Row: **Price, Wheeler, C. Williams.** *Replacement:* **Campbell** for Davies (66 min).
Tries: O'Driscoll, Gravell.
Conversion: Davies.
Penalties: Davies (2), Irvine.

REFEREE: F. Palmade (F.F.R.).

● Only the second occasion in which the Lions conceded four or more tries, the first being in first Test, when it was five. Louw and Germishuys were scoring their second tries in two Tests, and Botha reached 16 points in series. Davies, with 34 points from four matches, maintained record of scoring in every match for the Lions, and Gravell and O'Driscoll were getting on scoresheet for first time. Irvine, selected originally as wing before withdrawing with hamstring trouble, played for second time in two matches as full-back, with Scotland colleague Hay, originally selected as full-back, again playing his usual home international position as wing.

TOUR TALLY	P11	W9	L2		T	C	P	D	Pts
				For	29	13	32	6	256
				Agst	18	9	24	1	165

LIONS' LEADING SCORERS:
Tries: 5—Slemen; 3—Carleton, Holmes, Woodward.
Points: 47—Woodward; 34—Davies; 26—Ward; 25—Campbell, Slemen; 14—Renwick.
Most appearances:
8—Patterson, Renwick; 7—Carleton, Gravell, Price, Quinnell, Richards, Wheeler, C Williams.

MATCH 12

JUNIOR SPRINGBOKS 6pts, BRITISH ISLES 17pts
Wednesday, 18 June. Wanderers Ground, Johannesburg.
Weather: Sunny, warm, temperature in mid-sixties.
Crowd: 30,000, capacity.
Half-time: Junior Springboks 6, Lions 3.

A PERFORMANCE of character by the Lions, nervous after their second Test defeat. The forwards, a mixture of the Wednesday side plus four of the Test pack, controlled the game, and behind them, Dodge made his mark in his first game. Renwick dropped a neat goal in the fifth minute, two minutes before Orr left the field with a bloody trail of stud marks on his left thigh. He was replaced by Clive Williams. In the 18th minute, following flambuoyant play by the Junior Springboks, Geldenhuys burrowed through after a scrum to the Lions 10 yards out, and Cowley converted it. Ward and Irvine each missed penalties in this half and Beck was wide with three long ones for the Junior Springboks. In the third minute after half-time O'Donnell tackled Gerber into touch and injured his neck. He was taken to hospital, and Woodward came on to play left wing with Irvine moving to full back. In the 10th minute Irvine scored from a five yard scrum. Darius Botha, Naas's brother, and Beck and Gerber threatened danger, but in the last six minutes the Lions pulled well away. Ward gave Dodge a well-timed crash ball, and Rees scored from a flicked high pass to the right wing. Woodward converted, and in the second minute of injury time he ran 30 yards and though seemingly surrounded as he approached the left corner, he leaned forward, showed them the ball, pulled back, and turned infield where he put Dodge over.

Junior Springboks: T. Cocks (Natal); D. Botha (N. Transvaal), D. Gerber (Orange FS), C. Beck (W. Province), D. Jeffery (Orange FS); G. Cowley (E. Province), G. Visagie (Griqualand W); No 8: W. Claassen (Natal, Capt); Second Row: E. Jansen (Orange FS), S. Burger (E. Province), J. de V. Visser (W. Province), S. Geldenhuys (N. Transvaal); Front Row: F. du Toit (W. Province), E. Malan (N. Transvaal), J. Oberholser (N. Transvaal).
Try: Geldenhuys.
Conversion: Cowley.

British Isles: O'Donnell; Rees, Renwick, Dodge, Irvine; Ward, Robbie, No 8: Beattie; Second Row: O'Driscoll, Martin, Colclough, Squire (Capt.); Front Row: Price, Phillips, Orr. *Replacements:* C. Williams for Orr (7 min), Woodward for O'Donnell (43 min).
Tries: Irvine, Rees, Dodge.
Conversion: Woodward.
Drop: Renwick.

Referee: S. Strydom (Orange FS).

● Revival of fixture against virtual South Africa second XV, won 16–11 in 1962 and 15–12 in 1955. First match of tour without a penalty goal for either side, Lions now total as many tries as penalties. Renwick became seventh Lion to drop a goal, and Ward and Robbie—both injury reinforcements—became eighth half-back partnership starting a match on tour.

TOUR TALLY:	P12 W10 L2		T	C	P	D	Pts
		For	32	14	32	7	273
		Agst.	19	10	24	1	171

MATCH 13

NORTHERN TRANSVAAL 9pts, BRITISH ISLES 16pts
Saturday, 21 June. Loftus Versfeld, Pretoria.
Weather: Sunny, warm, temperature in mid-sixties.
Crowd: 68,000, capacity.
Half-time: N. Transvaal 0, Lions 16.

THE "Fifth Test", as it was labelled, was won surprisingly easily by the Lions, for whom all the locals predicted defeat. Quinnell's strained groin kept him out of consideration, so Squire moved to No 8, where he played beautifully, and the inclusion of Tucker made the back row a pacy Celtic fringe. Northern Transvaal's "Blue Bulls", joint Currie Cup holders including seven Springboks (four in the pack) and led by Naas Botha, couldn't harmonise their backs and forwards, and Botha missed two out of three drop-shots and all three penalty kicks. In the 16th minute Irvine kicked a penalty from two yards inside his own half; 11 minutes later Squire scored a pushover try; and in another six minutes Colclough rounded off a 40-yard inter-passing movement with O'Driscoll, Tucker and Campbell, for Campbell to convert. Just before half-time Irvine kicked his second penalty, from seven yards inside his own half. Northern staged a revival in the second half. Botha dropped a goal from 40 yards in the eighth minute and three minutes later he brought in Tjokkie van der Merwe on the burst, and the centre splintered the Lions' defence to score between the posts. Botha converted. There was a tense 20 minutes for the Lions, during which Darius Botha seemed to have touched down but the referee said he was unsighted and gave a 25 drop-out. Northern were awarded 10 penalties in the second half, the Lions none, but nothing could help Northern close the gap.

Northern Transvaal: P. Edwards; D. Botha, J. Knox, T. van der Merwe, P. van Zyl; H. E. Botha (Capt.), T. du Plessis; No 8: J. Marais; Second Row: T. Burger, L. Moolman, T. Stofberg, B. Geldenhuys; Front Row: C. Badenhorst, W. Kahts, J. Oberholzer.
Try: van der Merwe.
Conversion: H. E. Botha.
Drop: H. E. Botha.

British Isles: Irvine; Woodward, Gravell, Dodge, Hay; Campbell, Robbie; No 8: Squire; Second Row: Tucker, Colclough, Beaumont (Capt), O'Driscoll; Front Row: Price, Wheeler, C. Williams.
Tries: Squire, Colclough.
Conversion: Campbell.
Penalties: Irvine (2).
Referee: Capt. F. Burger (W. Province).

● Northern Transvaal's first defeat for 31 games, and the first time they had lost by more than four points to a touring side for 20 years (had held 1974 Lions to 12–16, 1968 lions to 19–22, and beaten 1962 Lions 14–6). Irvine, who had kicked two penalties and a conversion in 1974 match, maintained record of scoring in all four games in 1980, while Squire and Colclough were scoring first tries of tour. Naas Botha now totals 21 points in three matches against Lions, exceeded only by Woodward, Davies, Campbell, Ward and Slemen for Lions themselves.

TOUR TALLY	P13 W11 L2		T	C	P	D	Pts
		For	34	15	34	7	289
		Agst	20	11	24	2	180

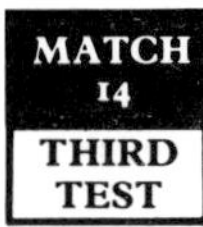
MATCH 14

THIRD TEST

SOUTH AFRICA 12pts, BRITISH ISLES 10 pts.
Saturday, 28 June. Boet Erasmus Stadium, Port Elizabeth
Weather: Intermittent torrential rain, overcast, temperature in mid-fifties.
Crowd: 47,000 in 55,000 capacity stadium.
Half-time. South Africa 3, British Isles 7.

THE Lions, needing to win to keep the series alive, had new caps in Dodge and Tucker, and for South Africa van Heerden returned in place of de Klerk. For the first time in the series, the Lions scored first, a second minute penalty by Campbell. Botha missed three penalties but equalised with one from 48 yards in the 23rd minute, but with 11 minutes remaining in the first half Hay gathered an attempted clearance by Serfontein and crashed over for a try from five yards. Botha dropped a goal in the fourth minute after half-time but six minutes later Campbell landed his second penalty. The Lions now led 10–6, and had several copper-bottomed chances to score tries in the next few minutes but missed them all. Dodge and Irvine knocked on and Patterson had a dab on his own with men to spare outside him. Even so the Lions were totally dominant in all phases until suddenly, with 10 minutes left, Germishuys threw in quickly to Stofberg while other forwards were streaming across the field, and Stofberg, though tackled by Woodward, passed back to Germishuys who ran 10 yards for his third try of the series. Botha converted brilliantly from near the left touchline to put South Africa in front for the first time and Campbell missed a chance to regain lead for the Lions with a penalty also from near touch on the left. Even Morné du Plessis admitted "The better team lost" but there was no excuse for the Lions, who won the line-outs, rucks and mauls but couldn't score the points.

SOUTH AFRICA: G. Pienaar (Orange FS); **R. Mordt** (Zimbabwe), **D. Smith** (Zimbabwe), **W. du Plessis** (W. Province), **G. Germishuys** (Transvaal); **H. E. Botha** (N. Transvaal), **D. Serfontein** (W. Province); No 8: **M.du Plessis** (W. Province, Capt); Second Row: **T. Stofberg** (N. Transvaal), **L. Moolman** (N. Transvaal), **J. L.van Heerden** (Transvaal), **R. Louw** (W. Province); Front Row; **M.le Roux** (Orange FS), **W. Kahts** (N. Transvaal), **R. Prentis** (Transvaal).
Try: Germishuys.
Conversion: Botha.
Penalty: Botha,
Dropped goal; Botha.

BRITISH ISLES: Irvine; Woodward, Gravell, Dodge, Hay; Campbell, Patterson; No 8: **Squire;** Second Row: **O'Driscoll, Colclough, Beaumont** (Capt), **Tucker;** Front Row; **Price, Wheeler, C. Williams.**
Try: Hay.
Penalties: Campbell (2).

REFEREE: J.-P. Bonnet (F.F.R.).

● First time Lions have gone 3–0 down since any series since New Zealand in 1966 and first time ever in South Africa. Their 10 points their lowest score in 14 matches on tour. Botha became first man to drop two goals during tour—no Lion has more than one—and now totals 29 points in four matches against Lions, exceeded for Lions in whole tour so far only by Woodward, Davies and Campbell. Germishuys maintained record of scoring in all three Tests, his three tries being as many as by any Lion in all matches except Slemen, who had returned home four weeks earlier. Hay's try was his first on tour, and he has now played five of his eight matches in Scotland position of wing, while Irvine, originally named as tour wing, has completed five matches at full-back since his arrival as a reinforcement. Campbell and Patterson, current Ireland half-backs, started a match together for the first time on tour, though they had played together twice after mid-match substitutions. They were tenth different partnership to start in 14 matches, the others being Davies with Holmes, Robbie and Patterson; Richards with Patterson (twice) and Holmes; Campbell with Holmes (twice) and Robbie; Ward with Patterson (twice) and Robbie. Lions again total more penalty goals than tries.

TOUR TALLY:	P14	W11	L3		T	C	P	D	Pts
				For	35	15	36	7	299
				Agst	21	12	25	3	192

LIONS' LEADING SCORERS:
Tries: 5—Slemen; 3—Carleton, Holmes, Rees, Woodward.
Points: 49—Woodward; 34—Davies; 33—Cambell; 26—Ward; 25—Slemen; 17—Renwick; 16—Irvine
Most appearances:
10—Price, C. Williams, 9—Colclough, Gravell, O'Driscoll, Patterson, Renwick, Wheeler, Woodward.

SOUTH AFRICAN BARBARIANS, 14pts BRITISH ISLES 25pts.
Wednesday, 2 July. Kings Park, Durban
Weather: Sunny, clear, temperature in mid-sixties.
Crowd: 33,000 in 40,000 capacity stadium
Half-time: Barbarians 6, Lions 19.

A RELAXED midweek frolic dominated by Hugo Porta, the brilliant Argentinian stand-off, but with the Lions, including only Irvine of their third Test team, proving they could hold together even with the series lost. Ward and Porta both hit posts with penalties before Ward opened the score with penalties from 30 and 15 yards. Davids, one of three coloureds in the Barbarians team, quickly replied with a try which Porta converted to equalise. A penalty by Ward and a try by Tomes converted by Ward made it 15–6, and Irvine added a try before half-time. Loane ran in from 30 yards in the third minute of the second half but Ward dodged round two men on the Barbarians line for a 21st minute try which he converted himself. Finally the bearded Buchanan leaped into the back of a Lions scrum on their line and was awarded a try, Porta's conversion hitting a post.

South African Barbarians: S. Mhlaba (SARA), C. Williams (SARFF), E. Tobias (SARFF), P. Oosthuizen (Stellenbosch Univ.), F. Davids (SARFF); H. Porta (Argentine), I. Buchanan (Zimbabwe); No 8 M. Loane (Natal, Australia) (Capt.); Second Row: P. Fourie (Pretoria Police), A. Markgraaff (W. TVL.), H. van Heerden (Natal), H. Mayers (W. Prov.); Front Row: T. Lupini (Diggers), C. Rogers (Zimbabwe), M. Mortassagne (Natal). *Replacement:* G. Visagie (Griqualand W) for Mhlaba (29 min)
Tries: Davids, Loane, Buchanan.
Conversion: Porta.

British Isles: Irvine; Rees, Morgan, Renwick, Carleton; Ward, Robbie; No 8: Beattie; Second Row: G. Williams, Martin, Tomes, Quinnell (Capt.); Front Row: Stephens, Phillips, Orr.
Tries: Tomes, Irvine, Ward.
Conversions: Ward (2).
Penalties: Ward (3).

Referee: C. Harrison (N. Zealand).

● New fixture. Tenth occasion in 15 matches Lions have exceeded 20 points, but first time for five matches. Ward's 17 points exceeded so far on tour only by his own 18 in first Test, and equalled by Campbell's 17 against Eastern Transvaal; Ward, with 43 points from four appearances, now second highest scorer on tour to Woodward (49 pts). Ward and Tomes were scoring their first tries of tour. Barbarians only the second non-Test team to score three tries against the Lions, following Orange Free State on May 24.

TOUR TALLY					T	C	P	D	Pts
	P15	W12	L3	For	38	17	39	7	324
				Agst.	24	13	25	3	206

WESTERN PROVINCE 6pts, BRITISH ISLES 37pts
Saturday, 5 July. Newlands, Cape Town
Weather: Cloudy, warm, temperature in low sixties.
Crowd: 44,000 in 50,000 capacity stadium.
Half time: Western Province 3, Lions 12.

AN IMPERIOUS forward display, and nearly faultless kicking by Campbell inflicted Western Province's biggest defeat this century. Campbell kicked 22 points and missed only one conversion. Province, without Springboks' captain Morné du Plessis and stand-off Robbie Blair, seemed only half a team against Lions' final Test selection. Campbell opened with dropped goals in the 11th and 15th minutes, sandwiching a penalty by Beck for Province. Then Irvine dropped a fine goal from 40 yards and Campbell added a penalty from the same distance in the second minute of first-half injury time. Province's front five had all played in that rumbustious match at Stellenbosch just before the first Test, and fighting broke out periodically, but after half-time the Lions took charge. Campbell kicked penalties in the second, ninth, and 15th minutes, and converted a try when Hay intercepted and ran 50 yards. The Lions second try came in the 23rd minute after some fine running by Carleton, beautifully finished by Irvine and converted by Campbell. Little Serfontein thumped a huge penalty from 45 yards in the 27th minute, but within four minutes Woodward, who had come on when Irvine retired with a hamstring niggle, scored after three rucks and a classic left-right-left movement. The crowds streamed away now—they had already seen enough.

Western Province: S. Naude; P. Oosthuizen, C. Ebersohn, W. du Plessis, P. Goosen; C. Beck, D. Serfontein; No 8: J.-P. Geldenhuys; Second Row: D. Johnson, H. Bekker, J. de V. Visser, R. Louw; Front Row: H. du Toit, R. Cockrell, H. van Aswegen (Capt.).
Penalties: Beck, Serfontein.

British Isles: Irvine; Carleton, Gravell, Dodge, Hay; Campbell, Robbie; No 8: Squire; Second Row: Tucker, Colclough, Beaumont (Capt.), O'Driscoll; Front Row: Price, Wheeler, C. Williams. *Replacement:* Woodward for Irvine (65 min).
Tries: Hay, Irvine, Woodward.
Conversions: Campbell (2).
Penalties: Campbell (4).
Dropped goals: Campbell (2), Irvine.
Referee: F. Muller (Eastern Province).

● Lions' highest score and biggest win of tour, and their biggest win ever over Western Province, joint Currie Cup champions, who had beaten 1938 and 1924 Lions. Campbell's 22 points made him highest scorer in one match on tour, also highest scorer on whole tour to date with 55 points to Woodward's 53. Campbell first Lion to drop two goals in any Lions match since Phil Bennett in 1974 third Test, and first to have dropped more than one goal on whole tour. Irvine became seventh tourist to have dropped one goal so far.

TOUR TALLY	P16	W13	L3		T	C	P	D	Pts
				For	41	19	43	10	361
				Agst.	24	13	27	3	212

LIONS' LEADING SCORERS:
Tries: 5—Slemen; 4—Woodward; 3—Carleton, Holmes, Irvine, Rees. *Points:* 55—Campbell; 53—Woodward; 43—Ward; 34—Davies; 27—Irvine; 25—Slemen; 17—Renwick. *Dropped goals:* 3—Campbell.

GRIQUALAND WEST 19pts, BRITISH ISLES 23 pts.
Tuesday, 8 July. de Beers Stadium, Kimberley
Weather: Warm, sunny, windy, temperature in low sixties.
Crowd: 8,500 in 12,000 capacity stadium.
Half time: Griqualand W. 9, Lions 7.

VICTORY enabled Beaumont's Lions to become only the second British Isles team this century to be unbeaten in provincial games in South Africa, but at the cost of Patterson suffering the eighth major injury when he tore ligaments in his right knee in the sixth minute, and was carried off to hospital. Fiery Griquas gave the Lions a torrid time, harrassing them unmercifully, and were leading entering the last 20 minutes. Beattie had opened the scoring with a Lions' try in the third minute but three minutes later Oosthuisen scored in the right corner following the move in which Patterson was injured, and Visagie converted. Penalties by Ward and Visagie completed the first-half scoring, Visagie made it 12–7 with a second penalty nine minutes after half-time, but then the Lions scored 13 points in as many minutes. Morgan dropped a goal from near the left touchline; Robbie regained the lead with a try; and Morgan scored between the posts, Ward converting. With seven minutes remaining Robbie dropped a goal from an indirect free kick, and finally Visagie kicked his third penalty and in injury-time chipped over a scrum, Hay was bowled over, and Koch touched down the bouncing ball.

Griqualand West: G. Rodwell; H. Lubbe, A. Gerber, J. Jooste, D. Prins; K. Erasmus, G. Visagie; No 8: C. Oosthuisen; Second Row: P. de Bruyn, P. van Zyl (Capt.), T. van Tonder, T. Koch; Front Row: J. Brown, B. O'Ehley, J. Harrison.
Tries: Oosthuisen, Koch.
Conversion: Visagie.
Penalties: Visagie (3).

British Isles: Hay; Rees, Woodward, Renwick, Morgan; Ward, Patterson; No 8: Beattie; Second Row: Quinnell (Capt.), Tomes, Martin, G. Williams; Front Row: Stephens, Phillips, Orr. *Replacement:* Robbie for Patterson (9 min.).
Tries: Beattie, Robbie, Morgan.
Conversion: Ward.
Penalty: Ward.
Dropped goals: Morgan, Robbie.
Referee: Dr L. Wessels (N. Transvaal).

● Griqualand West became only fourth team outside Tests to lead Lions at half-time, and certainly ran them closer than in 1974, when McBride's Lions won 69–16 with Tom Grace scoring four tries and Irvine converting eight. Griquas had drawn 8–8 with 1962 Lions and beaten the 1910 team. Morgan, playing his last game of tour for the Lions, and Robbie scored their first points for Lions, and also became the eighth and ninth Lions to have dropped one goal on tour. Lions again level on tries and penalty goals for the tour.

TOUR TALLY	P17	W14	L3		T	C	P	D	Pts
				For	44	20	44	12	384
				Agst.	26	14	30	3	231

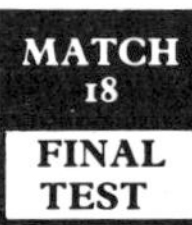
MATCH 18

FINAL TEST

SOUTH AFRICA 13pts, BRITISH ISLES 17
Saturday, 12 July. Loftus Versfeld, Pretoria.
Weather: Sunny, no wind, temperature in mid-sixties.
Crowd: 68,000, capacity.
Half-time: South Africa 3pts, British Isles 7.

THE LIONS capped their extraordinary tour with this against-the-odds victory, thus becoming the first Lions side ever to win a fourth Test in South Africa and avoiding the ignominy of being the only Lions to have been whitewashed by South Africa in Tests. The pattern of play in the first half was familiar: unrelenting pressure by the magnificent Lions forwards, mistakes by their backs, and attacking flurries by the Springboks. Campbell landed a penalty in the 32nd minute and Botha replied in kind two minutes later. In the 40th minute Williams burrowed over for a try from a maul on South Africa's line, but a four-point lead was scant reward for the Lions. If the backs had taken their chances they could have scored 15 points. Willie du Plessis scored a try to equalise in the fifth minute of the second half but Botha badly missed the conversion. He had earlier missed a drop at goal and a penalty, and though a home-town hero, he was booed and replaced as kicker by Pienaar, who was successful with penalties in the 10th and 13th minutes. Then the Lions scored two tries in three minutes. In the 15th Irvine darted over in the left corner and then O'Driscoll scored after dashes by Irvine and Gravell. Campbell's conversion ended the scoring.

SOUTH AFRICA: G. Pienaar (Orange FS); **R. Mordt** (Zimbabwe), **D. Smith** (Zimbabwe), **W. du Plessis** (W. Province), **G. Germishuys** (Transvaal); **H. E. Botha** (N. Transvaal), **D. Serfontein** (W. Province); No. 8: **M. du Plessis** (W. Province, Capt.); Second Row: **T. Stofberg** (N. Transvaal), **L. Moolman** (N. Transvaal), **J. L. van Heerden** (Transvaal), **R. Louw** (W. Province); Front Row: **M. le Roux** (Orange FS), **W. E. Malan** (N. Transvaal), **R. Prentis** (Transvaal)
Try: W. du Plessis.
Penalties: Botha, Pienaar (2)

BRITISH ISLES: Irvine; Carleton, Gravell, Dodge, Hay; Campbell, Robbie; No 8: **Squire;** Second row: **Tucker, Colclough, Beaumont** (Capt.) **O'Driscoll;** Front Row: **Price, Wheeler, C. Williams.**
Tries: Williams, Irvine, O'Driscoll.
Conversion: Campbell.
Penalty: Campbell.

REFEREE: J.-P. Bonnet (F.F.R.).

● Lions ensured that they finished tour with more tries than penalty goals—47 to 45—but they still totalled only seven tries and 11 penalties in Tests, while the whole tour (counting opposition scores) produced only 74 tries compared with 78 penalties. Campbell and Robbie became Lions' fourth half-back pairing in four Tests, following Ward and Patterson, Davies and Patterson, and Campbell and Patterson. O'Driscoll became first Lion to score tries in two Tests. Botha's penalty took his total points in five matches against Lions to 32, exceeded for Lions in whole tour only by Campbell, Woodward, Ward and Davies.

FINAL TOUR TALLY					T	C	P	D	Pts
	P18	W15	L3	For	47	21	45	12	401
				Agst.	27	14	33	3	244

THE LIONS: THEIR INTERNATIONAL BOARD CAPS

The Lions

Their International Board Cap Details

	P	W	D	L	T	C	P	D	Pts
Full-backs									
Bruce H. HAY (Boroughmuir, Scotland) Born 23-5-50, 5′10½″, 13 st 12 lb. Married. East Scotland sales representative for Gremer Chemicals.	17	2	2	13	1	—	—	—	4
	(Twelve caps as a wing)								
Rodney C. O'DONNELL (St Mary's Coll, Ireland) Born 16-8-56, 5′10″, 13 st 2 lb. Single. Manager of sales department, Smith's Templeogue Motors Ltd, Dublin.	5	4	0	1	—	—	—	—	—
	(Outstanding success with Ireland in Australia, 1979)								
Wings									
John CARLETON (Orrell, England) Born 24-11-55, 5′10″, 13 st. Single. Former maths and PE teacher at Park High School, Hindley, Lancs, but resigned to tour with Lions.	5	4	0	1	4	—	—	—	16
	(First England player to score three tries in a Home International since 1924)								
Michael A. C. SLEMEN (Liverpool, England) Born 11-5-51, 6′1″, 12 st 3 lb. Married, one boy. Teaches PE, biology and chemistry at Merchant Taylors', Crosby.	20	9	1	10	5	—	—	—	20
	(Two tries for Barbarians v 1978 New Zealanders)								

[Andy Irvine (Heriot's FP, Scotland) also selected as wing but withdrew injured on eve of tour]

	P	W	D	L	T	C	P	D	Pts
Utility back									
Peter MORGAN (Llanelli, Wales) Born 1-1-59, 5′10″, 12 st 5 lb. Single. West Wales sales representative for Fiat-Alliss.	2	1	0	1	—	—	—	—	—
	(Capped as replacement centre, then stand-off, after playing full-back for Wales XV v Rumania)								
Centres									
Ray W. R. GRAVELL (Llanelli, Wales) Born 12-9-51, 5′11″, 14 st. Married. Works for Manpower Services Commission in Llanelli.	18	14	0	4	1	—	—	—	4
	(Last capped 1979, his wing partners have scored eight tries in internationals)								
James RENWICK (Hawick, Scotland) Born 12-2-52, 5′8½″, 12 st 10 lb. Married, two boys. Linesman/engineer with South of Scotland Electricity Board, Galashiels.	35	10	2	23	5	1	2	—	28
	(Scotland's most capped three-quarter, including once as replacement wing)								

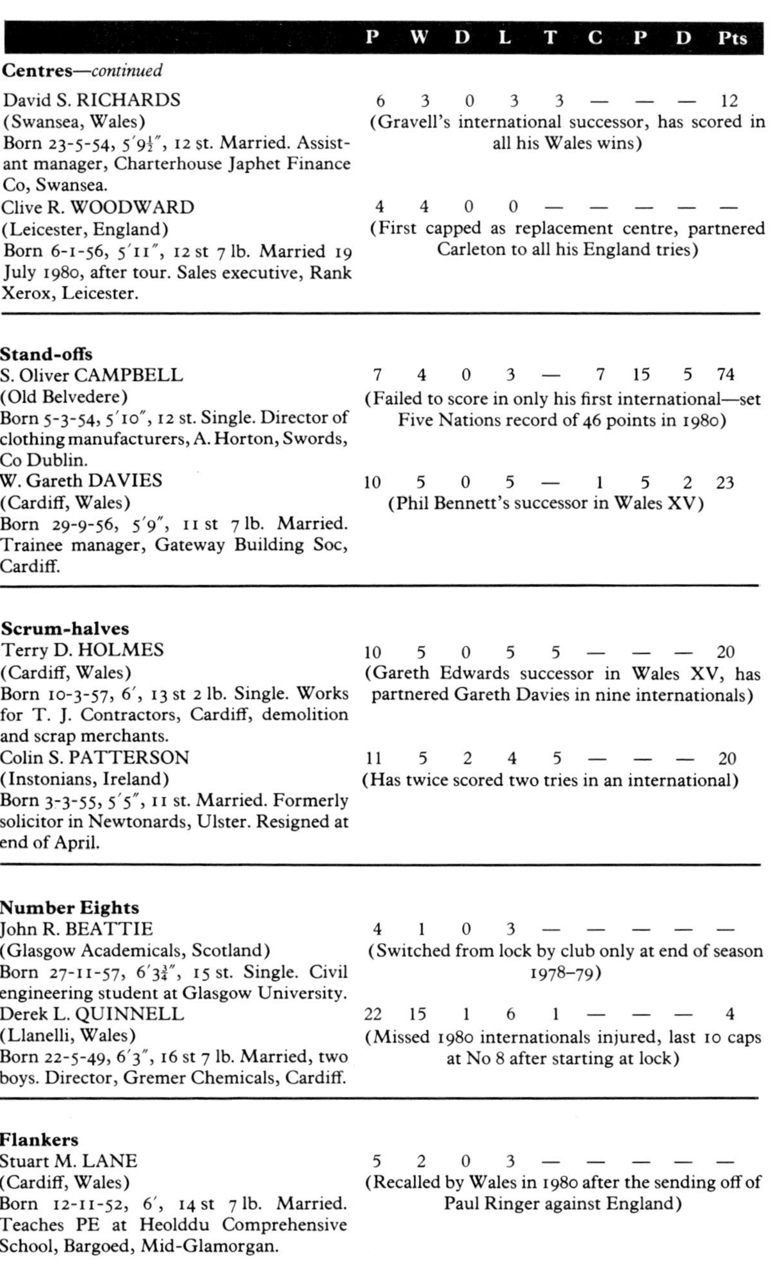

	P	W	D	L	T	C	P	D	Pts	
Centres—*continued*										
David S. RICHARDS (Swansea, Wales) Born 23-5-54, 5′9½″, 12 st. Married. Assistant manager, Charterhouse Japhet Finance Co, Swansea.	6	3	0	3	3	—	—	—	12	(Gravell's international successor, has scored in all his Wales wins)
Clive R. WOODWARD (Leicester, England) Born 6-1-56, 5′11″, 12 st 7 lb. Married 19 July 1980, after tour. Sales executive, Rank Xerox, Leicester.	4	4	0	0	—	—	—	—	—	(First capped as replacement centre, partnered Carleton to all his England tries)
Stand-offs										
S. Oliver CAMPBELL (Old Belvedere) Born 5-3-54, 5′10″, 12 st. Single. Director of clothing manufacturers, A. Horton, Swords, Co Dublin.	7	4	0	3	—	7	15	5	74	(Failed to score in only his first international—set Five Nations record of 46 points in 1980)
W. Gareth DAVIES (Cardiff, Wales) Born 29-9-56, 5′9″, 11 st 7 lb. Married. Trainee manager, Gateway Building Soc, Cardiff.	10	5	0	5	—	1	5	2	23	(Phil Bennett's successor in Wales XV)
Scrum-halves										
Terry D. HOLMES (Cardiff, Wales) Born 10-3-57, 6′, 13 st 2 lb. Single. Works for T. J. Contractors, Cardiff, demolition and scrap merchants.	10	5	0	5	5	—	—	—	20	(Gareth Edwards successor in Wales XV, has partnered Gareth Davies in nine internationals)
Colin S. PATTERSON (Instonians, Ireland) Born 3-3-55, 5′5″, 11 st. Married. Formerly solicitor in Newtonards, Ulster. Resigned at end of April.	11	5	2	4	5	—	—	—	20	(Has twice scored two tries in an international)
Number Eights										
John R. BEATTIE (Glasgow Academicals, Scotland) Born 27-11-57, 6′3¾″, 15 st. Single. Civil engineering student at Glasgow University.	4	1	0	3	—	—	—	—	—	(Switched from lock by club only at end of season 1978–79)
Derek L. QUINNELL (Llanelli, Wales) Born 22-5-49, 6′3″, 16 st 7 lb. Married, two boys. Director, Gremer Chemicals, Cardiff.	22	15	1	6	1	—	—	—	4	(Missed 1980 internationals injured, last 10 caps at No 8 after starting at lock)
Flankers										
Stuart M. LANE (Cardiff, Wales) Born 12-11-52, 6′, 14 st 7 lb. Married. Teaches PE at Heolddu Comprehensive School, Bargoed, Mid-Glamorgan.	5	2	0	3	—	—	—	—	—	(Recalled by Wales in 1980 after the sending off of Paul Ringer against England)

	P	W	D	L	T	C	P	D	Pts	
Flankers—*continued*										
John B. O'DRISCOLL (London Irish, Ireland) Born 26-11-53, 6'2½", 15 st 12 lb. Married. Doctor at Westminster Hospital, London.	7	5	0	2	1	—	—	—	4	(London's only Lion)
Jeff SQUIRE (Pontypool, Wales) Born 23-9-51, 6'3", 15 st 12 lb. Married. Manager, Pontypool branch, Gateway Building Soc.	16	10	0	6	1	—	—	—	4	(Wales captain 1980, first capped at No 8 for two matches as successor to Mervyn Davies)
Colm C. TUCKER (Shannon, Ireland) Born 22-9-52, 6'1", 15 st 10 lb. Married. Sales manager, Murphy's Brewery, Limerick.	3	0	1	2	—	—	—	—	—	(Surprise selection, capped in 1980 only as substitute, but in Munster XV which beat 1978 All Blacks)
Locks										
William B. BEAUMONT (Fylde, England) Born 9-3-52, 6'3½", 17 st. Married. Director of family textile firm, J. Blackledge and Son Ltd, Chorley.	26	10	1	15	—	—	—	—	—	(Captain who led England to first Grand Slam for 23 years, and led North XV who beat 1979 New Zealanders. England's most capped lock)
Maurice J. COLCLOUGH (Angouleme, England) Born 2-9-53, 6'5", 17 st 5 lb. Single. Director of firm renting out amusement games, and managing director of Holiday Charente, firm hiring out holiday cruisers in West France.	6	5	0	1	—	—	—	—	—	(Biggest man in side, commutes from France to play for England and Sussex)
Allan J. MARTIN (Aberavon, Wales) Born 11-12-48, 6'4½", 16 st 5 lb. Married, one boy, one girl. Owner Allan Martin Sports shop, Port Talbot, and director, Treorchy Enterprises (Sportswear) Ltd.	31	22	1	8	1	3	5	—	25	(Needs two more caps to beat Brian Price as most capped Wales lock)
Alan J. TOMES (Hawick, Scotland) Born 6-11-51, 6'5", 17 st. Single. Works study engineer for Northern Gas, based in Newcastle.	16	3	2	11	2	—	—	—	8	(Missed season's opening international against Ireland because of suspension)
Props										
Philip J. BLAKEWAY (Gloucester, England) Born 31-12-50, 5'11", 16 st. Married, one boy, one girl. Director, Francis Blakeway, Ltd, Gloucester, wholesale fruit merchants.	4	4	0	0	—	—	—	—	—	(Tight-head, missed whole of 1978–79 season with broken bone in neck)
Graham PRICE (Pontypool, Wales) Born 24-11-51, 5'11", 16 st. Married, two girls. Engineer with Fibreglass Ltd, Cwmbran, Gwent.	28	20	0	8	2	—	—	—	8	(Tight-head, ever-present for Wales since scoring on international debut v France, 1975)

Props—*continued*

Player	P	W	D	L	T	C	P	D	Pts	Notes
Fran E. COTTON (Sale, England) Born 3-1-48, 6′1½″, 16 st 12 lb. Married, one girl. Training adviser to Distributive Industries Training Board in North West, based in Sandbach.	30	13	0	17	1	—	—	—	4	(Loose-head, but has won 21 caps as tight-head. Became England's most capped prop forward, when he overtook Ron Jacobs in Scotland match, 1980)
Clive WILLIAMS (Swansea, Wales) Born 2-11-49, 6′, 16 st 2 lb. Married, one girl. Plasterer with J. E. H. Ltd, Newton, Porthcawl.	6	4	0	2	—	—	—	—	—	(Loose-head, missed season injured after 1977 Lions tour of New Zealand)

Hookers

Player	P	W	D	L	T	C	P	D	Pts	Notes
Alan PHILLIPS (Cardiff, Wales) Born 21-8-54, 5′11″, 14 st. Married, 2 August 1980, after tour. Director, H. and A. Phillips, window and office cleaners, Porthcawl.	5	3	0	2	—	—	—	—	—	(Scored 19 tries for Cardiff in 1975–76, claimed as world record for a hooker)
Peter J. WHEELER (Leicester, England) Born 26-11-48, 5′11″, 13 st 10 lb. Married, one boy. Insurance broker, Hogg Robinson, UK Ltd, Leicester.	20	10	1	13	—	—	—	—	—	(Leicester's cup winning captain, former goal-kicker at club level, twice exceeding 100 points in a season)

SUPPLEMENTARIES (in order of playing)

Player	P	W	D	L	T	C	P	D	Pts	Notes
Wing (for Irvine on eve of tour) H. Elgan REES (Neath, Wales) Born 5-1-54, 5′7″, 12 st 4 lb. Married, one girl. Sales executive for P. D. Langstone and Sons Ltd, Swansea, safety equipment and protective clothing manufacturers.	8	5	0	3	4	—	—	—	16	(International successor to Gerald Davies, Wales' most capped threequarter)
Flanker (for Lane) Gareth WILLIAMS (Bridgend) Born 6-11-55, 6′4″, 15 st 4 lb. Married, one boy. PE teacher, Maesteg Comprehensive School.	—	—	—	—	—	—	—	—	—	(Five Wales B caps, but a Lion before a full international. Summoned from Wales secondary tour of US and Canada. Two Welsh Cup wins with Bridgend)
Prop (for Blakeway) Ian L. STEPHENS (Bridgend) Born 22-5-53, 5′11″, 16 st 2 lb. Married, one girl, one boy. Formerly a casemaker with E. C. Cases of Taff's Well, but resigned to join Wales tour of US and Canada.	—	—	—	—	—	—	—	—	—	(One Wales B cap, but—like Gareth Williams—a Lion before a full international, summoned from Wales secondary tour, and two Welsh Cup wins with Bridgend)
Stand-off (cover for Campbell and Davies) Tony J. P. WARD (Garryowen, Ireland) Born 9-10-54, 5′7″, 12 st 4 lb. Married. Trained as PE teacher, but now runs Tony Ward Sports, a shop in Limerick.	9	2	2	5	—	4	20	3	77	(Not a current Ireland player, having lost place on 1979 Australia tour to Campbell, who in 1980 exceeded 38-points-in-a-championship record Ward shared with Roger Hosen, Phil Bennett and Steve Fenwick)

	P	W	D	L	T	C	P	D	Pts
Scrum-half (for Holmes) John C. ROBBIE (Greystones, Ireland)	5	0	0	5	—	—	3	—	9
Prop (for Cotton) Phil A. ORR (Old Wesley, Ireland)	24	7	2	15	—	—	—	—	—
Wing (for Slemen) Andrew R. IRVINE (Heriot's FP, Scotland)	37	12	2	23	9	16	38	—	182
Centre (for Richards) Paul W. DODGE (Leicester, England)	10	5	1	4	—	—	1	—	3
Scrum-half (cover for Robbie when Patterson injured) Steve J. SMITH (Sale, England)	14	7	1	6	2	—	—	—	8

Scrum-half (for Holmes)
John C. ROBBIE
(Greystones, Ireland)
Born 17-11-55, 5′9″, 11 st 7 lb. Married, one boy. Management trainee in traffic dept of Arthur Guinness Son and Co, Dublin.

(Ireland's last scrum-half but one before Patterson, last capped 1977, summoned from club tour of Zimbabwe. Scored 17 points for Cambridge in 1978 University Match)

Prop (for Cotton)
Phil A. ORR
(Old Wesley, Ireland)
Born 14-12-50, 5′10″, 16 st. Married. Assistant manager of Orrwear Ltd, Dublin, manufacturers of jeans, trousers and protective clothing.

(Ireland ever-present since first cap in 1976)

Wing (for Slemen)
Andrew R. IRVINE
(Heriot's FP, Scotland)
Born 16-9-51, 5′10″, 12 st 4 lb. Married, two girls. Chartered Surveyor, associate partner in Jones, Lang, Wootton in Edinburgh. (Originally selected as wing, but withdrew on eve of tour.)

(Scotland's most capped back, with 33 of his caps at full-back. Has scored in 26 internationals)

Centre (for Richards)
Paul W. DODGE
(Leicester, England)
Born 26-2-58, 6′1″, 13 st 7 lb. Engaged. Bookbinder for Syston Printing and Bookbinding Co.

(Eight successive caps till starting 1980 internationals apparently as fourth choice England centre, not recalled till injuries to Tony Bond and Nick Preston. Leicester Cup winning colleague of Wheeler and Woodward)

Scrum-half (cover for Robbie when Patterson injured)
Steve J. SMITH
(Sale, England)
Born 22-7-51, 5′10″, 13 st. Single. Area training advisor for the Distributive Industry Training Board, based at Sandbach, Cheshire.

(First capped 1973, recalled 1979–80 after three-season absence and scored both his tries in Grand Slam campaign)

Management
Manager
Syd MILLAR
(Ballymena, Ireland)

P	W	D	L	T	C	P	D	Pts
37	12	3	22	—	—	—	—	—

Born 24-5-34. Married, two boys, one girl. Managing director of Scott (Toomebridge) Ltd. Ireland caps from 1958–70. Lions tours, Australia and New Zealand 1959, S. Africa 1962 and 1968, played nine Tests. Coach to 1974 Lions in South Africa.

(Played 22 successive matches for Ireland from 1958–63)

	P	W	D	L	T	C	P	D	Pts
Assistant manager/coach Noel A. A. MURPHY	41	16	2	23	5	—	—	—	15

(Cork Constitution, Ireland)
Born 22-2-37. Married, five boys, one girl. Director of Musgrave Ltd, cash-and-carry firm in Republic of Ireland. Ireland caps from 1958–69, Lions tours Australia and N. Zealand 1959 and 1966, played in eight Tests. Former Ireland coach.

(Played with Millar in 19 internationals and two Lions Tests, Ireland's most capped flanker till overtaken by Fergus Slattery in 1980)

The Lions

Previous Tours

	P	Tests	W	D	L	Tries	Con	Pen	Drop	Pts
New Zealand and Fiji 1977										
HAY	11	—	10	0	1	5	—	—	—	20
	(All games at full-back, two tries v Counties/Thames Valley)									
IRVINE	19	4	15	0	4	11	8	9	—	87
	(Finished top try-scorer despite playing all games at full-back, including five as substitute. Five tries v King Country/Wanganui, and 25 points v S/Mid Canterbury—N. Otago)									
REES	11	—	10	0	1	8	—	—	—	32
	(A Lion before a Wales cap)									
QUINNELL	14	2	12	0	2	2	—	—	—	8
	(Six matches as flanker, including both Tests)									
SQUIRE	15	1	12	0	3	3	—	—	—	12
	(Five matches at No 8, including one as replacement)									
BEAUMONT	10	3	7	0	3	2	—	—	—	8
	(Late injury reinforcement, was in Test team within three weeks of first game in New Zealand)									
MARTIN	14	1	11	0	3	—	—	2	—	6
	(Lost Test place after first Test)									
COTTON	16	3	13	0	3	—	—	—	—	—
	(Ten matches as tight-head, but loose-head in all his Tests)									
PRICE	15	4	11	0	4	—	—	—	—	—
	(The only current Lions forward to play in all four Tests in 1977)									
C. WILLIAMS	9	0	8	0	1	1	—	—	—	4
	(Severely injured knee after two-thirds of tour and missed whole of following domestic season)									
ORR	12	1	10	0	2	1	—	—	—	4
	(Loose-head prop in first Test but then lost place to Cotton)									
WHEELER	13	3	10	0	3	1	-	-	-	4
	(Succeeded Bobby Windsor as No 1 hooker after first Test)									
South Africa 1974										
IRVINE	15	2	14	1	0	5	26	27	1	156
	(Lions' highest scorer on record in a South African tour, including 22 points v Rhodesia and 20 v SARA Leopards. Ten games at full-back but both Tests on wing)									

	P	Tests	W	D	L	Tries	Con	Pen	Drop	Pts
South Africa 1974—*continued*										
COTTON	14	4	13	1	0	—	—	—	—	—
	(Twelve matches as tight-head)									
New Zealand 1971										
QUINNELL	10	1	9	0	1	1	—	—	—	3
	(Uncapped by Wales at time, the only current Lion to have been a Lion when try worth only three points)									

The Lions in South Africa 1980 (P18, W15, L3, F401, A244)

	Played	Tests (*incl Test won)	Included in overall total: Matches as replacement	Included in overall total: Matches when replaced	Won	Lost	Tries	Con	Pen	Drop	Pts
Backs											
HAY	11	3*	0	0	9	2	2	—	—	—	8
(Played only first three and last-but-one match in selected position of full-back, rest on left wing. Succeeded Slemen as Test team wing)											
O'DONNELL	6	1	0	1	5	1	—	—	—	1	3
(First Test full-back, but dropped for second. Injured neck in Lions' 12th match)											
CARLETON	10	3*	0	1	8	2	3	—	—	—	12
(Nine matches on right wing, one on left. Played in five of first seven matches)											
SLEMEN	5	1	0	0	4	1	5	1	—	1	25
(Scored in his first four matches, and remained top try-scorer though returning home after first Test because of pregnant wife's illness)											
MORGAN	7	0	0	0	7	0	1	—	—	1	7
(One match at full-back, three at centre, three on left-wing, and briefly at stand-off when Davies was hurt in first match. Did not play in Saturday side after third week)											
GRAVELL	11	4*	1	0	8	3	1	—	—	—	4
(Came on as replacement wing when Carleton was hurt in first Test, selected at centre for last three)											
RENWICK	11	1	2	0	10	1	1	2	2	1	17
(Centre in first Test, but only appearance in Saturday side after that was as replacement)											
RICHARDS	7	1	0	1	6	1	1	—	—	—	4
(Played in six successive matches, three at stand off, up to first Test, before dislocating shoulder against Transvaal)											
WOODWARD	11	2	2	0	9	2	4	5	8	1	53
(Varied between centre and right wing, one Test at each with two games as replacement left wing. Unexpectedly led tour scorers from second match till last Saturday but one)											
CAMPBELL	7	3*	1	0	5	2	—	6	13	3	60
(Ruled out of eight of first nine matches with hamstring trouble, scored on every appearance except when late replacement for Davies in second Test)											
DAVIES	4	1	0	2	3	1	1	3	7	1	34
(Appearances restricted by shoulder and knee trouble. Scored in every game he played)											
HOLMES	4	0	0	2	4	0	3	—	—	—	12
(Also restricted by shoulder and knee trouble. Scored tries in his first three matches)											

	Played	Tests (*incl Test won)	Included in overall total: Matches as replacement	Included in overall total: Matches when replaced	Won	Lost	Tries	Con	Pen	Drop	Pts
PATTERSON	10	3	2	1	7	3	1	—	—	—	4
	(Appeared, twice as replacement, in eight of first 11 matches, badly injured knee in last match but one)										
Forwards											
BEATTIE	8	0	0	0	8	0	2	—	—	—	8
	(Seven matches at No 8, one at flank. Lost place in Saturday side after second week)										
QUINNELL	9	2	1	0	7	2	2	—	—	—	8
	(Moved from No 8 to flank after losing place in second Test. Briefly leading try-scorer with two in second match of tour)										
LANE	1	0	0	1	1	0	—	—	—	—	0
	(His active participation ended with cartilage trouble after 50 sec. of opening match of tour, without his touching the ball)										
O'DRISCOLL	11	4*	0	0	8	3	2	—	—	—	8
	(The only Lion to score tries in two Tests)										
SQUIRE	11	4*	0	0	8	3	1	—	—	—	4
	(Six matches at flank, five at No 8, including last four when superceding Quinnell)										
TUCKER	9	2*	0	0	8	1	—	—	—	—	0
	(Graduated from midweek pack to last two Test sides)										
BEAUMONT	10	4*	0	0	7	3	—	—	—	—	0
	(Played in every Saturday match, but never in midweek)										
COLCLOUGH	11	4*	0	0	8	3	1	—	—	—	4
	(Graduated from midweek side to play eight matches as Beaumont's partner)										
MARTIN	8	0	0	0	8	0	—	—	—	—	0
	(Dropped from Saturday side after second week)										
TOMES	7	0	0	0	7	0	1	—	—	—	4
	(Played midweek matches only, never partnered Beaumont)										
BLAKEWAY	1	0	0	1	1	0	—	—	—	—	0
	(Lasted just 70 minutes of rugby before recurrence of rib trouble ended his tour)										
PRICE	12	4*	0	0	9	3	2	—	—	—	8
	(The Lion actually selected for most matches—Clive Williams having been a replacement twice)										
COTTON	4	0	1	1	4	0	—	—	—	—	0
	(Played tight-head as replacement, otherwise loose-head, his tour ended with heart trouble in sixth match)										
C. WILLIAMS	12	4*	2	0	9	3	1	—	—	—	4
	(Once played in five successive matches, once in four, all matches at loose-head)										
PHILLIPS	7	0	0	0	7	0	—	—	—	—	0
	(Another to play in midweek matches only, never in same side as Beaumont)										

	Played	Tests (*incl Test won)	Included in overall total: Matches as replacement	Included in overall total: Matches when replaced	Won	Lost	Tries	Con	Pen	Drop	Pts
WHEELER	11	4*	0	0	8	3	1	—	—	—	4
(Played in every Saturday match and one in midweek)											
Supplementaries											
REES	6	0	0	0	6	0	3	—	—	—	12
(Five matches on right wing, first only in Saturday side. Scored in his first two)											
G. WILLIAMS	6	0	0	0	6	0	1	—	—	—	4
(Played only once in Saturday side)											
STEPHENS	5	0	0	0	5	0	—	—	—	—	0
(Another to play only in midweek matches)											
WARD	5	1	0	0	4	1	1	4	11	1	48
(Scored in all but one match, including record 18 pts in first Test, but then dropped to midweek side)											
ROBBIE	7	1*	1	0	7	0	1	—	—	1	7
(The only Lion to play in a Test and not lose on tour. Scored all his points when replacement for Patterson against Griqualand West in last but one match)											
ORR	5	0	0	1	5	0	—	—	—	—	0
(One appearance only in Saturday side)											
IRVINE	8	3*	0	1	6	2	4	—	4	1	31
(Equalled Phil Bennett's world record 210 pts in all internationals, with penalty in second Test, try in fourth, 15 pts in South Africa Tests 1974, 6 in New Zealand Tests 1977, and 182 for Scotland. Started one match in originally tour-selected position of wing but finished all eight at full-back. Scored in seven matches, played in eight of last ten including six in succession)											
DODGE	5	2*	0	0	4	1	1	—	—	—	4
(Scored in midweek side on first appearance, thereafter a permanent Saturday Lion)											
SMITH	0	—	—	—	—	—	—	—	—	—	—
(Just a "quiz question of the future" as the man who flew out to sit on subs' bench at final Test)											
TOTALS							47	21	45	12	401
OPPOSITION							27	14	33	3	244

- Morgan, Renwick, Beattie, Martin, Rees, Gareth Williams, and Orr guested for South African Barbarians beaten 43–14 by Junior Springboks in final Test curtain-raiser, leaving only Holmes, Tomes, Cotton, Phillips, Stephens, and Robbie—plus Lane, Blakeway and Smith—as unbeaten in South Africa, 1980. Beattie, Renwick and Morgan scored the Barbarians' tries and Renwick's was converted by the Argentinian stand-off Hugo Porta.

- Slemen is the lowest highest try-scorer in Lions' history on South African tours, though there were two more matches when A. J. W. Hinshelwood finished top try-scorer with only six in 1968. By contrast on the 1974 tour, J. J. Williams scored six tries in one afternoon, against a South West Districts XV at Mossel Bay, opposition the 1980 Lions did not meet. Campbell with 60 points is not the lowest highest points-scorer on a Lions South Africa tour, A. C. Pedlow having been top with only 58 points in 1955, these though included eight tries which at 1980's values would give him eight more points—66. The 12 dropped goals were a record high, and the ratio of only just over one try per penalty goal was easily a record low. Though the 1974 Lions totalled 56 penalty goals in 22 matches they scored 107 tries—almost two tries per penalty—the 1968 team totalled 55 tries compared with 42 penalties, while no previous team had kicked more than 24 penalty goals.

LEADING TOUR SCORERS

Tries: 5—Slemen; 4—Irvine, Woodward; 3—Carleton, Holmes, Rees.
Points: 60—Campbell; 53—Woodward; 48—Ward; 34—Davies; 31—Irvine; 25—Slemen.
Dropped goals: 3—Campbell.

TEST MATCH RECORD

P4	W1	L3		Tries	Con	Pen	Drop	Pts		Tries	Con	Pen	Drop	Pts
			For	7	2	11	1	68	**Agst**	11	6	6	1	77

BRITISH TEST SCORERS:

Tries: O'Driscoll (2), Price, Gravell, Hay, C. Williams, and Irvine
Conversions: Davies, Campbell
Penalty goals: Ward (5), Campbell (3), Davies (2) and Irvine
Dropped goal: Ward
Leading total Test scorers: 18 pts—Ward; 11—Campbell; 8—Davies and O'Driscoll; 7—Irvine
Test substitutions: First—Gravell for Carleton; **Second**—Campbell for Davies
Total players called upon—24, including different half-back partnership in each of the 4 Tests

SOUTH AFRICA TEST SCORERS:

Tries: Germishuys (3), Louw and W. du Plessis (2), van Heerden, Serfontein, Stofberg, and Pienaar
Conversions: Botha (6)
Penalty goals: Botha (4), Pienaar (2)
Dropped goal: Botha
Leading total Test scorers: 27 pts—Botha; 12—Germishuys; 10—Pienaar; 8—Louw and W. du Plessis
Test substitutions: Second—Burger for Louw.
Total players called upon—18

TOUR SUBSTITUTIONS (13)

v Eastern Province—Quinnell for Lane, Renwick for Davies (Morgan switching)
v SARA Invitation—Cotton for Blakeway
v Orange Free State—Patterson for Holmes
v SARFF Invitation—C. Williams for Cotton
First Test—Gravell for Carleton
v Transvaal—Renwick for Richards
v E. Transvaal—Patterson for Holmes
Second Test—Campbell for Davies
v Junior Springboks—C. Williams for Orr, Woodward for O'Donnell (Irvine switching)
v Western Province—Woodward for Irvine (Hay switching)
v Griqualand West—Robbie for Patterson

Opposing sides had SEVEN substitutions

TOUR CAPTAINS

10—Beaumont; 5—Quinnell; 2—Hay; 1—Squire

Index

Note: this index covers Chapters 1–14, but excludes the match reports and other appendices.

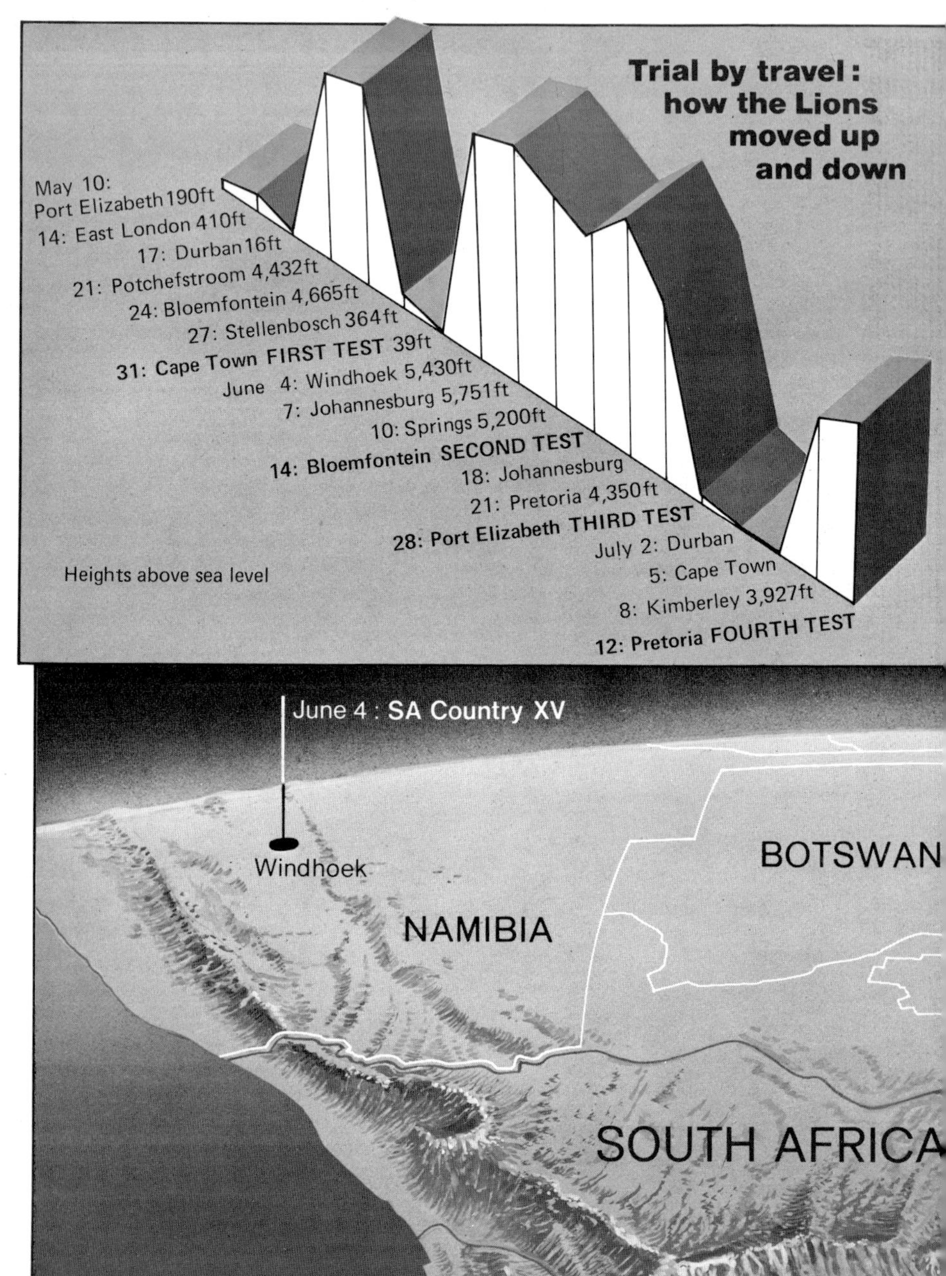
Trial by travel: how the Lions moved up and down
May 10: Port Elizabeth 190ft
14: East London 410ft
17: Durban 16ft
21: Potchefstroom 4,432ft
24: Bloemfontein 4,665ft
27: Stellenbosch 364ft
31: Cape Town FIRST TEST 39ft
June 4: Windhoek 5,430ft
7: Johannesburg 5,751ft
10: Springs 5,200ft
14: Bloemfontein SECOND TEST
18: Johannesburg
21: Pretoria 4,350ft
28: Port Elizabeth THIRD TEST
July 2: Durban
5: Cape Town
8: Kimberley 3,927ft
12: Pretoria FOURTH TEST
Heights above sea level
June 4 : SA Country XV
Windhoek
NAMIBIA
BOTSWAN
SOUTH AFRICA
May 27 : SARF Federation
May 31 : FIRST TEST
July 5 : Western Province
Stellenbosch
Cape Town